HARLEM

HARLEM

The Crucible of Modern African American Culture

LIONEL C. BASCOM

 PRAEGER™

An Imprint of ABC-CLIO, LLC

Santa Barbara, California • Denver, Colorado

Library of Congress Cataloging-in-Publication Data

Names: Bascom, Lionel C., author.
Title: Harlem : the crucible of modern African American culture / Lionel C. Bascom.
Other titles: Crucible of modern African American culture
Description: Santa Barbara, California : Praeger, an imprint of ABC-CLIO, LLC, [2017] | Includes bibliographical references and index.
Identifiers: LCCN 2016031523 (print) | LCCN 2016034763 (ebook) | ISBN 9781440842689 (hardcopy : alk. paper) | ISBN 9781440842696 (ebook)
Subjects: LCSH: Harlem (New York, N.Y.)—Civilization. | Harlem (New York, N.Y.)— Intellectual life—20th century. | Harlem Renaissance. | Harlem (New York, N.Y.)— Politics and government—20th century. | African American arts—New York (State)— New York—20th century. | African Americans—New York (State)—New York— Intellectual life—20th century. | African Americans—New York (State)—New York— Politics and government—20th century. | African Americans—New York (State)— New York—Biography. | African Americans—Intellectual life—20th century. | New York (N.Y.)—Intellectual life—20th century.
Classification: LCC F128.68.H3 B37 2017 (print) | LCC F128.68.H3 (ebook) | DDC 974.7/1—dc23
LC record available at https://lccn.loc.gov/2016031523

ISBN: 978–1–4408–4268–9
EISBN: 978–1–4408–4269–6

21 20 19 18 17   1 2 3 4 5

This book is also available as an eBook.

Praeger
An Imprint of ABC-CLIO, LLC

ABC-CLIO, LLC
130 Cremona Drive, P.O. Box 1911
Santa Barbara, California 93116-1911
www.abc-clio.com

This book is printed on acid-free paper ∞

Manufactured in the United States of America

"For us, Africa isn't so much a lost continent
as it is an imaginary one."

Eric V. Copage, *Black Pearls*[1]

"The desire and yearning of my soul is for an African nationality. I want a people that have a tangible, separate existence of its own ... and where am I to look for it? You will tell me our race have equal rights to mingle in the American republic ... We have more than the rights of common men; we have the claim of an injured race for reparations. But I do not want it, I want a country, a nation of my own ..."

George Shelby in *Uncle Tom's Cabin* by Harriet Beecher Stowe, 1853[2]

Contents

Introduction

Stowe's tragic slave character, George Shelby, is as real to me as my own, elusive African heritage. Shelby is both a fiction and symbolically real to me. Shelby is a fiction because slaves of 1852 did not always have last names, and generally, were called by an assigned first name like Gullah Jack or pet names like Chicken George. Still, Shelby belonged to the first and last generations of Africans brought here, stripped of all tribal and cultural markings, music, drums, and funeral rituals, and then set adrift to fend for himself for generations.

He became a Negro, an abstraction, one that was as made up as Stowe's George Shelby's identity was invented.

The worst of these indignities was the loss of African birth names, the one thing heirs might have used to trace their origins back to an African past. I belong to this lost tribe of George Shelby, the tragic American Negro.

Sometime after the end of slavery and a few short years into the twentieth century, a peculiar, unprecedented kind of social alchemy began brewing among black people from all over the world, especially those who started gathering in New York. They found each other uptown in Harlem where they also discovered an opportunity to become self-aware for the first time in history for the so-called American Negro. Although they came from many different parts of the world, the Deep South, Africa, the Caribbean and else where, they learned to speak and communicate with each other as black men, not as oppressed men. It was an intoxicating time in our history.

In general, the period is most often called the Harlem Renaissance, an era between the 1920s and the early 1970s, by my reckoning. The Harlem Renaissance is almost always described as the sudden flowering of artistic expression discovered in Harlem by a clique of singing, dancing musical Negroes, a handful of black painters, some poets and novelists. While almost no one can say when it began, most histories say that it died in 1929, disappearing just as suddenly as it had first appeared.

This is romantic fiction, not the history of what perhaps was the most progressive era of African American history.

The term *Harlem Renaissance* is a construct about an idea, not a period of time, which captures both a popular and imagined understanding of an abstraction about black people in America. The term did not occur in the era it generally describes, the early years of the 1920s. According to Ernest J. Mitchell II, the phrase Harlem Renaissance did not appear in print until the 1940s to describe a series of historical events first noticed in Harlem that may have begun as early as 1900 and lasted through the 1970s. During those years, it was variously called the New Negro Movement, the Negro Renaissance, the Harlem Renaissance, and Black Modernism.

According to Mitchell, the term *Harlem Renaissance* entered mainstream discourse through the popular black press in the 1960s like *Freedom Ways*, a quarterly review of the Negro Freedom Movement that was characterized by the freedom bus rides into the Deep South by civil rights workers. "Harlem symbolizes a radical awakening on a national and world scale," Alain Locke wrote in his book *The New Negro*.[1]

In an essay titled "Our Little Renaissance," written by Locke in 1927, the Howard University scholar narrowed his definition and scope of this idea.

> If then it is really a renaissance, and I firmly believe it is, we are still in the hill-town stage, and the mellowness of maturity has not yet come upon us. [...] The Negro Renaissance is not ten years old; its earliest harbingers cannot be traced back to the beginning of the century; its representative products to date are not only the work of the last three or four years, but the work of men still in their twenties [...], he is quoted as saying in the Critical Temper of Alain Locke by Jeffrey Stewart.[2]

Harlem was not heaven. It was a haven where images of ignorant darkies, watermelon-eating, little pick-ninny girls, Aunt Jemima, Jim Crow and the so-called Negro, all began to fade. Those old images of "darkies" were replaced by a new construct of strident, confident, educated, New Negroes, something unseen in American daily life. This book tracks this evolution beginning late in the nineteenth century and follows its rise from the black exodus from feudal American in the South to the birth of Harlem as a cultural center. It was in this crucible called Harlem that the image and character of modern African American culture thrived and finally began to develop.

In *Harlem: The Crucible of Modern African American Culture*, I attempt to examine the accuracy of the established image of Harlem during the Renaissance period—roughly between 1917 and the 1960s—as heaven for migrating Negroes.

In 1939, Bruce Nugent wrote a carefree, colorful sketch of Harlem, writing for the Federal Writers' Project.

> Boom and prosperity swept over Harlem, magically heightening its already remarkable capacity for enjoyment and entertainment. ... Money flowed in and out of pockets as easily as laughter escaped lips. The air was alive with the beat of drums and the trill of clarinets, the clinking of never-emptied glasses and the rumble of luxurious cars rolling from fashionable avenues to stop before the more lively and colorful of the after-hour Harlem places of amusement. Hundreds of honkey-tonks and cabarets sprang up. The ever-growing crowds spilled into the thousands of speakeasies and gin-mills, which were already multiplying like mushrooms ... dim red or blue light glowed from the windows of apartments that seemed to rock with the shuffle of feet, as house-rent parties spewed their patrons into the adjacent hallways and side streets. Everywhere there was good feeling and impromptu jazz spirit.
>
> There was no [classy] magazine which did not have contributions by or about Negroes. No poetry reading, literary gathering, cocktail partly, underworld group, gang war, creditable business, labor organization, art gallery, religious society, physical culture sect, love cult, or Yogi philosophy school was complete without having been graced by the inclusion of some member of this now strangely prevalent minority group.[3]

"To make a round of the cabarets and the honky-tonks that studded Harlem would have taken months," Nugent said. "This is generally what comes to mind when the era of Harlem's so-called renaissance is remembered."[4]

This is a popular sketch of that time, not a comprehensive recollection that ignores rigorous, vibrant political, social, and progressive movements that sprang up about the same time and thrived for decades in Harlem. It was this air of fraternal brotherhood and community organizing that gave birth to the largest civil rights organizations in American history, labor unions, unprecedented legal battles in the highest court in the nation and a clergy elite who eventually wielded great sway in the pulpits of small towns everywhere and in national arenas on behalf of black constituents.

Along with the revelers who flowed in and out of Harlem, came hardworking migrants, old and young, refuges of long-standing oppression. College-educated intellectuals, progressive ministers, writers, agitators, journalist, and lecturers also came to Harlem in search of opportunities and they mingled with former tenant farmers, cotton pickers, maids, and farmhands, who had migrated earlier for better lives up North. These progressives formed various organizations determined to erase negative images of Negroes as bumbling, ignorant second-class citizens. They drew massive crowds of followers in lavish parades in Harlem, speeches where throngs of black people filled Madison Square Gardens or the streets of Harlem to hear these leaders give thunderous speeches. These men and women flirted with socialism, communism, antiunion agitators, and government insurgents who had labeled them unpatriotic in a nation that had always treated them worse than second-class citizens.

Before the era of Malcolm X in the 1960s, the cry of equality "by any means necessary" was on many lips in Harlem of the 1920s, 1930s, and later decades when Malcolm joined these other, older voices. The dream of the Rev. Doctor Martin Luther King Jr. was also the unrequited dream of many leaders in Harlem who urged common men on the streets to learn the art of self-defense in a nation that would lynch a black man quicker than they could snatch away his right to vote.

This book challenges claims that the aims and goals of leaders of Harlem's renaissance failed. This view completely ignores the many political and social movements of the Harlem Renaissance period that left indelible influence on the evolution of African American culture.

By what measure did Renaissance leaders fail? Harlem was never a monolithic community. Separately, Harlem leaders of different political, labor, or religious movements, led different factions of followers. Some had followers that numbered in the tens of thousands around the world who had rallies that only Madison Square Gardens could hold while others caught the attention of only a few dozen followers who met in storefront churches or in library meeting rooms. These movements and causes were well covered by black-owned, nationally circulated newspapers and magazines published in Harlem. In different ways, their activities collectively were responsible for eventually ending segregation in the armed forces, legal segregation in public facilities, and their leaders drafted plans that eventually led to the first sweeping civil rights legislation. Their efforts abolished segregation in the armed forces. Writers first discovered by Harlem publishers and published in black-owned magazines only went on to win coveted national book awards and joined the ranks of America's best short story writers, black or white. What some called assimilationist, a derogatory label for sell out in the early years of the twentieth century, would later be seen as accomplished artists in mainstream circles, not just in black venues. Today, artists prized by large audiences are praised as crossover artists, not sell outs. The trek into mainstream acceptance by black artists, writers and leaders can be traced to Harlem where their work was first conceived and showcased.

This book begins with the epic story of the greatest exodus of blacks in American history called the Great Migration. It began when millions of blacks uprooted themselves from lives on plantations in the Deep South and they migrated northward after the Civil War. After nearly 300 years of slavery, slaves were free to roam, relocate, or remain on plantations where their families had been enslaved. Millions of emancipated slaves struggled to survive after slavery. Once protected by owners who prized their free labor, these former slaves became the victims of widespread terrorism by white vigilante groups like the Ku Klux Klan at the end of the Civil War. Many became tenant farmers in the sharecropping system where they on worked land they did not own but were allowed to sell a portion of what they grew at the end of each growing season. The system was rife with dishonest landowners who routinely failed to share profits with black farmers. When crop failures through drought and the infestation of insects struck the South, whole families of tenant farmers fled the South for northern cities like New York. It was not a migration at all, it was an American exodus.

By the 1920s, whole communities of Southern blacks had relocated to New York. In Harlem, these people formed neighborhood organizations where they resumed using the same barbers, beauty salons, dentists, and tailors they had patronized in the South. When these working-class people fled their rural homes, they left behind the educated teachers, politicians, and professionals in those Southern communities. Eventually, these intellectuals migrated to Harlem too.

Other groups came to New York from impoverished farming and fishing communities in the Caribbean. In Harlem, they formed social and political networking organizations like the National Urban League, the New Negro Movement, the March on Washington Movement, the National Association for the Advancement of Colored People, and the Universal Negro Improvement Association (UNIA) and the African Communities League and the socialist Liberty League. In nationally circulated newspapers and magazines published in Harlem, they began to uplift the idea and image of Negroes who were reinventing themselves in New York. These leaders condemned the images of the black mammies and Sambo's of the South. Using different strategies to achieve similar goals of civil rights, fair labor, and housing, these leaders began to voice and disseminate their progressive and radical ideas in a national press that was first headquartered in Harlem.

These leaders were no ordinary Negroes. They were armed with undergraduate and doctorate degrees from a wide variety of colleges, including Harvard, Fisk, and Howard universities. These scholars traveled and studied in Europe and the United States where they acquired academic and political allies. They established magazines and newspapers in Harlem that remain in print today that had circulations climbing beyond 200,000 subscribers in the 1920s. They formed the first all-black labor union and founded newspapers, including one called *The Messenger*, which the U.S. Justice Department claimed had become "the most dangerous of all Negro publications.

Black self-help groups, some whose recruits numbered in the tens of thousands, also published reformist newspapers. They included intellectuals like W.E.B. Du Bois, a founding member of the NAACP, socialist like Hubert Harrison sometimes known as the black Socrates and bodacious women like writer Zora Neale Hurston. An army of young lawyers were recruited and brought to Harlem by the NAACP, including a future justice of the U.S. Supreme Court. From a storefront office in Harlem and led by the best black legal minds in American, the NAACP Education and Legal Defense Fund set out to dismantle widely used segregation laws that had been in place since the days of reconstruction.

From another office in Harlem, organizers attacked segregation on another front, confronting government sanctioned discrimination by federal contractors. When the president of the United States baulked

CHAPTER ONE

From Exodus to the Rise of Harlem as a Cultural Center

"The terms in which people speak about the Negro Problem have nothing to do with human beings," writer James Baldwin said in an article published in a 1964 edition of *Transition* magazine. "There seems to be some extraordinary assumption ... that Negroes are either saints or devils, that the word Negro describes something and it doesn't. There is no such thing as a Negro, but there is such a thing as a boy or a man or a woman," he said, "but when you say 'the Negro Problem,' you create a big monolith, and beneath this wall are thousands of millions of human being lives which are being destroyed because you want to deal with an abstraction."[1]

If I had read this in my Brooklyn high school, I would have immediately been able to relate to Baldwin, a Harlem native whose rage sat well with my generation. When Baldwin spoke, he spoke for a generation of colored boys just like me who no longer wanted to be seen as just another poor, colored boy in America. Unfortunately, I did not read Baldwin in my high school. It would be many years after I left New York, joined the Navy, and was nearly a man that I found Baldwin on my own and began to read about the many visionaries like him who once had also made Harlem home. These were independent thinking men who gathered together in the basements of Harlem churches on 135th Street or Lenox Avenue before I was born, where they could hear inspiring speeches of revolutionary front men from all over the world. All of them seemed to have two things in common: all were black, and they had come to Harlem where they gathered crowds.

While Harlem was still famous for its rich nightlife and theaters like Smalls Paradise, the Baby Grand and the Palm Cafe, and The Apollo when I was a boy, Harlem was also notorious as the hotbed of political radicalism in my youth where impromptu speeches on the street were still common. In the 1920s, Harlem was also home to large circulation of newspapers and black magazines such as *The Crisis*, *Opportunity*, *The Voice*, *The Messenger*, or *Negro World*. Harlem was also famous as a breeding ground for "race men," leaders with elaborate schemes, policies, and movements aimed at uplifting the tarnished image of black people in America. Some race men called themselves "New Negroes" and leaders like the radical Marcus Garvey, Howard University professor Alain Locke, publisher Charles S. Johnson, and ministers like Reverend Adam Clayton Powell Sr. sought ways to reinvent the image of what writer Ralph Ellison called the lost tribe, the American Negro.

"After the Egyptian and Indian, the Greek and Roman, the Teuton and Mongolian," *The Crisis* editor W.E.B. Du Bois said, "the Negro is a sort of seventh son, born with a veil, and gifted with second-sight in this American world, a world which yields him no true self-consciousness, but only lets him see himself through the revelations of the other world," he wrote in *The Souls of Black Folk*. "It is a peculiar sensation, this double-consciousness, this sense of always looking at one's self through the eyes of others, of measuring one by the tape of a world that looks on in amused contempt and pity. One ever feels his two-ness—an American, a Negro ... two thoughts, two un-reconciled strivings; two warring ideals in one dark body, whose dogged strength alone keeps it from being torn asunder," he said. "The history of the American Negro is the history of strife, this longing to attain self-conscious manhood, to merge his double self into a better and truer self."[2]

The idea that not even Malcolm X was able to say my name chewed away at my self-esteem as a teenage boy. He said we were so-called Negroes. It was an unresolved problem that boiled over in my own household because my father called himself Negro and sometimes, colored. I wanted to be a black man and called myself black, but my father was repulsed by the word *black* and more turned off at my stance to use the word *black* to describe his son. My classmates in school who were from Hungary, Poland, Syria, Scotland, and even American Jews in New York suffered no such identity crisis that any hyphen could fix. There were no Negro-Americans.

Negroes were culturally orphaned, wanders in a multicultural nation of people who could easily trace themselves back centuries to western or eastern European villages, Asian dynasties, or the Celtic sailors who stumbled into Nova Scotia before the days of Columbus.

Born in a small New England, working-class town and later schooled in New York City, I could not even claim the black heritage of Southerners whose families still maintained Southern ties in North Carolina, Georgia, even the godforsaken state of Mississippi. The black families I was raised around came from Maine or Boston, like my father. They baked codfish, stewed chicken, and ate boiled dinners. Down home to my relatives went as far south as Rhode Island, not the Deep South depicted in Stowe's *Uncle Tom's Cabin.*

The influx of particular kind of slaves in America began with the advent of "rice Negroes" almost 235 years before the end of slavery with the arrival of a Dutch ship to Virginia. They would later be identified as Gullah, a scion of slaves who were captured and brought to America specifically because they knew how to cultivate and grow rice crops.[3]

"Sails furled, flag drooping at her rounded stern, she rode the tide in from the sea. She was a strange ship, indeed, by all accounts, a frightening ship, a ship of mystery," wrote J. Saunders Redding, a black writer describing the landing of a slave ship to North America in 1619. Redding's observation documents the arrival of a slave ship to the English settlement called Jamestown. "Whether she was trader, privateer or man-of-war, no one knows. Through her bulwarks black mouth cannon yawned. The flag she flew was Dutch; her crew a motley [bunch]. She came, she traded, and shortly afterwards was gone. Probably no ship in modern history has carried a more portentous freight. Her cargo? Twenty slaves," Redding wrote in his book, *They Came in Chains: Americans from Africa.*[4] If accurate, Redding's narrative captures something larger than the arrival of the first slaves to the New World; it also marks the seeding of African American culture.

"There is not a country in world history in which racism has been more important, for so long a time as the United States," said historian Howard Zinn in the opening pages of his book, *A People's History of the United States, 1492–Present.*[5] "And the problem of 'the color line' as W.E.B. Du Bois put it in the 1920s, is still with us. Slavery developed quickly into a regular institution and became the basis for the standard labor relation of blacks to whites in the New World. With it developed that special racial feeling—whether hatred, or contempt, or pity, or patronization that accompanied the inferior position of blacks in America for the next 350 years—that combination of inferior status and derogatory thought we call racism," Zinn said.

Unshackled by civil war that freed millions of black slaves by the year 1865, living generations of former slaves, their children and grandchildren, then began an historic cultural migration to flee feudal America in the South. It was a journey into the future that would take the greater part of the next century.

Stripped of their bonds, ex-slaves were left culturally, socially, and economically naked at the close of a war. Slaves found themselves free but unprotected by paternalism and protections against violence by masters who had valued them as personal property. Millions of emancipated slaves and their families suddenly became prey to widespread economic and social discrimination, vigilante violence, and a justice system that saw them as anything but equals. Laws passed in almost every Southern state aimed to control and restrict the lives of blacks. The widespread segregation that ensued effectively barred Negroes from voting, purchasing property, access to adequate public schooling, employment, and to the other necessities needed for any meaningful pursuit of happiness that was guaranteed by the Constitution.

By the end of World War I, millions of black tenant farmers and laborers who could not vote in Mississippi, Virginia, South Carolina, and other Southern states, boarded railroad trains by the thousands each week bound for new lives in northern cities.

This move from life on the plantations in the South to futures in urban cities became one of the great sagas in modern American history. It was a tale of two countries, two Americas, one black, the other white, one free, the other perpetually seeking freedom. It was an exodus that seemed to have been plucked whole from the pages of second book of the Old Testament in the Bible, the universal story of the Israelites escape from Egypt. Shaking off the taint of slavery and the stench of a corrupt reconstruction, these black farmers, fishermen, and their wives set off to do for themselves what President Abe Lincoln's army and a nation of laws had failed to achieve for them through the Emancipation Proclamation. They left cotton fields in Georgia, orange groves in Florida, and tenant farms of Arkansas to begin the impossible task of reconstructing their lives at the turn of the twentieth century, just three decades after the emancipation. They took jobs in meatpacking plants, donned the uniforms of railroad porters, and red-capped baggage handlers. Bean pickers from South Carolina became housemaids in Chicago, autoworkers in Detroit, and sewing-machine operators in the garment district of New York City.

Their exodus became known as the Great Migration and was first chronicled in the pages of a magazine called *Survey Graphic*, a journal that covered social change throughout the world. A special Harlem edition of the magazine was published in 1925, edited by Howard University professor Alain Locke.

"A railroad ticket and a suitcase, like a Baghdad carpet, transport the Negro peasant from the cotton-field and farm to the heart of the most complex urban civilization," Locke wrote. "Here in the mass, he must and does survive a jump of two generations in social economy and of a century and more in civilization. Like camp followers who traipsed from place to place behind an advancing army, the black poets, students, artists, professionals, and thinkers came too."[6] This black migration was numerically smaller than the migration of European immigrants who had come to America from villages in Ireland, Italy, Germany, and Russia in earlier decades. However, the impact black migrants had on the cities where they landed were no less significant, Locke said.

The influx of so many Negroes almost immediately transformed sections of cities such as Harlem and the South Side of Chicago into something more than city blocks that had suddenly become "unaccountably full of black people." This represented a dramatic change in American demographics that transformed cities. Communities of different kinds of black people, who found themselves together with other black people all suddenly empowered with the strength of having common goals with their neighbors.

Previously, ex-slaves were strictly under the thumbs of Southern authorities by black laws enacted throughout the South between 1865 and 1897. These restrictive laws were passed everywhere and were bolstered as the laws of the land when the U.S. Supreme Court institutionalized them in a famous Louisiana court decision, *Plessy v. Ferguson* in 1896.

Homer Plessy had been arrested in Louisiana for refusing to sit in a "colored" section of a train. He lost the case in an appeal to the high court, which ruled in 1896 that separate but allegedly equal public facilities for blacks and whites were constitutional. This institutionalized segregation became law throughout the United States.

At the beginning of the twentieth century, blacks everywhere were refused service at restaurants, movie houses, public beaches, libraries, bathrooms, hotels, and public accommodations of all kinds. This deep-seated discrimination was practiced in the North as well as the South. But it was most stringent in the South where black laws based on the *Plessy* court decision were passed legitimizing this kind of bigotry.

The so-called Negro, forced to pay taxes in the Southern communities where they lived, could be arrested for even trying to use public bathrooms, train cars, schools, colleges, libraries, or movie houses that were reserved for "whites only." These were generally called Jim Crow laws, named after a second-rate, white minstrel show actor named Thomas Dartmouth who popularized a slow-talking, ragged blackface character in the 1830s who became known as Jim Crow. Appearing in blackface with various foolish sidekicks like Jim Dandy, Zip Coon, and Sambo, Dartmouth's Jim Crow shows played in London, Dublin, and opened in New York in 1832. By 1838, the name Jim Crow itself became a slur for the way blacks were treated in America.

By 1914, on the strength of the *Plessy* decision, every Southern state had passed Black Codes, or Jim Crow laws.

CHAPTER TWO

Raisins in the Sun

A dainty, light-skinned, little man from Philadelphia embodied a peculiar scion of black intellectual in America. Alain Locke, sometimes called the architect of a period in black history that became known as the Harlem Renaissance, became the quintessential image of this kind of new Negro.

A professor at Howard University in Washington, DC, Locke traveled north to New York in the winter of 1924 to preside over a dinner sponsored by a magazine called *Opportunity*, owned and financed by the National Urban League in Harlem. The National Urban League, which has played so pivotal a role in the twentieth-century freedom movement, grew out of that spontaneous grassroots movement for freedom and opportunity that came to be called the Black Migrations. The brutal system of economic, social, and political oppression the white South quickly adopted after the *Plessy* decision transformed what had been a trickle of African Americans northward into a flood. Those newcomers to the North soon discovered they had not escaped racial discrimination by fleeing north.

Locke came to New York to preside over what would become the first of many events where black writers would be introduced to some of the most influential publishers in the world. Soft spoken, Locke was still a commanding speaker. That winter, he spoke at the Civic Club dinner downtown to claim a small piece of literary turf in New York for himself and a small group of black leaders who had proclaimed themselves as the inner circle of what they called the New Negro Movement.

For some, the event marked the formal launch of the New Negro Movement Locke had come to promote, what others said it was the beginning of the Harlem Renaissance, that sudden blooming of Negro visual, performing and literary art in New York.[1] This small clique realized that seismic cultural changes occurring in Harlem had created an unprecedented opportunity to use art to recast the Negro as a deserving, worthwhile American, no longer to be seen as just the downtrodden descendants of slaves. It was a righteous idea that would be carried out in fits and starts over the next three or four decades but not always by these noblemen who had conceived it.

The so-called Harlem Renaissance Locke attempted to nurture is an elusive phenomenon sometimes difficult to pinpoint along the continuum of American or African American history. Shots are fired at the start of war and the start of that war can easily be calculated by tracing who fired that first shot. Legislation is passed or rejected by winning or losing votes and the passage or failure of law too can be calculated by merely counting those votes. What happened in Harlem and when it began is a more difficult task and the dates depend largely upon whom you ask.

It is now clear to me that the so-called Harlem Renaissance was not merely the sudden and brief blossoming of black creative expression in New York City. It was probably an aesthetic, a state of mind that flowed on many levels simultaneously, producing good and bad art, music, poetry, and literature that was sometimes useful propaganda as well as art, sometimes not so useful. Some of it was predominately a black thing for blacks, but much of it grew beyond the boundaries of race and culture, becoming all-American jazz, American short stories with American characters who happened to be black, transcending the clichés of gender and ethnic literature of previous generations.

"Like other historical watersheds, the Harlem Renaissance has no easily demarcated beginning or ending," notes Dallas scholar Matthew Henry. "Certainly, much of its influence has been felt in the arts to this very day," Henry wrote in a 1999 edition of the *Richland College Navigator*.

"It is safe to say that after the end of the First World War, there emerged for African Americans an optimism (that was) unprecedented in American history. Between 1910 and 1930 ... a host of talented young artists ... also converged upon Harlem. This helped fuel an era of artistic exuberance exemplified by black writers who satirized their social, economic and intellectual peers, and who laughed at themselves and their neighbors."

What had been called a sudden explosion of self-expression was really the result of a slow process of self-actualization. While art seemed to take center stage, there was a simultaneous outburst of political doctrines, there was the formation of civil rights organizations like the Urban League, and there were a number of novels and musicals published and performed alongside the labor unrests and political organizing. There were a burst of published short stories and poems about black life in America by black writers, some of which were all products of a process that had taken centuries to develop in the same way a volcano suddenly erupts after years of lying dormant. Poets, historians, philosophers, folklorists, ministers, street orators, politicians, and composers heard the same bang and they all had different explanations for what had occurred in Harlem.

What was also known as the Jazz Age to some was Bible prophecy coming true for others, blacks arriving in Harlem fulfilled some sort of Promised Land prophesy. One white man called it nigger heaven.[2] While some called it a renaissance in Harlem, others proclaimed it marked the coming of this New Negro Movement for which Alain Locke became one of the many to voice its varied doctrines. The freedom engendered by the great numbers who had gathered there made it seem like a sudden explosion.

Born in 1886, Locke taught philosophy at Howard University and was educated at Harvard. He wore expertly tailored suits and carried himself with the dignity of the scholar the world came to know. Locke, the first and at the time the only American Negro to get a Rhodes' scholarship at Oxford, was a fitting masters of ceremony for the august occasion over which he presided that cold night in March at the Civic Club. Locke belonged to the gentry of educated blacks in America, the "Talented Tenth" as another scholar with similar credentials called this scion of black men.[3] It described more than the intellectual abilities of this small cadre of predominantly fair-skinned, college-educated black men and women like Locke. It denoted the pedigree of upper-class Negroes who saw themselves as superior to masses of mostly darker skinned, uneducated blacks. They became the self-appointed, designated black leaders of the race.

It was from these ranks that self-anointed race leaders emerged and felt it their right to speak for all black people in America. It was to this gentry that the rest of society turned when they needed or wanted to talk to or about Negroes in America. Other Negroes, not of this breed, upset this arrangement by drawing crowds of their own, particularly on streets like Lenox Avenue or 135th Street in Harlem. Some could pack Madison Square Garden with throngs of ordinary black men and women eager to hear their revolutionary speeches.

Locke had quietly come to New York that night to deliver more than just a polite speech at the *Opportunity Magazine* dinner. The dinner was held to celebrate publication of the first novel of Jessie Fauset, who worked for another scholar, W.E.B. Du Bois, as literary editor for *The Crisis*, the magazine Du Bois had started in Harlem. Part of Locke's mission was to announce the birth of the New Negro to the nation. Therefore, it was no accident that the small audience assembled to hear Locke that night contained media giants who could put Locke's words into print in the most widely read newspapers and magazines in the world.

Locke and the black scholars he represented were the real oddities in American culture at the time. The hotel clerks, burly dockworkers down on the Hudson River piers, or house cleaners were more representative of thousands of beleaguered Negroes living in Harlem uptown then. Locke and Du Bois had less in common with this horde of the working class than with the Europeans Locke had studied with at Oxford and at the University of Berlin.

But when he rose to make his remarks that evening, this fastidiously dressed academic had become the unwitting ambassador of a raucous movement that even the most astute intellectual of his group could not sway or exert any control over.

Jervis Anderson, a staff writer for *The New Yorker* magazine, noted that "Locke's fine suit and manners together with his education and his upper-middle class background, made him an unlikely enthusiast of a movement in proletarian writing, one estranged from the sensibilities of his own class and upbringing."[4] The Harlem that Locke seemed to speak of and for that night was really much more than the exotic community of bars, cabarets, and prostitutes that downtowners had begun to notice and enjoy.

Harlem had become what writer Ralph Ellison called an outpost of American optimism. Locke and the other intellectuals who realized this too, used the occasion of this dinner to proclaim themselves spokesmen for what he had rightly called "the first fruits of the Negro Renaissance."

"The old Negro had long become more of a myth than a man," Locke would later write in a series of essays and a book he also called *The New Negro*. "The old Negro, we must remember was a creature of moral debate and historical controversy. He has been a stock figure perpetuated as an historical fiction partly in innocent sentimentalism, partly in deliberate reactionism ... so in the mind of America, the Negro has been more of a formula than a human being, something to be argued about, condemned or defended, to be 'kept down,' or 'in his place,' or 'helped up,' to be worried with or worried over, harassed or patronized, a social bogey or social burden. The New Negro had somehow wrestled himself free of this image, breaking the grip of prejudice," Locke wrote.[5]

This invention of the New Negro was perceived as a spiritual emancipation from the restrictive black laws that kept Negroes in the same place they had always been in for centuries. As if by magic, Locke said, the twin yokes of fear and intimidation suffered by the old Negro were suddenly broken in the first two decades of the twentieth century by the mere force of determination and a great exodus north so many had undertaken, he realized.

The New Negro Movement and the Harlem Renaissance were political and cultural reflections of the same yearning for authentic changes in the Negro's self-image and self-expressions. Locke seemed to be touting both of these things in his speech that night.

"The days of aunties, uncles and mammies is equally gone," Locke wrote. "Uncle Tom and Sambo have passed on. . . . The popular melodrama has about played itself out, and it is time to scrap the fictions, garret the bogeys and settle down to a realist facing of facts," Locke wrote.[6]

As eloquently as Locke's pronouncements seemed to his audience that night, his sentiments quickly drew fire in the very center of the cultural and political community he claimed to represent. The New Negro whose existence he had announced that night was not all that new. The phrase itself was a moniker, which he had borrowed from more militant factions of the black community, including a man named Marcus Garvey and from radical newspaper editors who used it as a rallying cry against lynching, segregation, and the widespread discrimination in employment and housing. The so-called New Negro Movement and the Universal Negro Improvement Association (UNIA)[7] Movement that Garvey had invented were both declarations of independence on behalf of black Americans, but they were just on opposite ends of the same political spectrum.

Locke was preaching assimilation by suggesting a new Negro was just another worthy American waiting for white America to recognize his worth through artistic achievement, one writer of the time said. Locke knew this message coming from an educated Negro like himself, delivered with all of the tact and polish a moderate like him could muster, could easily be popularized by the editors at *Vanity Fair*, *The Nation*, and *Esquire* magazines with just a nod of acceptance from the editors who came to dinner that night. "The New Negro Movement which Locke represented was an educated, middle-class response to the same changes that drew the masses to Garvey's ideas and programs," says Amrijit Singh, a writer for the *Oxford Companion to African American Literature*.[8]

This excitement was not limited to Harlem. Downtown columnists like Carl Van Vechten began writing about Harlem's nightlife, cultural activities, and other events in the *New York Times*. Locke oversaw publication of the *Harlem Number of Survey Graphic* in 1925. Other mainstream newspapers also began writing stories about Harlem and in no time at all, Harlem was in vogue.

"So, well-meaning, vapid whites from downtown New York came by bus, subway, or in limousines, to see for themselves these Negroes who wrote poetry and fiction and painted pictures," wrote Levi Hubert, a WPA folklorist. "They came to listen, and to marvel. Over cups of tea, Park Avenue and Central Park West went into raptures over these geniuses, later dragging rare specimens of the genus Homo Africanus downtown for exhibition before their friends. Bustling, strong-minded matrons, in Sutton Place, on The Drive, even on staid Fifth Avenue, sent out informal notes and telephone invitations."

"There will be present a few artistic Negroes. It's really the thing. They recite with such feeling, and when they sing—such divine tones. Imagine a colored person playing Debussy and Chopin."[9]

Uptown, black millionaires and business people who now lived in Harlem too hosted literary salons and poetry readings on the same block where gambling kingpin and associate of New York mobsters, Casper Holstein's Turf Club was located. Literary study groups sprang up in cafes and furnished flats.

The poetry that was read here wasn't always the polished verse that appeared in *Opportunity* or *The Crisis*. The clubs uptown played experimental rags, unknown melodies were invented on the spot and played on Stride pianos, and singers whaled about the plight of being wronged by lovers and leavers. These were the real voices of Harlem and the authentic content of what they said was intoxicating.

It was seen everywhere from the pews of store front churches to the cabarets and newsstands where any number of magazines and newspapers written by blacks about other blacks all over the world could be purchased by anyone. The music, the dances, and the civic organizations all belonged to them. Collectively, all of these things were images of black life in America as it really was and lots of people, black and white, were moved by its authenticity.

This realism and the willingness of a few to embrace it would later help erase long-standing stereotypes of contented, docile, or ignorant blacks in the decades between the 1920s and 1950. Publishing it, painting it, and making it into music for public consumption marked the first time real black idioms, dialects, and the different ways American black folks were portrayed accurately. The real images of countrified men and women new to the city, rent parties, and janitors who comingled with the words of emerging blues singers like Ethel Waters and Bessie Smith were new in America. Stories and books about them were being written by black writers and read by millions of mostly white readers in the pages of *The Atlantic*, *Harpers*, *Scribner's*, *The Nation*, and other magazines.

"Harlem rocked," as Arna Bontemps said in his introduction to *Not without Laughter*, a novel by Langston Hughes. "Bessie Smith and Ethel Waters sang in dark underground places where one could buy gin in those prohibition years," Bontemps said. "Afternoons as well as midnights, kids on Lenox and Seventh Avenues invented camel walks, black bottoms, and Charlestons. It was the next thing to Camelot to be young and a poet in the Harlem of those days . . . Langston was strolling among his kind like a happy prince whose time had come."[10]

CHAPTER THREE

A History of New York Activism

Although always restricted to specific sections of the city, Negroes have lived in New York City since 1626, according to *New York Panorama: A Portrait of Harlem*[1] that was commissioned and sponsored the Federal Writers' Project of 1937 and written by two novelists, Richard Wright and Claude McKay.[2] Wright and McKay would become literary lions of both the Harlem Renaissance period and later in wider American literary circles.[3]

In 1930, according to the census, 327,706 Negroes lived in New York, the largest single concentration of Negroes anywhere in the world. Throughout the centuries, black residents of New York exhibited progressive, antiestablishment, and radical leanings.

In the early years of the city, Negroes in New York understood the benefits of fraternal lodges, churches, and mutual aid societies in their social and educational life. This trend began in the nineteenth century and continued well into the next century when the number of blacks grew. With slavery outlawed in the state in 1827, the city's Negroes were largely free men. To capitalize on their growing numbers, most belonged to the New York African Society for Mutual Relief. When they were refused membership in all-white lodges, the Negroes quickly banded together, forming their own lodges like the Philomathean Lodge of the Grand Order of Odd Fellows. In a merging of abolition groups, the Moral Reform Societies was formed in the mid-1840s. As these freemen gained a strong foothold for their own civil rights in New York, their participation in abolitionist activities grew from intermittent outbursts to planned movements.

"A number of New York Negroes were ardent and prominent workers in the abolitionist cause," the writers' project guide to New

York said. "In 1827, nearly four years before the appearance of William Lloyd Garrison's *Liberator,* a group gathered in the home of M. Boston Crummell and launched the first Negro newspaper in America, *Freedom's Journal,* under the editorship of John Russwurm and the Rev. Samuel E. Cornish. This journal not only helped to shape the ideas of Negroes on the burning question of slavery, but also appealed to many anti-slavery whites and influenced the policies of the abolition societies that were organized soon after."[4]

In subsequent years, several protest publications were launched by New York Negroes. These included *The Genius of Freedom, The Mirror of Liberty* and several sarcastic pamphlets, including one promoting the work of the Vigilance Committee, a group organized by the New York Reform Society and credited with aiding hundreds of slaves through the Underground Railroad. These fugitives included former slave Frederick Douglass, who found shelter in New York with Dr. Reese Ruggles, one of the early organizers of the network of safe houses and farms collectively called the Underground Railroad. Douglass went on to become one of the most famous antislavery advocates of his time, giving antislavery speeches throughout the United States and Europe.[5]

A class of prominent black agitators, orators, and publishers had firmly established themselves in New York by the 1840s. These included Anti-Slavery Society lecturer Samuel Ringgold Ward, son of fugitive slaves; J.W.C. Pennington, author of *A Text Book of the Origin and History of the Colored People,*[6] Charles Bennett Ray, who published the weekly *Colored American.* These New York dissenters were joined by two of the most famous antislavery agitators in history, Harriet Tubman, who brought slaves out of border states and Sojourner Truth, who became prominent in the antislavery struggle and later in the woman's suffrage movement. In 2016, the U.S. Treasury Department acknowledged Tubman's struggles by putting her image on the face of the U.S. $20 bill.

The names of New York-based protesters against slavery during this time read like the Who's Who list of the antislavery movement. James Birney, who freed slaves in Kentucky, became secretary of the American Anti-Slavery Society in New York; Horace Greeley, editor of the *New York Tribune,* worked side by side with black activist in New York. Others included: Richard Hildreth, historian and author of the first antislavery novel *The Slave: or Memoirs of Archy Moore;*[7] Charles A. Dana, editor of *The New York Sun*; Sydney Howard Gay, an agent of the Underground Railroad and editor of the *Anti-Slavery*

Standard, a weekly newspaper; William and John Jay, two prominent lawyers and antislavery jurists; Theodore Weld, one of the most tireless workers in the Anti-Slavery Society, according to public records; Angelina Grimke, a frequent speaker at the antislavery auxiliaries in New York; and the Tappan brothers, Arthur and Lewis, philanthropists and generous contributors to the antislavery movement activities in New York. These efforts were quelled by the passage of the Fugitive Slave Act that prompted proponents of slavery to begin sending slaves found in New York back to the South, forcing this hotbed of antislavery activity in New York to relocate to Canada and Europe.

The plight of blacks in New York during this period grew steadily worse, resulting in several race riots beginning in 1900. Hundreds of blacks were lynched throughout the United States. This prompted a surge in black leadership everywhere, but it was particularly strong in New York where black businessmen banded together and the *Colored American* newspaper was launched in New York by Fred R. Moore. As unemployment among blacks who had to compete for jobs with newly arrived immigrants rose, the Negro in New York began to move steadily northward uptown toward Harlem. The experience, taste, and temperament for protests moved North too as New York-born Negroes mingled with the sudden influx of Southern Negroes fleeing Southern roots for northern cities like New York. When nine black Alabama teenagers were accused of raping two white women on a train in 1931, a long effort to defend and free them began in Harlem, according to Wright and McKay.[8] The Scottsboro Boys, as the case was called, led to a landmark set of legal cases involving all white juries, rushed trials, disruptive lynch mobs, and frame-up cases against black defendants in many states.

One of the chief proponents to abolish slavery came from former slave Timothy T. Fortune, editor of several influential newspapers in New York. In 1884, Fortune wrote a scathing critique of the widespread racial devastation he saw in the South in the years following the Civil War and later during the Reconstruction years. The essay, titled "Black and White, Land, Labor, and Politics of the South," was published in the *New York Globe* where Fortune was the managing editor.[9] Writing with meticulous detail, Fortune laid out the economic slavery he saw throughout the South decades after the Emancipation Proclamation had allegedly ended legal slavery.

What Fortune described shed new light on more than a half century of homegrown terrorism that fueled what historians called "the Great Migration" of blacks from the South to the North. Fortune's commentary brings into sharp focus a neglected legacy of slavery—an exodus only rivaled by biblical lore. The great exodus was peopled by generations of refugees of slavery left to languish in the South after the war at the hands of former masters and their families in the South. Abandoned by federal troops and the law, these former slaves were left unprotected from violence and economic exploitation for decades after slavery.

The flight from the South began sometime in the nineteenth century when the first generation of freed slaves and their descendants realized they could not survive life in the post-war South. Like the ancient Israelites who fled Egypt, black families fled to North to escape a feudal legacy. A colleague at Temple University once speculated that it was this exodus that marked the true beginning of what would later be called the Harlem Renaissance.

After the Civil War, Fortune wrote:

The government of the United States confiscated as "contra-band of war" the slave population of the South, but left it to the unrepentant rebel a far more valuable species of property. The slave, the perishable wealth, was confiscated to the government and then manumitted (released) it; but property in land, the wealth which perishes not nor can fly away, and which had made the institution of slavery possible, was left as the heritage of the robber who had not hesitated to lift his iconoclastic hand against the liberties of his country. The bar of feudal Europe would have been paralyzed with astonishment at the leniency of the conquering invader who should take from him his slave, subject to mutation, and leave him his landed possessions which are as fixed as the Universe of Nature.

He would ask no more advantageous concession. But the United States took the slave and left the thing which gave birth to chattel slavery and which is now fast giving birth to industrial slavery; a slavery more excruciating in its exactions, more irresponsible in its machinations than that other slavery, which I once endured.

The chattel slave-holder must, to preserve the value of his property, feed, clothe and house his property, and give it proper medical attention when disease or accident threatened its life. But industrial slavery requires no such care. The new slave-holder is only solicitous of obtaining the maximum of labor for the minimum of cost. He does not regard the man as of any con-sequence when he can no longer produce. Having worked him to death, or ruined his constitution and robbed him of his labor, he turns him out upon the world to live upon the charity of mankind or to die of inattention and starvation. He knows that it profits him nothing to waste time and money upon a disabled industrial slave. The multitude of laborers from which he can recruit his necessary laboring force is so enormous that solicitude on his part for one that falls by the wayside would be a gratuitous expenditure of humanity and charity which the world is too intensely selfish and materialistic to expect of him.

Here he forges wealth and death at one and the same time. He could not do this if our social system did not confer upon him a monopoly of the soil from which subsistence must be derived, because the industrial slave, given an equal opportunity to produce for himself, would not produce for another. On the other hand the large industrial operations, with the multitude of laborers from which (economist) Adam Smith declares employers grow rich, as far as this applies to the soil, would not be possible, since the vast volume of increased production brought about by the industry of the multitude of co-equal small farmers would so reduce the cost price of food products as to destroy the incentive to speculation in them, and at the same time utterly destroy the necessity or the possibility of famines, such as those which have from time to time come upon the Irish people.

There could be no famine, in the natural course of things, where all had an opportunity to cultivate as much land as they could wherever they found any not already under cultivation by someone else. It needs no stretch of the imagination to see what a startling tendency the announcement that all vacant land was free to settlement upon condition of cultivation would have to the depopulation of over-crowded cities like New York, Baltimore and Savannah, where the so-called pressure of population upon subsistence has produced a hand-to-hand fight for existence by the wage-workers in every avenue of industry.

This is no fancy picture. It is a plain, logical deduction of what would result from the restoration to the people of that equal chance in the race of life which every man has a right to expect, to demand, and to exact as a condition of membership of organized society. The wag (rogue) who started the "forty acres and a mule" idea among the black people of the South was a wise fool; wise in that he enunciated a principle which every argument of sound policy should have dictated . . . the forty acres could only be property if it was cultivate; and not to simply designed to impose upon the credulity and ignorance of his victims. But the justness of the "forty acre" donation cannot be controverted.

In the first place, the slave had earned this miserable stipend from the government by two hundred years of unrequited toil; and, secondly, as a free man, he was inherently entitled to so much of the soil of his country as would suffice to maintain him in the freedom thrust upon him. To tell him he was a free man, and at the same time shut him off from free access to the soil upon which he had been reared, without a penny in his pocket, and with an army of children at his coat-tail some of his reputed wife's children being the illegitimate offspring of a former inhuman master was to add insult to injury.[10]

Eight years later in 1892, Fortune sheltered an exile from Memphis in New York who had literally fled that city to escape a lynch mob that burned down her business and sought her as a fugitive who had safely taken flight to the safety of New York.

Ida B. Wells-Barnett was part owner of the *Memphis Free Speech*. The newspaper printed a story denouncing the lynching of three of Wells's friends accused of raping three white women in May 1892. The article angered Memphis whites largely because Wells's story exposed the often used but seldom proven claim that rapes of white women by black men was epidemic. Memphis whites stormed the newspaper offices after the story ran, ransacked it looking for Barnett and destroyed the newspaper's press. She had fled to New York and found crusading journalist Timothy Fortune, who was the editor of *The New York Age*. Fortune ran Barnett's lynching exposé in the *Age* on June 25, 1892.

Southern Horrors: Lynch Law in All Its Phases

By Ida B. Wells-Barnett

The greater part of what is contained in these pages was published in the *New York Age,* June 25, 1892, in explanation of the editorial which the Memphis whites considered sufficiently infamous to justify the destruction of my paper, *The Free Speech*. . . . Requests have come from all parts of the country that [the story] be issued in pamphlet form. The noble effort of the ladies of New York and Brooklyn . . . enabled me to comply with this request and give the world a true, unvarnished account of the causes of lynch law in the South.

... It is with no pleasure I have dipped my hands in the corruption here exposed. Somebody must show that the Afro-American race is more sinned against than sinning.... The awful death-roll that Judge Lynch is calling every week is appalling, not only because of the lives it takes, the rank cruelty and outrage to the victims, but because of the prejudice it fosters and the stain it places against the good name of a weak race. The Afro-American is not a bestial race. If this work can contribute in any way toward proving this ... and at the same time arouse the conscience of the American people to a demand for justice to every citizen, and punishment by law for the lawless, I shall feel I have done my race a service. Other considerations are of minor importance.

IDA B. WELLS, New York City, Oct. 26, 1892

The Offense

[On] Wednesday evening May 24, 1892, the city of Memphis was filled with excitement. Editorials in the daily papers of that date caused a meeting to be held in the Cotton Exchange Building; a committee was sent for the editors of The Free Speech, an Afro-American journal published in that city, and the only reason the open threats of lynching that were made were not carried out was because they [the editors] could not be found. The cause of all this commotion was the following editorial published in the *Free Speech* May 21, 1892, the Saturday previous.

"Eight negroes lynched since last issue of the Free Speech, one at Little Rock, Ark., last Saturday morning where the citizens broke into the penitentiary and got their man; three near Anniston, Ala., one near New Orleans; and three at Clarksville, Ga., the last three for killing a white man, and five on the same old racket—the new alarm about raping white women. The same program of hanging, then shooting bullets into the lifeless bodies was carried out to the letter. Nobody in this section of the country believes the old thread-bare lie that Negro men rape white women. If Southern white men are not careful, they will overreach themselves and public sentiment will have a reaction; a conclusion will then be reached which will be very damaging to the moral reputation of their women."[11]

The Negro Problem

Eleven years later in 1903, leading black intellectuals wrote a collection of essays assessing the economic and social status of the Negro in

America. In one essay, *New York Age* editor Timothy Fortune said one of the problems Negroes had yet to deal with is the assimilation of mixed race Negroes like himself into life among mainstream America. He said it was a scandalous wound left and long neglected in these early days after slavery. That assimilation process would continue to taint blacks, even during the heyday of the renaissance when blacks seeking acceptance in mainstream, white society were branded as assimilationists, an epithet. Today, those writers, musicians, and entertainers who assimilated would be called cross over artist, not race traders.

What was scandalous about this question of assimilation? It was a code name when used by black folks to identify a race trader, someone ashamed of being black. Truthfully, it was a widely discussed topic behind closed doors in Harlem salons when a mixed-race man or woman was suspected of passing or trying to pass themselves off as being white. It was scandalous because passing as white had always been an indelible, unforgivable crime during slavery in white communities. Quietly, every black and white knew that mixed-race citizens were most likely the product of rapes and forced prostitution of black women during slavery. Obviously the progeny of a mixed-race family himself during slavery, Fortune said integrating millions of light-skinned blacks into mainstream American would take at least another century.

The whispers in Harlem and elsewhere about mixed-race persons was the genesis for the classic tale of the tragic mulatto, a stereotypical fictional character of nineteenth- and twentieth-century American literature. Typically, the mulattoes were assumed to be unhappy because they failed to fit into a white or a black world. While no accurate census figures were available for the number of mulatto citizens there were in 1892, some figures claimed as many as one-third of a black population in some parts of the country were mixed-race citizens. Fortune predicted the tragic mulatto would be the genesis of a new breed of American, a strain that would not be assimilated into mainstream life for at least a 100 years. Was this the "New Negro" Fortune's contemporaries like Alain Locke or Du Bois were forecasting?

Was the tragic mulatto to become the embodiment of a spiritual emancipation of the Negro? Was this the evolutionary leap writer Ralph Ellison would later tell a U.S. Senate subcommittee would be seen in large numbers one day in Harlem? Remember, that Ellison said, "We are a new racial type blended right here on this continent ... what makes us Negroes is not race so much as our having shared a special cultural and political experience in the institution of slavery."[12]

One hundred-and-five years after Fortune's essay was published, the son of an American Jewish woman and an African man, Barack Obama, became the first acknowledged president of the United States of racially mixed parentage. Fortune was a visionary.

As Harlem grew to become an almost natural hotbed of political and social organizing activities. A confluence of black organizations, both national and local, that organized in Harlem brought various schools of thought and action to the community. These ranged from organizations favoring passive resistance, colonization, salvation through art and joy to legal, political, and economic action organizations.

Among these, the National Association for the Advancement of Colored People was organized in 1909 and set up shop in Harlem. The following year, W.E.B. Du Bois became director of publicity and research and the editor of *The Crisis*, an independent magazine sanction but not controlled by the organization. According to Wright and McKay:

> In his words, the aim of the association was to create an organization so effective and so powerful that when discrimination and injustice touched one Negro, it would touch 12,000,000 ... an organization that would work ceaselessly to make Americans know that the so-called Negro problem is simply one phase of the vaster problem of democracy in America, and that those who wish freedom and justice for their country must wish it for every black citizen.[13]

In subsequent years, the organization and its zeal for legal defense of blacks became known throughout the nation. Over time, the most prominent legal defense team ever assembled to tackle civil rights causes gathered in Harlem and would eventually take on and win landmark decisions before the U.S. Supreme Court.

Almost simultaneously, the National Urban League was organized in 1911 and set up shop in Harlem to assist tens of thousands of Southern migrants relocating to Harlem. The organization was initially organized to investigate social conditions among arriving blacks under the auspices of many Negro social workers. "More than any other social agency, the league has fought for a better community life among Negroes, better housing conditions, and against crime, disease and unemployment," Wright and McKay said.[14] In 1918, the New

York Urban League was set up as a separate branch of the national organization to fight for better working conditions, exposing unfair labor practices, fostering unionism, and aiding in the education of workers in the lower and unskilled ranks.

The organization also launched *Opportunity Magazine*, a publication devoted to interpret the changing social and economic life for blacks throughout America. In subsequent years, the magazine recruited black writers through literary prizes and lured them to come to Harlem too where they formed well-known collectives of black artists.

Joining this organizing activity, the National Negro Congress was organized in Harlem to safeguard the social, economic, and political equality of blacks. This federation of black organizations unified member groups to become a watchdog of trade unions.

By the late 1930s, black fraternal organizations became the most dominant form of organizing in Harlem. "They are motivated by the need for mutual aid and companionship," Wright and McKay said. "There are Negro Elk, Odd Fellow, Mason, Pythian, Woodmen and Philomathean lodges in Harlem whose large membership makes possible the maintenance of mountain homes, bands, athletic leagues and summer camps."[15]

The Brotherhood of Sleeping Car Porters was the strongest national organization formed in Harlem as early as 1929 with a national membership of 6,000 members throughout the United States and headquartered in Harlem. In 1929, this first black union organization became affiliated with the American Federation of Labor and in 1936, it was granted an international charter.

"Since the depression and the inception of the Committee for Industrial Organizations, there is hardly a trade or profession in Harlem that is not organized," Wright and McKay said. "Barbers, clerks, laundry workers, newspapermen, bartenders, teachers and domestic workers have all formed unions for mutual protection," defenses blacks outside of New York did not generally have but knew about because of the proliferation of a vibrant black press in New York. "Most of these unions were affiliated with the Negro Labor Committee, a representative central body that gives common guidance to Harlem's trade union activities."[16]

Harlem drew scholars of all stripes and colors and when they left New York years after their arrivals, they left a legacy of their work behind too for others to study. One of those legacies began as one branch of the massive New York Library system, the 135th Street branch. It grew into the Schomburg Center for Research in Black Culture.[17] In 1937, the collection had amassed 18,000 books, 1,500 manuscripts, numerous engravings, and specimens of primitive African art. Named after Afro-Puerto Rican scholar Arturo A. Schomburg, the center grew to five divisions: the Jean Blackwell Hutson General Research and Reference Division, the Manuscripts, Archives and Rare Books Division, the Moving Image and Recorded Sound Division, and the Photographs and Prints Division. In 1998, the Schomburg Collection was considered to hold the rarest and most useful Afro-centric artifacts of any public library in the United States, according to curators of the collection. As of 2006, it was viewed as the most prestigious archive for African American materials in the country, according to Elaine Woo, author of *A Champion of Black History*. As of 2010, the collection stood at 10 million objects and is housed in several buildings beyond the original 135th library building.

As if anticipating the thesis of this book, novelists Richard Wright and Claude McKay made a startling prediction in writing *New York Panorama: A "Portrait of Harlem"* in 1937.

"It has been said that the Negro embodies the romance of American life," they wrote. "If that is true, the romance is one whose glamor is overlaid with shadows of tragic premonition. The question of what will ultimately happen to the Negro in New York is bound up with the question of what will happen to the Negro in America."[18]

Harlem not only became Mecca, it became Mega Mecca, where exceptions to what was happening to blacks in America ripened and often became excessive and exaggerated. "Harlem flowered into a unique amusement center, and Broadway extended itself into the many side-streets," Bruce Nugent wrote in "On Harlem," as a writer for the Federal Writers' Project in 1939. "Excess was the order of the day. Satanist Aleister Crowley's devil-worship cult flourished. Bootlegging became the first industry of the land. Carl Van Vechten wrote about the Gramercy Park set and discovered Langston Hughes," Nugent wrote. "Negroes found their own interest in themselves reviving, encouraged as it was by white trailblazers. Radical news pamphlets and magazines devoted to 'the race' struggled into greater visibility. Being black began to be fashionable. ... Boom and prosperity swept over Harlem, magically heightening its already remarkable capacity ..."[19]

At 21, Arna Bontemps made his way from Los Angeles to Harlem in the fall of 1924 full of romantic dreams, he said in a remembrance written for *American Scholar* in the spring the following year.

"The first danger I recognized that fall ... was that Harlem would be too wonderful for words. Unless I was careful, I would be thrilled into silence. When we were not too busy having fun, we were shown off and exhibited and presented in scores of places, to all kinds of people," he said, "and we heard their sighs of wonder, amazement, sometimes admiration when I was whispered or announced that here was one of the 'New Negroes'."[20]

Bontemps, who authored several novels, books for juveniles and later headed the library at Fisk University, had only been out of college for six months and came to New York in search of work. Patrons of poets like the young Bontemps told him his mission was to somehow capture and bottle the authentic wildness of the Negro temperament. "The 'New Negro' was to recapture this definite, though sometimes dim quality in poetry, painting and song, by this means he must transmit it to all of America. Through us, no less, America would regain a certain value that civilization had destroyed," he wrote. "The idea intoxicated us. ... And the miracle of the whole notion was that it came so near taking root. Our group came within an inch of giving America ... at least a certain new aesthetic value. ..." But then the depression hit and the New Negroes of Harlem were not spared, Bontemps recalled. "Something was wrong. When the depression came and artists of every kind began to feel the pinch, the Harlem group was not excluded. New Negroes were scattered from Boston to Florida, from Pleasantville to Carmel-by-the-Sea, from Alabama to the pearly gates."[21] The Harlem of his youth began to wither over the next decade, and Harlem deteriorated into a slum. Still something significant from that experience lingered from that experience.

Bontemps and many other well-educated Negroes like himself were celebrated in Harlem because nowhere else on earth had such a gathering of black men and women occurred. "In an era when almost no blacks went to college, an elite group of African-American intellectuals (like Bontemps) were making significant contributions to American literature, music, and the arts," according to *The Journal of Blacks in Higher Education*. "They were redefining race relations in a still virulently racist American society."[22]

When Bontemps moved into an apartment on Fifth Avenue and 129th Street, he had unwittingly stepped into what Pulitzer Prize-winning author David Levering Lewis called a "forced phenomenon, a cultural nationalism of the parlor, institutionally encouraged and directed by the leaders of the national civil rights establishment for the paramount purpose of improving race relations in a time of extreme national backlash in large part by economic gains won by African Americans during the Great War."[23] This was the capsulized description of the Harlem Renaissance that most histories of the period deliberately missed or ignored in favor of the more raucous, fun-loving view that Bruce Nugent describes so well.

Like soldiers in an educated cadre of graduates like Bontemps, W.E.B. Du Bois called upon some 10,000 college-educated blacks in America at the time to provide leadership for Negroes. He dubbed them the "Talented Tenth" in a 1903 essay and later in an article written for *Booklover's Magazine*. Those who came to New York were promptly deployed to the broad avenues of Harlem. "The Talented Tenth were to sacrifice their personal interests and endeavors to provide leadership for the African American community," according to Juan Battle and Earl Wright, writing in the *Journal of Black Studies*.[24] Du Bois said the leadership, ideologies, and tactics of these men and women would spread throughout black communities in a few brief years and eventually lead black Americans out of feudal times that existed for them in the early decades of the twentieth century.

CHAPTER FOUR

The Arrivals

The history of the period in the early decades of the twentieth century, we now generally call the Harlem Renaissance, was in fact, no renaissance at all. The term implies the rebirth of a dormant movement or culture. African American culture had not yet been fully formed in Harlem or anywhere in the early decades of the century. It was being formed in what had first been noticed in those early decades. What was implied might more aptly be called the seeds of a long-feared social insurrection by Negroes that was sparked by circumstances of perfect storm proportions.

One of those conditions was the unrequited dream of owning land in the South. It was nearly impossible for black farmers to own land in the South. Working as farmers generally meant suffering the endless debt of sharecropping where blacks farmed land in return for a share of profits. Those profits rarely materialized. Still, most Southern blacks worked on farms they did not own in the South when another circumstance befell them in the 1890s. A boll-weevil insect blight damaged cotton crops beyond repair, making cotton farming impossible. About the same time, the South was ravaged by widespread terrorism waged against blacks by white hate groups that made living there dangerous for any black man, woman, or child.

A booming economy in the North meant jobs were plentiful, so the lure to flee the South was powerful. These circumstances created a surge to relocate that sent millions of former sharecroppers North, and Harlem was a favorite destination. Despite many literary claims about the period, this migration northward was not sudden although to many, it seemed sudden when it was first discovered around 1920. Generally, most texts say the Harlem Renaissance, or the New

Negro Movement of the period is arguably a defining moment in African literature. It was also a critical time in the social history of American blacks. Most texts covering the period generally favor highlighting this time as a period of enlightenment for black artists. But this choice is a narrow view of a widely diverse, important period in African American history. It was first seen and well documented by both black- and white-owned newspapers, magazines, and social movement leaders who lived in Harlem or Lower Manhattan. Howard University Scholar Alain Locke was among the earliest to note and write about Harlem in his 1925 essay, "The New Negro" but he was not the first. Key to the philosopher's observation was the idea that a "New Negro" was evolving in Harlem just north of Central Park somewhere between 130th and 145th Streets who had turned away from stereotypical images of ex-slaves. In Ralph Ellison's view, this idea went beyond sloganeering. While some wrote sonnets about what they saw in Harlem during those years, many who flocked there in those early decades of the century were social architects, political organizers, and community activists and not just the poets, band leaders, or piano players who began to call Harlem home.

Twenty-five years later in 1950, Locke wrote that those early years had seen the growth of "a movement that never surpassed the 'gawky' and 'pimply' stage of adolescence, one that had essentially failed in its attempt to achieve universal, objective approaches in its creation." "Overall, he concluded that perhaps he and others had 'expected too much of the Negro Renaissance',," Locke said, quoting an article in *Phylon*, the Atlanta University journal.[1] By 1950, the idea that this New Negro Movement had mainly been a brief, sudden flowering of a black artistic movement had been enshrined in major histories of the period, an unfortunate error which I found prevalent even half a century after Locke had declared the movement, he defined it, as a failure. "In his zeal to capture the younger generation's declaration of cultural independence," Jonathan S. Holloway said, writing in *The Journal of Blacks in Higher Education*, "Locke largely ignored much of the political activity that also defined this era. ... This was also an era of avant-garde political and social activism," noted Holloway, whose leaders developed and touted popular theories at the time about their activities that have also been ignored in favor of Locke's more fanciful, popular notions of a monolithic, artistic movement.[2]

When an undocumented, unknown slave escaped bondage in the American South and migrated to the Northeast, this act of an individual started what became known as the "Great Migration." This migration, first begun in the desperate attempt to flee slavery, eventually fueled an intellectual, social, and personal pursuit too—the long-standing quest for identity by every black man, woman, and child in America. In Harlem, that quest was anchored by a wide array of civic, religious, and radical fraternal organizations started by prominent black leaders who succeeded in establishing what we now know as modern African American culture.

"Why did so many Africans, southerners and West Indians flock to Harlem? They came for the same reasons that whites were also drawn to Harlem of the 1920s," Professor Manning Marable said in an interview for a Columbia University website called Columbia 250. "But ... African Americans ... were looking in part for sites where they could establish cultural institutions and construct notions of community that were spaces that they could call their own."

"And so churches, which had long been established in New York City, such as Abyssinian Baptist Church, relocated to Harlem," the late Columbia University professor of public affairs, history and African American Studies said. "Others followed suit in the nineteen-teens and twenties. So by the early 1920s, after World War I, there were a series of cultural institutions, of churches, civic associations, theater groups, clustered all around West 135th and increasingly 125th" and "the community had become thoroughly identified with African American people," Marable said.[3]

Marable said it was the establishment of the many churches or those which relocated and fraternal associations which called Harlem home that helped African Americans to begin planting the seeds of cultural identity using organizing tactics and self-help strategies long denied to their ancestors in other parts of the country. This was true down South too where blacks had to create their own communities. When their members migrated North, their institutions were reinvented again in Harlem. With this in mind, one might say there was a renaissance in Harlem of many older communities that were first established in the South, the Caribbean, and Africa and later duplicated in Harlem. While the establishment of similar communities was successful in other Northern and midwestern cities, Harlem attracted leaders whose ideas were useful for decades after Harlem no longer seemed to be in vogue. Nevertheless, the seeds for future cultural, social, and racial progress had been planted and Harlem became Camelot to many of us. To some, including novelist Ralph Ellison and my older brother and I, Harlem had an undeniable mystique for us as black men unlike any other place I have lived.

"It isn't often mentioned ... but Harlem is a place where there is a community of Negro styles," Ellison said, testifying before a U.S. Senate subcommittee on Executive Reorganization in 1966. "Harlem has its elegant side. Harlem is a place where you see the transformation of the southern idiom into a northern idiom. This is exciting in itself. Harlem is a place where our folklore is preserved and transformed," the novelist said. "It is the place where the body of Negro myth and legend thrives. It is a place where our styles, musical styles, the many styles of Negro life, find continuity and metamorphosis," said Ellison who spent most of his life in and on the borders of Harlem.[4]

"This is very important," he said, testifying on a federal panel called *The City in Crisis.* "Harlem is where a southern Negro who has a little luck, who has a little talent, can actually make himself into the man or woman of his dreams, because Harlem is a base. . . . It enhances ... what you already have, and this is inventive, this is creative."[5]

Significantly, Ellison recognized what few in his era noticed although many of the men and organizations you will read about here tried in their own unique ways to create a unique community. He said what happened in Harlem in those early decades of the last century and beyond was evolutionary, something that had not occurred before in modern times or at least not in the modern memory for black people in America.

Against the greatest odds, the Negro was reinvented in Harlem where the so-called New Negro was gradually transformed into the African American species. "We are a new racial type blended right here on this continent ... what makes us Negroes is not race so much as our having shared a special cultural and political experience in the institution of slavery," Ellison said.

"One of the things that gave rise to the Negro's transformation in Harlem is the same thing that helped slaves resist and escape slavery, the black church. The Negro church is our strongest institution," Ellison said. It was true in the South and it remained true in Harlem. "It was a moral support of the discipline against provocation which we Negroes have developed over the years."[6]

The avant-garde political and social activism Holloway noted in his 1995 *Journal of Blacks in Higher Education* essay began with the arrivals of activists and their organizations to Harlem late in the nineteenth and the early decades of the next century.

The luminaries generally credited with fostering a renaissance in Harlem like poet Langston Hughes, bandleader Duke Ellington, or Paul Robeson arrived in New York to find a community of others like themselves already established in the community and they were armed with a wide variety political and social agendas.

The Abyssinian Baptist Church was founded by 12 black women and 4 men, prosperous traders from Abyssinia (modern Ethiopia) early in the nineteenth century.[7] They fled segregated seating in the First Baptist Church of New York in 1808 and founded the Abyssinian Baptist Church that year. One-hundred years later in 1908, the church moved to Harlem from Lower Manhattan. These became known as "The Powel Years" after Pastor Adam Clayton Powell Sr. became the 17th pastor of Abyssinian in 1908. By 1920, the church had more than 2,000 members who built the existing church building on West 138th Street between Lenox and Seventh Avenues. According to the church, Powell brought his "social gospel" to the pulpit, which blended social activism with Powell's progressive leadership. It involved the church in a wide variety of community service that included the causes of the National Association for the Advancement of Colored People (NAACP) and its leadership in Harlem.

New arrivals to the streets of Harlem found the pages of widely read national newspapers and magazines owned and published by Harlem blacks. *The Crisis* was the official magazine of the NAACP, a leading social and political publication charged with keeping "a Record of the Darker Races." Edited by commentator and Harvard scholar William E.B. Du Bois, *The Crisis* was launched in 1910 from a Harlem storefront and covered a wide variety of issues related to blacks, including lynching, the "Great Migration" and related stories that reached more than 100,000 readers during its most popular years in the 1920s under Du Bois.

The stories written by fledgling writers of a literary movement, which flourished in the early 1920s found room in the pages of *The Crisis* as well as rival *Opportunity: A Journal of Negro Life* and several other publications published in New York. Launched in 1923, founding editor of *Opportunity* Charles S. Johnson aimed to "lay bare Negro life as it is." Under Johnson's leadership, *Opportunity* sought research, essay, short stories, and poetry written by then unknown poets such as Langston Hughes. Countee Cullen and Claude McKay, short story writer Dorothy West, and novelist Zora Neale Hurston. Most notably, *Opportunity* launched the writing careers of many writers through a literary contest judged by some of the most powerful editors in New York. Other Harlem publications also sponsored literary contests and attracted new talent to their publications about the same time.

Migrants new to Harlem were influenced by more politically radical publications like *The Messenger*, *The Negro World*, and the *New York Age*. These publications were edited by radical socialist, agitators, and self-defense advocates. Labor leaders A. Philip Randolph and Chandler Owen had edited a publication first meant only for black hotel workers called *Hotel Messenger*. The hotel workers' magazine ceased publication immediately after Randolph and Owen published a scathing story exposing corrupt union officials. *The Messenger* was launched in 1917 with political news and commentary with a socialist message and was popular in Harlem.

The Crisis, a monthly magazine, was founded in 1910 and it chronicled racial tensions and riots everywhere. Most notably, they covered race riots that broke out all over the country in the summer of 1919 when racially motivated riots occurred in more than three dozen cities that summer. The period was called "Red Summer" by NAACP field secretary James Weldon Johnson.

During this time, Randolph's newspaper defended the right of blacks to defend themselves and the newspaper published poet Claude McKay's now iconic poem, "If We Must Die." *If we must die—let it not be like hogs hunted and penned in an inglorious spot*, it began. It was a call to arms for blacks to fight back when attacked by mobs of white racists. This was protest literature meant to incite *The Messenger* readers into action, not to soothe them.

The Messenger was certainly a radical, widely circulated publication edited by Randolph and Owen, who was also a lecturer at the Rand School of Social Science. The school was Socialist's breeding ground for radicalizing and politicizing class consciousness in students.*The Messenger* was a natural place to express these ideas. The editors were drumming up followers for a mass movement that would later join labor unions and Socialist party organizations for political actions. A measure of how influential *The Messenger* was in New York was demonstrated when the newspaper took responsibility for rallying 25 percent of the Negro vote in the 1918 election to support the Social Party's Negro candidate for Congress in New York, the Reverend George Frazier Miller.

In rallying voters behind Miller, the newspaper wrote an editorial with the headline:

The Cause of and Remedy for Race Riots:
Revolution must come. By that we mean a complete change in the organization of society. Just as absence of industrial

democracy is productive of riots and race clashes, so the introduction of industrial democracy will be the longest step towards removing the cause. When no profits are to be made from race friction, no one will longer be interested in stirring up race prejudice. The quickest way to stop a thing or to destroy an institution is to destroy the profitableness of that institution. The capitalist system must go and its going must be hastened by the workers themselves.[8]

These denouncements were not limited to white establishment leaders. They were also leveled at black leadership in Harlem who held lucrative jobs during World War I. In January 1918, the newspaper advocated a race pride revolt against existing Negro leaders, saying they were guilty of "ignorance of the laws of society" and "ignorance of the methods by which to achieve" goals for black people.

Taking up this cause and many others like advocating self-defense against attacks by police and vigilante groups, made Randolph a ripe target for a young lawyer in the U.S. Justice Department named J. Edgar Hoover. For decades, Hoover, who later because the first director of the Federal Bureau of Investigation, tried to unsuccessfully charge Randolph, Du Bois, and many other black editors throughout the United States with sedition, saying their publications used speech to incite people to rebel against the United States. Hoover's attempts failed because sedition is a charge that can only be brought during war time and Hoover's timing never showed Randolph or Du Bois had breached that legal barrier despite repeated attempts by Hoover to charge them.

Hoover, who would go on to investigate almost every black leader to gain national prominence for most of the twentieth century, did successfully go after the one man who almost became the king of Negroes, particularly those in Harlem.

A Jamaican, Marcus Garvey arrived in New York in 1916 and quickly became acquainted with powerful, public black speakers in the city such as Hubert Harrison, the West Indian American writer, orator, educator, critic, and radical socialist. Harrison took to speaking on street corners in New York shortly after he arrived and by the spring of 1916, Garvey too took up public lecturing starting in a churchyard downtown to promote economic, political, and social freedom for black people. To further his causes, Garvey launched *The Negro World* and by 1920, he convinced Harrison to edit the newspaper. For the brief time that Harrison was principal editor,

Negro World and he became a leading voice for race-conscious Negro radicals. Garvey had unwittingly joined a small band of Harlem radicals so diverse and single minded, they rarely banded together and often fought against each other's ideas in the pages of their own newspapers and magazines. This internal turmoil turned Harlem into the crucible that forged the best of these ideas into political actions.

"Crucibles are often also used to remove impurities from a substance, so that only the pure matter remains," according to an essay posted on ClassicsNetwork.com critiquing Arthur Miller's stage classic *The Crucible*. "We burn a hot fire here; it melts down all concealment?" Miller wrote.[9]

Harlem was the trendy crucible of an ever-changing black culture. Agitators like Du Bois, Randolph, and Garvey stoked fire into it with the radical rhetoric each spewed out in *The Crisis*, *The Messenger*, and *Negro World*. Their columns thrashed nonbelievers black and white in their praise of socialism, black nationalism, and protests against lynching. Like the abolitionist publications before them and the Black Power advocacy that would come in later decades, these men preached the gospel of the New Negro while they trashed the old, consolatory urgings of leaders like Booker T. Washington, one of the most sought-after black leaders by white authorities of his time.

The New Negro was epitomized by singer Paul Robeson. A Columbia University law school graduate and an all-American football player at Rutgers, Robeson was the son of a slave. Charming, well-spoken, and seen in the company of the most sophisticated Americans black or white, Robeson represented an emerging figure in American culture—the New Negro. Robeson was a first-generation African American and he typified the image of the *New Negro*, a new term widely used by a large number of Harlem progressives. The New Negro was no common man or woman, but rather a hybrid, new, privileged member of an emerging racial and political entity that saw Harlem and all the activity they found there as an opportunity to uplift themselves and an entire race by example. It was this new class of Negro, untarnished by slavery that was first recognized in New York and popularized in the writing and speeches heard throughout Harlem of the 1920s.

The New Negro Movement was at the core of this so-called Harlem Renaissance and was itself a larger, diverse movement that grew in strength and popularity during the same period. Its members belonged to a number of different, loosely organized, multifaceted political and social movements. It was not just a grass roots literary or cultural movement either. It was essentially, a collective of varied personalities and groups who each garnered different followers in New York and later throughout the country. It was not a single-minded organization such as the NAACP or the Urban League where members met regularly, crafted platforms, and carried out long-term plans. Like members of the fictional Mystic Knights of the Sea of a popular *Amos 'n' Andy* radio show some unwitting New Negroes were genuinely bamboozled by a handful of pseudo leaders who tried to lead a cultural renaissance in Harlem that some now say failed. Some of their ideas worked but one of their most ambitious goals—to uplift the Negroes' image in the eyes of all Americans—failed, according to some critics but I think these critics comingled the goals of the New Negro with those who led a short-lived artistic movement whose rank and file artists jumped ship near the end of the decade. Like the Kingfish of Mystic Knights of the Sea, they had sought solidarity but offered only sentimentality when the black people they claimed to represent, demanded racial cohesion and most of all, sincerity. As one scholar put it, the New Negro Movement was really one movement and many at the same time although its advocates were slow to recognize other advocates from different factions.

Among other notable New Negroes was a lean, immaculate man named Charles Johnson, the conservative Urban League editor of *Opportunity* magazine who had come to New York from Virginia to edit the magazine and would later become the first black president of Fisk University in Nashville.

Another was Du Bois, the bold, sometimes harsh Harvard-trained intellectual who presided over the founding and early years of the NAACP in Harlem and a popular magazine still in print, *The Crisis*. Du Bois's most celebrated work was *The Souls of Black Folk*, which extolled the virtues of an elite cadre of highly educated, skilled black intellectuals he dubbed the "Talented Tenth." In Du Bois's mind, it was this select band of some 10,000 college educated, sophisticated souls that would finally lead the working class Negro to his rightful place into mainstream American society. It was largely fiction since the two groups rarely mingled.

James Weldon Johnson belonged to this new guard of black leadership. A colleague of Du Bois's in the NAACP, J. W. Johnson wrote the controversial novel *Autobiography of an Ex-Colored Man* around 1912, the account of a black man who passes for white to escape racism and death. A. Philip Randolph, the socialist street orator and union organizer, was among this collection of former stock boys, nurses, homosexuals, intellectuals, immigrants, elevator operators,

Harvard-trained PhDs, even a dethroned Harlem dictator named Marcus Garvey that called themselves new Negroes. Du Bois and Randolph despised Garvey. But all were New Negroes of their own making, new because their separate campaigns against racism and segregation were new.

Like the flamboyant Garvey, the soft-spoken editor Charles Johnson, the sometimes aloof Du Bois, J. W. Johnson, and many others were all calling for Negro solidarity, but calling for it in different ways. Some saw the language of the New Negro as shifty, shadowy, and stories about them resembled trickster tales of the past. Others said the New Negro saw the opportunity in this so-called renaissance in Harlem, the chance to reinvent the image of Negroes and used that invention to further their goals of fostering greater racial equality. These were all noble and varied ideas that attracted a wide variety of New Negroes who did not even pretend to like each other. While some like Charles Johnson were cautious conservatives, many more were strident, outlandish, and bolder than most people ever expected to see from the Negroes in their towns, churches, or barbershops. Young Negroes like Langston Hughes openly praised white novelist and critic Carl Van Vechten's novel about Harlem *Nigger Heaven*, while other New Negroes such as Du Bois and his colleagues berated it in their magazines just for using the word *nigger* in the title. These intellectual and cultural differences were battles waged bitterly among all these New Negroes who gathered their separate flocks first in Harlem and later wherever they could attract followers. While it is rarely mentioned in most Harlem histories, this dissention spurred a melding process that had to aid each of their causes in some way. All of this debate over not just what to call the so-called Negro but, more importantlt, but debate over how to acquire a healthy stream of self-respect was happening throughout the community as more and more New Negroes gathered their followers in Harlem to reinvent themselves there. What they could not or dared not to be in their hometowns, they could easily be by slipping into new Negro skin once they arrived in Harlem. For example, a woman named Gladys Bentley came from Pennsylvania to Harlem to join these New Negroes. Bentley became a shameless, homosexual entertainer at age 16 once she found the A Train and 135th Street in Harlem. Donning her signature white tuxedo and top hat, Bentley was an entertainer who performed raunchy song and dance routines at rent parties anywhere and performed regularly at Jungle Alley, a joint on 133rd Street between Lenox and Seventh Avenue.

Another member of this emerging class of Negro was a nurse named Mabel Staupers who came to Harlem from Barbados. In the city, she organized the first hospital in Harlem where black doctors could admit and treat their own patients. Healthcare, like everything else in America in the first half of the century, was segregated. Black patients could not go to just any hospital and expect to be admitted or treated. Staupers set up the Booker T. Washington Sanitarium, Harlem's first in-patient medical facility for black patients with tuberculosis and one of the few facilities in any Northern city that admitted patients sent there by black physicians. Winner of the NAACP's Spingarn Medal, Staupers won this award for being instrumental in integrating the Army Nurse Corps and for tearing down racial quotas that limited the number of black nurses allowed into the armed forces during and after World War II.

CHAPTER FIVE

Negrophilia

Colorful images of frolicking Negroes in Harlem became the most popular descriptions of the community, and this kind of exotic feature story did not go unnoticed by white columnists and reporters at downtown newspapers. Reporters from the *New York Herald Tribune*, *The New York Times*, and other widely circulated publications in the city met Locke and other blacks like him at events like the 1924 Civic Club awards dinner. They began writing stories about Harlem, saying things like America was "on the edge if not already in the midst, of what might not improperly be called a Negro Renaissance."[1] Downtown columnists such as Carl Van Vechten became sincerely interested in uptown culture too. He joined the company of Baltimore writer H. L. Mencken and other writers from magazines such as *The Smart Set* and *Vanity Fair* whose interests in Harlem were fueled by a need to find new, exotic trends. Negroes in Harlem, the Spanish of East Harlem, and the Yiddish theater downtown, were all deemed colorful realms by these New York writers looking for fads.

If Harlem was not in vogue when they discovered it, it did not take long for this trendy community to find stories about itself in the reviews, gossip columns, and society pages.

Van Vechten and scores of other white writers were escorted to uptown spots nightly in the 1920s where they could eat ethnic food and drink liquor unavailable downtown during the years of alcohol prohibition and vetted entertainment of all kinds. Clubs uptown had new, exciting bands like Louis Armstrong and his Hot Seven, white musicians like Eddie Condon, or a jazz guitarist and a banjo-playing blues man like Lonnie Johnson, all played at the Savoy Ballroom in Harlem regularly.

As more stories about Harlem ran in downtown magazines, whites began to flock to Harlem, suffering from what one scholar called Negrophilia. Ironically, it would be a book by Van Vechten, not the black literati who ferried him around, that would become one of the most famous Harlem books about the period. It was called *Nigger Heaven*.[2]

In it, Van Vechten good-naturedly pokes fun at the elitist blacks he rubbed elbows with nightly, probably offending some but not all who had called Van Vechten a friend. The characters he wrote about were thinly disguised New Negro men and women.

In a letter to Literary Guild editor Carl Van Doren, who also judged the *Opportunity Magazine* literary awards, Harlem schoolteacher Aubrey Bowers emphasized the real dilemma Van Vechten's novel represented.

"How many magazines or publishers would accept Negro stories from a Negro point of view? They might accept a Negro's work if he would consent to denigrate his race and pander to the American idea that a Negro is a clown, a child, or a brute. But then he would not really be a Negro writer, he would be a liar," she said. This was just one of the many controversies over the fact that whites had discovered Harlem.

"White people began to come to Harlem in droves. For several years they packed the expensive Cotton Club on Lenox Avenue," Hughes said in his autobiography, *The Big Sea*. "But I was never there because the Cotton Club was a Jim Crow club for gangsters and wealthy whites." He said the club management did not even pretend to be cordial to black patrons unless they were celebrities like dancer Bill Robinson, known around the world as Bojangles.

As Harlem nightlife became more popular, Hughes said resentment over the influx of whites grew. "Now the strangers were given the best ringside tables to sit and stare at the Negro customers—like amusing animals in a zoo," Hughes added.

He said dancers at the Savoy saw an opportunity to capitalize on the situation by showing off dances and acrobatic routines to amuse the white dancers. "Some of the Lindy-hoppers had cards printed with their names on them and became dance professors teaching the tourists."

This same aim-to-please attitude influenced Harlem writers too and more than a few began writing "to amuse and entertain white people," Hughes recalled. In the process, he said, they distorted their material "and left out a great many things they thought would offend their American brothers of a lighter complexion."

"All of us know that the gay and sparkling life of the so-called Negro Renaissance of the '20s was not so gay and sparkling beneath the surface as it looked. I had a swell time . . . but I thought it wouldn't last long. For how long could a large and enthusiastic number of people be crazy about Negroes forever? But some Harlemites thought the millennium had come. I don't know what made Negroes think that— except . . . they were mostly intellectuals doing the thinking. The ordinary Negroes hadn't heard of the Negro Renaissance."[3]

Zora Neale Hurston was perhaps the bluntest in sizing up the accomplishments of the black literati to which she belonged and ridiculed at the same time.

"The decade just past was the oleomargarine era in Negro writing," she wrote in a long article. "Oleomargarine is the fictionalized form of butter. Margarine is yellow, it is greasy, it has a taste that paraphrases butter. It even has the word 'butter' printed on the label often. In short, it has everything butterish about it except butter," the sometimes-irascible Hurston said.

"And so the writings that made out they were holding a looking-glass to the Negro had everything in them except Negroness. Some of the authors meant well. The flavor was in them. They had a willing mind, but [were] too light [in the] behind.

"From all this I learned that most white people have seen our shows but not our lives. If they have not seen a Negro show they have seen a minstrel or at least a blackface comedian and that is considered enough. They don't know us. . . . The great majority of us live our lives . . . unconcerned about other people. So any literature that proposes to point out to the world fourteen million frustrated Negroes is also insincere. There is certainly more outspoken racial prejudice in the South than elsewhere, but it is also the place of the strongest inter-racial attachment. The situation is so contradictory, paradoxical and what not, that only a southerner could ever understand it," she said.

She concluded, "And Northern Negroes, unless they have spent years in residence and study, know no more about Negro life in the south than Northern white folks do. Thus a great deal of literary postures and distortions has come from Negro pens."[4]

I found Hurston's laments in a typeset but unpublished story written for *American Mercury* magazine in an archive at the Library of Congress in Washington. It was slated to run in 1936 but it was never published. An anonymous, handwritten note scrawled across the top simply said: "Not printed. I don't know why."

The years Hurston identified in her essay were 1924 to 1934, the same year the *Opportunity Magazine* awards dinners began at the Civic Club. It is also the decade most often used to pinpoint the beginning and end of the Harlem Renaissance period.

Hurston is clearly attacking the New Negro writers, not the wider, raucous Harlem school of young writers to which she belonged. These writers championed the use of black folklore, dialect, and black idioms in their short fiction and novels. The New Negro espoused race pride but ignored these folk traditions choosing Victorian models of writing, art, and music instead. This riled many younger writers who had initially been lured by New Negro leaders to come to New York where they promised to use their influence to help the young artists who came. They touted artistic forms that suited their political agenda and ignored those which did not.

"This unofficial literary program of the Harlem Renaissance tended to break completely with folktales," wrote Leonard Diepeveen, a literature professor writing in an issue of the journal, *American Literature*. "Part of this break was made in order to emphasize the 'New Negro': the race had moved on to more contemporary issues. But Black folklore also was peculiarly tied to the past; Black folklore contained many more references to recent (within the past seventy-five years), historically verified oppression and humiliation as did folklores of most other races and cultures."

For this reason, Diepeveen said, this kind of literature, old or new versions of it, did not seem to promote the type of art the Harlem Renaissance (leaders) wanted and was dubbed a low art form not worthy of their time or attention. "Only a few writers . . . wanted these materials to be used, but (Langston) Hughes was the most prophetic: Certainly there is, for the American Negro Artist who can escape the restriction . . . a great deal of unused material ready for his art. During the Harlem Renaissance the material was left unused," Diepeveen said.[5]

When Diepeveen speaks of Harlem's Renaissance, he seems to be referring to those same few years, which Hurston and most histories for the period have set aside for the renaissance period. Those years coincide with the beginning of the New Negro Movement and a larger, political and social renaissance that would last for decades well into the 1960s.

In a random survey of dozens of mainstream magazines published between 1920 and the early 1960, more than 80 short stories, poems, and essays were written by the writers and intellectuals connected to the Harlem school of writers. These appeared in mainstream magazines as well as in black magazines like *The Crisis* and *Opportunity*. In another survey that I conducted years before I wrote *Crucible*, I found more than 40 short stories by one Harlem Renaissance writer alone whose work appeared twice a month in the *New York Daily News* between 1940 and 1961. Her name was Dorothy West, a writer originally from Boston who was among the first to win an *Opportunity* magazine award and she later became one of the most successful arrivals to Harlem in the 1920s. Arriving as a winner for an Opportunity writing award, she would later win a long-term contract to write fiction for the *New York Daily News* largest daily circulated newspaper in the world with more than 2 million readers, West acquired short period of fame, but only after she left New York in 1940 to live on Martha's Vineyard. While she had always been known as the youngest member of the Harlem Renaissance era writers, she would become iconic 40 years later when the most famous First Lady of the United States discovered and published her second novel, *The Wedding*. Decades later, after I discovered and published a short story West wrote but had never published, *My Baby*. The story was included in the Best American Short Stories 2001. By my reckoning, Dorothy West was iconic too for another reason. Her short stories were probably more widely read as the crossover artist she became than any other black writers of the Harlem Renaissance period who stories were read by millions of *Daily News* readers.

Dozens of other writers associated with this renaissance were intellectuals, con men, ex-cons, poets, essayists, college professors, elitists, folklorists, and paroled felons who had all gravitated to Harlem over the same 40-year period and made contributions to a now famous literary movement that was spawned in Harlem.

In their writings, they expressed distinctly different and varied ideas about life in America and especially life in Harlem. Written in the decades between 1920 and 1960, this work illustrates the many creative differences, which existed among Harlem writers. This tension and the opportunities to write about it inspired an eclectic group of then young writers to split into factions. West uniquely chose to critique the black elite, the class she had come from as the daughter of a wealthy Boston fruit merchant. Like her contemporaries Wallace Thurman, Hurston, and Hughes, West ventured outside the boundaries of acceptable black writing and dared to criticize the shallowness of wealthy blacks, educated blacks. This belied the aims of the new Negroes, who had championed writers like West, Hughes, Thurman, and their contemporaries when they first came to New York.

Other writers wrote sentimental novels and books about unrequited love; the plight of being black in America or bleak poems about discrimination and the exploitation black migrants found in the city many believed would be the promised land. This worked quietly acknowledged the existence of homosexuals in their midst along with the "dicty" (stuck up) Negroes Van Vechten had written about, who seemed to want to be seen as white, not as colored or any kind of Negro. They wrote about nameless, faceless sleeping car porters, domestics who cleaned other people's houses, and the owner of splendid brownstones in Harlem. Their protagonists were cleaning ladies and janitors who dreamed of being businessmen with secretaries and important letters to write. This variety of work heeded a warning Hughes wrote in the summer of 1926 about black art in general and black writers specifically.

"We younger Negro artists who create now intend to express our individual dark-skinned selves without fear or shame. If white people are pleased, we are glad," Hughes declared. "If they are not, it doesn't matter ... If colored people are pleased, we are glad. If they are not, their displeasure doesn't matter either."[6] West had quietly joined these renegades.

This declaration was biting the hand that had certainly fed Langston Hughes, and it seemed to specifically target New Negro leaders such as Alain Locke and W.E.B. Du Bois, editor of the influential NAACP magazine *The Crisis* as censors of black writing. Locke and Du Bois had been early champions of his poetry just a few years earlier, but now Hughes was warning them not to impinge upon his or the artistic freedom of other writers who had racial issues they intended to air in print. This manifesto was clearly an affront to old-guard intellectuals such as Locke and Du Bois.

The idea of contemporary black writing "to Du Bois, meant high cultural forms rather than vernacular expressions, and stories set in Strivers' Row parlors instead of Lenox Avenue cabarets," wrote Steven Watson in his book *The Harlem Renaissance: Hub of African-American Culture 1920–1930.*[7] Writer Countee Cullen echoed Du Bois's lament in a 1928 edition of *Opportunity* magazine. "Decency demands that some things be kept secret; diplomacy demands it. The world loses respect for violators of this code."[8]

This code was apparently strictly enforced and violators were threatened with intellectual banishment. This was driven by the politics of propaganda, an element that is seldom associated with literary factions in Harlem, but it was common knowledge at the time.

Dallas scholar Matthew Henry notes that "most of the studies of the Harlem Renaissance, or of the individual artists and writers associated with it, suffer from a form of historical amnesia: they rarely discuss the political climate of this period outside the context of the race problem, they rarely engage the political nature of the art produced, and they often ignore the influence of radical ideologies."

As the renaissance and its significance spread after 1900, numerous political camps emerged in Harlem. They influenced what was published in a number of small literary and cultural magazines.

Du Bois's editorial attacks on radical Marcus Garvey and others whose policies he opposed were widely read in *The Crisis*. The magazine was used regularly to tout or attack political campaigns or policies Du Bois did not endorse. In 1918, for example, Du Bois wrote editorials encouraging Negroes to support American troops during World War I, despite the fact that the American military was still segregated. Still, Du Bois asked blacks to "forget our special grievances and close ranks" with whites in fighting for democracy. This stance was immediately attacked by black socialists for being too accommodating.

Matthew Henry said that "Du Bois began rejecting poetry and articles that might be considered disloyal by the government, especially the Justice Department, which at the time had its eye closely (focused) on the activities of Harlem's radicals and the black press." This included Du Bois and the NAACP, although Du Bois may not have been aware of the surveillance at the time.[9]

While Du Bois was a patriotic American and advocated for the rights of blacks to participate in the national debate, not ceded from it like Garvey, he thought blacks should work to get along, not oppose American institutions. It was noticeable that he opposed any criticism of government agencies and the magazine he edited was noticeably silent about the well-known segregation policies of several white-owned clubs in Harlem like the Cotton Club. This kind of hypocrisy did not go unnoticed by Hughes, Hurston, and other younger writers who did more than break this New Negro code of silence. They defied it.

Led by Wallace Thurman, Hurston, and Hughes, this group of dissidents described themselves as the "Niggerati." They conceived and launched an idea for a new magazine in an apartment on 136th Street they all frequented regularly. They called the magazine *Fire!!!* because it was supposed to burn up old-fashioned ideas about what they should and should not be writing. They formed an editorial board in the summer of 1926 that included writers Hurston,

Hughes, Thurman, Gwendolyn Bennett, John Davis, Richard Bruce, and painter Aaron Douglas. Thurman served as editor.

The group published a single issue of *Fire!!!* Devoted to younger Negro artists in November of 1926, it cost about $1,000 and was published just 32 months after that first Civic Club dinner that was presided over by Alain Locke.

Matthew Henry says, "There is … a bohemian impulse behind *Fire!!!,* and it is evident that its editors were intentionally challenging the Victorian morality of the older generation. Thurman was apparently the most vocal in his protestations—after all the submissions … had been made, he announced to his partners that they now needed a way to get Fire !!! banned in Boston so as to ensure its success." The potential for this existed because the magazine had selected a wide variety of writing and subjects to offend just about any Victorian-minded critic. A story called "Cordelia the Crude" by Thurman was about prostitution. "Smoke, Lilies and Jade" by Bruce was a mystical fantasy about a bisexual love triangle. This was salacious material in 1926.

Hurston debuted a play in *Fire!!!* she called "Color Struck." It begins in a segregated railroad car and features black, white, and mulatto characters, all speaking in dialects common to Southern blacks.

"Who you gointer walk de cake wid," a girl character asks.

"Nobody, ah reckon," says Effie. "John and Emma gointer win it. They's the bestest cake walkers in dis state."[10]

In another short story by Hurston called "Sweat,"[11] she again uses Southern characters who abuse their women this time and they speak in vulgar ways. These characters originated in an oral literary tradition, which the more genteel school of Harlem Renaissance writing of the New Negro had no interest in promoting.

In a seething commentary, Thurman used *Fire!!!* to again praise *Nigger Heaven*, a book by the white critic Carl Van Vechten, which Du Bois and so many others had denounced for simply using the racial epithet in print.

Thurman wrote, "Some time ago, while reviewing Carl Van Vechten's … Nigger Heaven, I made the prophecy that Harlem Negroes, once their aversion to the nigger in the title was forgotten, would erect a statue on the corner of 135th Street and Seventh Avenue, and dedicate it to the ultra-sophisticated Iowa New Yorker," talking about Van Vechten.[12]

"So far my prophecy has failed to pan out, and superficially, it seems as if it never will, for instead of being enshrined for his pseudo-sophisticated, semi-serious, semi-ludicrous effusion about Harlem, Mr. Van Vechten is about to be lynched, at least in effigy."

"I for one, and strange as it may sound, there are others, who believe that Carl Van Vechten was rendered sincere during his explorations and observations of Negro life in Harlem, even if he remained characteristically superficial. ... In writing *Nigger Heaven* the author wavered between sentimentality and sophistication. That the sentimentality won out is his funeral. That the sophistication stung certain Negroes to the quick is their funeral." Thurman added "The so-called intelligentsia of Harlem has exposed its inherent stupidity. And *Nigger Heaven* is a best seller. Why Negroes imagine that any writer is going to write what Negroes think he ought to write about is too ridiculous to merit consideration."[13]

Another essay in *Fire!!!* called "Intelligentsia" written by Arthur Huff Fauset seemed to also specifically target Locke and his New Negro contemporaries.

"Of all the doughty societies that have sprung up in this age of Kluxers [Ku Klux Klan] ... the one known by that unpronounceable word, 'Intelligentsia' is the most benighted. The war seems to have given it birth, the press nurtured it, which should have been warning enough, the public accepted it, and now we all suffer."

"According to the ultra-advanced notions of the great majority of this secret order if it were not for the intelligentsia, this crippled old world would be compelled to kick up its toes and die on the spot. Were it not for these super-men all the brilliance of the ages and the inheritance, which is so vital to the maintenance of the spark of progress, would vanish and pass away. In other words, if the intelligentsia were to stick their divinely appointed noses a little higher into the ethereal regions and withdraw themselves completely from the tawdry field of life that field would soon become a burial ground for the rest of humanity."

"This is the rankest folly. The world owes about as much to the rank and file of this society (the Talented Tenth) as a Negro slave owes to Georgia," Fauset said. "Besides a few big words added to the lexicon and one or two highfalutin' notions about the way the world should run, the contribution of intelligentsia to society is as negligible as gin at a Methodist picnic. ... Sift the chaff out of intelligentsia," he said, "and you will find that the residuum is about fifty-six one hundredths of one per cent. For the rest, the society is made up of nonproducers and bloodsuckers," wrote this author in *Fire!!!* Arthur Huff Fauset was the brother of Jessie Redmon Fauset, the novelist first honored at the 1924 Civic Club dinner presided over by Alain Locke. "If the New Negro movement had been a religion, and not the political construct it became, *Fire!!!* and its authors would have been excommunicated," Thurman said.

The story of *Fire!!!* the publication has one final, ironic twist. The editors managed to sell only a few hundred copies. Financed primarily by a promise to pay made by Thurman, he died an impoverished man. Zora Neale Hurston too died in poverty, working as a housecleaner and maid back in Florida where she was buried in an unmarked grave. Like West, her reputation would only be revived later in life long after she died and she was nearly forgotten about until writer Alice Walker rescued Hurston's reputation. Several hundred of unsold copies of *Fire!!!* were destroyed in a fire that broke out in the basement of an apartment house where they were stored. This unhappy event turned volume 1, number 1 of *Fire!!!* into a collector's item that drew the fame the New Negro Movement had sought for black authors in the first place.

CHAPTER SIX

Almost Made King

Street orator Hubert Harrison first noticed a fellow West Indian in a crowd where Harrison often spoke one afternoon in 1917. It was an historic meeting. The man was Marcus Garvey, a Jamaican, relatively new to the city. Harrison invited Garvey to join him up on a makeshift stage set up on Lenox Avenue. In no time, the name Marcus Garvey began to rise in prominence everywhere in the community because of his speeches, not just as a mimic of the charismatic Hubert Harrison, but as a self-styled, dynamic Black Nationalist speaker. Like Harrison, Garvey called himself a New Negro.

A heavyset, dark-skinned man, Garvey arrived in New York in 1916 and was quick to admire Harrison's ability to speak so forcefully to large crowds anywhere in the city. An agnostic from Saint Croix, Harrison could draw crowds when he proclaimed his own atheism, expound on secular humanism, social progressivism, or free thought.

Garvey called himself a black Zionist too and was an advocate for creating a separate homeland for disenfranchised blacks, not just blacks in Harlem but black people everywhere. He patterned this idea after a similar movement he discovered and admired among Jews in New York City. Jews at the time sought a homeland in the Middle East, which later became the Jewish state of Israel. Garvey wanted black people to return to Africa from where they and their ancestors had been taken as slaves. Garvey set out on a world mission from Harlem to return blacks to Africa. Their chance meeting on Lenox Avenue in 1917 and subsequent appearances by Garvey and Harrison together, blossomed into a professional relationship and the two men became colleagues. Harrison helped Garvey cobble together the mechanics of a fledgling cause at the time to create a new black state in Africa. Garvey had carried the seeds of a similar idea to New York from a financially broke organization he had started two years earlier in Jamaica. He called it the Universal Negro Improvement Association or the UNIA. With Harrison's help in New York, he invented the UNIA in America. Over the next 11 years, the UNIA would become the first and largest Black Nationalist Movement in American history. It would dwarf the later movements of the Rev. Dr. Martin Luther King, the Nation of Islam, and other black power movements.

Garvey preached black liberation and Africa for Africans in his speeches. He attempted to establish worldwide economic enterprises, financed by enthralled black listeners wherever he spoke in the United States. He toured and mounted massive rallies, once attracting 35,000 people to Madison Square Garden. At these rallies, he raised millions of dollars in donations to finance what became a private empire. By most accounts, he attracted millions of followers to an entity he patterned after the British monarchy and he initially ruled it out of a tawdry Harlem office.

In his own time, Garvey became a true martyr. His fledgling ambition to launch an empire seemed to happen overnight with the help of a few followers like Harrison and ironically by a would-be assassin's bullet that missed its mark.

"In the world of the twenties, personalities quickly became notable and were fastened upon by admirers, detractors and the merely curious," according to the Universal Negro Improvement Association Papers Project now based in Los Angeles. "But even by the standards of the day, Garvey's rise from obscurity was spectacular."[1]

The heavyset Garvey was a captivating speaker. Garvey and Harrison became popular about the same time as another stepladder speaker in Harlem, Asa Philip Randolph, a socialist labor leader. All were popular speakers who attracted large crowds on Lenox Avenue. Their brand of fiery rhetoric had become a natural part of the landscape of Lenox by the time Garvey came to the city. Good political speeches could always attract crowds in Harlem, a tradition that dated back to the days before the great migration when Harlem was largely a Jewish, Irish, and Italian community.

It was a tradition that lasted well into the 1960s when another charismatic speaker named Malcolm X from the Nation of Islam drew the same kinds of crowds that Harrison and Garvey gathered in Harlem. This too was no accident but an extension of a long-held tradition. Malcolm X was born Malcolm Little, the son of Earl Little, a Baptist minister and long-standing member of Garvey's UNIA. Earl Little had worked as an organizer and president for the UNIA organization in the Omaha, Nebraska, division. His wife, Louise, served as division secretary. When Malcolm X came to Harlem in the 1960s, his speeches too had been inspired by the Garvey speeches his father had brought him to hear as a small boy living in Nebraska.

By the time Garvey started speaking, Harrison and Randolph had already "converted the black community of Harlem into a parliament of the people," wrote the UN project editors, who now maintain more than 30,000 documents from Garvey's era in archives at University of California AfricanAmerican Studies Center.[2]

"The World War I era was the time of the rise of 'the ebony sages' who laid the foundation in those years for what would eventually come to be known as the Harlem Renaissance. Garveyism was found ... in barber shops and basements, tea shops and railroad flats" where "art and education, literature and the race question were discussed with an abandon that was truly Bohemian," the UNIA project editors wrote.

As a boy, Garvey carried the nickname "Ugly Mug" in Ann's Bay, Jamaica, where he was born in 1887, the UNIA said. He was educated under a British system that allowed students to advance into upper grades based on their abilities, not race or family wealth. Although Garvey acquired a strong formal education, he did not attend college. Instead, he worked as a printer and later as a sailor and traveled to Europe and Central America when labor troubles in Kingston forced him to leave the country in 1909.

Garvey embarked on an odyssey for him to escape racism and the oppression he found everywhere he went. His first encounter with discrimination began in Jamaica where dark-skinned blacks like Garvey developed deep resentments for whites and a large mulatto population of slave descendants, according to his own writing in archives of the University of California.

Garvey had first organized the UNIA in Kingston, according to archival sources in California. He arrived in the United States in 1916 hoping to raise funds for the association, which he originally wanted to model after an American organization started by Booker T. Washington, founder of the Tuskegee Institute. Garvey came to America hoping to obtain Washington's assistance but Washington died before Garvey arrived. Garvey reorganized the UNIA anyway in Harlem, using members of an established history club as founding members. Together, they opened a small, sparsely furnished office at

56 West 135th Street and aggressively began to raise funds. An incident at that office sparked Garvey's meteoric rise to power and the establishment of his own self-styled monarchy allegedly over millions of subjects in American.

"One day, a lone, disgruntled follower, protesting that he'd been duped by the organizers, dashed excitedly into Garvey's office and shot the ... leader, grazing his forehead," according to Roi Ottley in *The Negro in New York: An Informal Social History*. "Garvey rushed hysterically into the street with the blood of a martyr streaming down his face. The incident was given much space in the local press, and he was a made man," Ottley said.[3]

One year later, he launched a weekly newspaper called *The Negro World*, appointing his new friend Hubert Harrison as editor. Garvey used the newspaper as a widely circulated platform to promote a controversial back-to-Africa program. He also began promoting a shipping company he called the Black Star Line. He planned to use it to transport disgruntled blacks back to Africa.

A fellow Jamaican, journalist and novelist Claude McKay said, "He thundered phrases that were authoritative if not wise, but the Negro people were ripe for such a prophet. Girding for a supreme war effort, America had little time to devote to the growing problems of its large Negro minority. Harassed in the South and rebuffed in the North, the southern Negroes eagerly swallowed the sayings and the projects of Garvey."[4] These were radical ideas that did not appeal to educated blacks who wanted justice, but wanted it within the framework of American ideals. Instead, his ideas and dreams attracted the marginalized poor.

In just a few weeks, with his ideas in print and circulated widely across the nation, the *Negro World* became a leading newspaper in Harlem and elsewhere in America where the Garvey message was being disseminated. Within a few months, the *World* had a circulation of 75,000 and could be read in numerous cities and countries, publishing Spanish and French language editions.

"These were slogans Garvey broadcast in a thousand different ways to move the mind of the Negro people," McKay wrote. "There was magic in his method. It worked miraculously. The Negro masses acclaimed the new leader. The black [communities] clamored to hear his voice and competed with one another for his lectures."[5]

Subscription money for the newspaper poured in. To raise more funds, the UNIA struck African Redemption medals. In fund-raisers, donors who pledged $50–$100 were given bronze crosses, silver cross went to subscribers who donated $100–$500, and gold crosses went to subscribers who pledged amounts between $500 and a $1,000. The coffers of the Universal Negro Improvement Association swelled. Today, Garvey's ability to reach followers might easily be compared to the Move On.org campaign that gathered up the followers of President Barack Obama in 2008 that swept Obama into office. Had the Internet existed in his time, Garvey's Negro World potentially could have gone viral universally. While the campaigns of Obama and Garvey were wildly different, Garvey and Obama both had accomplished something long feared by authorities not willing to share real power—the potential to incite large groups of black people to take up their own causes. This potentially made Garvey one of the most dangerous black men in America.

In a short time, Marcus Garvey became a leader who had created his own empire and paid for his own coronation in Harlem with the nickels and dimes of tens of thousands of readers who followed his weekly sermons in the *World*.

The activities of the UNIA and Garvey did not go unnoticed by one of the most powerful, rising white men in Washington, DC, a young lawyer in the U.S. Justice Department named J. Edgar Hoover.[6]

Garvey was an enigma in America, but not in Harlem. He seemed to voice what most Harlemites felt. Black Americans, like Jamaicans, not only experienced racism but there was also working cast system in Harlem between Du Bois's light-skinned blacks and Garvey's dark-skinned blacks. Black newspapers as a rule ran ads for skin-lightening creams, hair-straightening pomades, revenue the *World* refused. As his organization grew, Garvey dramatized his disdain for this cast system by surrounding himself with all things black. He bought a house and painted it black. He launched the Black Star Line and opened a chain of grocery stores that employed only dark-skinned blacks, who all wore black crosses.

In no time, the ranks of his organization outgrew the offices on 135th Street. Three blocks away on 138th Street, Garvey built a magnificent new building and called it Liberty Hall, a grand zinc-roofed hall that took up a whole block between Lenox and Seventh Avenues and could hold 6,000 people at one time.

Marcus Garvey had become the black messiah in America.

His words had clearly inspired young Malcolm Little who later became Malcolm X, the venerable leader who joined the Nation of Islam in the 1960s. In *The Autobiography of Malcolm X*, Malcolm remembered his father's UNIA membership, and said, "The image of him that made me proudest was his crusading and militant campaigning with the words of Marcus Garvey ... it was only me that he sometimes took with him to the Garvey U.N.I.A. meetings which he held quietly in different people's homes."[7]

But Garvey was still somewhat of an oddity, according to Wilbert Miller, a Jamaican who joined Garvey's organization in Harlem. "To many, he was a clown; a jester who wanted to play at being king but to hundreds of thousands of Negroes, he was a magnificent leader and martyr to a great cause," Miller said.

Miller, an interior designer who lived on 140th Street, remembered the first speech he heard Garvey give, reciting it from memory years later to a WPA writer:

He recounted Garvey said, "Wherever I go, whether it be France, Germany, England or Spain, I am told that there is no room for a black people. The other races have countries of their own and it is time for the 400,000,000 blacks of the world to claim Africa for themselves. Therefore, we shall demand and expect of the world a Free Africa. The black man has been serf, a tool, a slave and peon long enough. I see Ethiopia stretching forth her hands unto God, and methinks I see the Angel of God taking up the standard of the Red, the Black, and the Green, and sayings; Men of the Negro race, Men of Ethiopia, follow me."[8]

Miller recalled, Garvey

had such a magnetic personality that people flocked to see him wherever he went and when he appeared on any platform to speak, he'd have to wait sometimes five or ten minutes before the loud ovations and sounds of applause subsided. Then he would stride majestically forward in his cap and gown of purple, green and gold, and the hall, arena, square, or whatever it was, would become magically silent.[9]

Garvey gave one of these speeches before thousands of UNIA delegates at Madison Square Garden. They came to New York in August 1920 from UNIA chapters that Garveyites had organized in countries around the world. The exact number of delegates varies but range from 2,000 to 25,000, depending upon the historical source. This too is reminiscent of Obama's very strong grass roots organizing community employed for each of his successful presidential bids, ignored and widely criticized by the two Republican candidates in two elections, where they were defeated by the successful grass root nature of the Obama campaign.

"Imagine, huge spacious Madison Square Garden," Miller said, "rocking with the yells of 25,000 frenzied Negro patriots demanding a free Africa, from the Strait of Gibraltar to the Cape of Good Hope—A Negro republic run exclusively by and for Negroes," Miller told a WPA interviewer for the Federal Writers' Project in New York. "Doesn't sound real, does it? Well, it happened."[10]

By all accounts, Liberty Hall was splendidly decorated with the banners of the various delegations who had come that year for this occasion. Prominently displayed everywhere were the red, black, and green flags of the new African republic Garvey was proposing to build. A colorful, 40-piece band, a choir of 50 voices, and several quartettes entertained the assembly during the event, which lasted for 20 days.

During the proceedings, Marcus Garvey himself read the Declaration of Rights. It contained 54 demands. Claiming a world-wide UNIA membership of between 2 million and 6 million, Marcus Garvey proclaimed them "as free citizens of Africa, the motherland of all Negroes." It was a declaration of black independence.

Those demands included:

"Be it known to all men . . . that we believe in the supreme authority of our race in all things racial; that all things are created and given to man as a common possession; that there should be an equitable distribution and apportionment of all such things, and in consideration of the fact that as a race we are now deprived of those things that are morally and illegal ours, we believe it right that all such things should be acquired and held by whatsoever means possible.

"Whereas, the lynching, by burning, hanging or any other means, of human beings is a barbarous practice, and a shame and disgrace to civilization, we therefore declare any country guilty of any such atrocities outside the pale of civilization.

"We believe all men should live in peace, one with the other, but when races and nations provoke the ire of other races and nations by attempting to infringe upon their rights . . . the attempt in any way to free one's self or protect one's rights or heritage becomes justifiable."[11] This of course is now reminiscent of Malcolm X's now famous "by any means necessary" pronouncements in speeches related to black liberation.

In language fit for a king, Garvey had organized his kingdom of followers into the first unofficial monarchy on American soil.

Naturally, he installed himself as the "provisional president of Africa" and presided over the "court of Ethiopia," a body he fashioned after the British monarchy. His aides were awarded the titles of duke, duchesses, ladies-in-waiting, knight commanders of the sublime order of the Nile and other names. These titles were conferred upon his most trusted aides who made up the new government to run the Universal Negro Improvement Association, Inc. and the African Communities' League, Inc. of the World from Harlem.[12]

As any government being formed between two world wars, Garvey's kingdom had its own army. He called it the African Legion. The African Legion had full line of commissioned officers, a nurse's corps, a quartermaster staff, and commissioners of each brigade. The number of Egyptian sphinx symbols and gold buttons officers wore determined an officer's rank.

The organization also held regular classes in etiquette, rituals of the UNIA, black history, and military tactics for boys and girls.

Garveyites were well known in Harlem because of the parades they staged on Seventh Avenue on Sundays that were sometimes miles long. In them, Marcus Garvey and his entourage wore ornate garb. This self-styled potentate sometimes rode in an open, horse-drawn carriage naturally pulled by black horses. He dressed up in the colorful military regalia that started with a dark-blue uniform that could be mistaken as black, a black-feathered hat, and gold braid that his African Legion wore too. President Garvey and his high-ranking officers each wore gold swords. The president's carriage was flanked by a royal guard made up of the highest-ranking officers of his Legion on one side and members of The Black Cross, the women's nursing corps on the other.

His Grace Arch Bishop George Alexander McGuire, Primate of the African Orthodox Church, became chaplain general of Garvey's army. On one occasion, Garveyites held a "special form of Divine Service" performed by the new chaplain. In the ceremony, they canonized Jesus as the "Black man of sorrows," and declared that his mother, the Blessed Virgin Mary, had been a black woman.

Garvey raised millions of dollars to run this elaborate, officially unacknowledged monarchy. In the winter of 1919 alone, Wilbert Miller said, more than half a million dollars worth of stock in the Black Star Line was sold to blacks all across America. One all-black college in Louisiana reputedly raised $7,000 alone to help defray the cost of buying three Black Star Line ships. Miller said Garveyites emptied the national fund on one occasion to purchase ships. Three of them were called the *Yarmouth*, the *Maceo* and the *Shadysiah*.

According to *The New York Times*, the UNIA also established a shipping firm that staffed these ships with an all-black crew. The *Yarmouth*, according to the newspaper, was used to haul a $3 million worth of liquor from Brooklyn to Cuba, which had to be shipped out of the country before prohibition started on January 15, 1920. Hundreds of similar offshore enterprises operated by "rum runner" entrepreneurs like Garvey cropped up during this period. Unfortunately, "that whisky was too much temptation for the crew, who got drunk and put in at Norfolk, where the ship was seized under the prohibition law," according to the *Times*.[13]

A campaign to purchase a fourth ship was advertised in the *Negro World*. Garvey planned to call it the *Phillis Wheatley*, naming after the African American poet. The ship was supposed to sail between Cuba, St. Kitts, Barbados, Trinidad, Demerara, Dakar, and Monrovia. A much-publicized inspection of the ship repeatedly promised by Garvey in his newspaper never happened. In fact, the *Phillis Wheatley* never sailed. This incident made UNIA insiders suspicious and during the Madison Square Garden convention, they sent a delegation to His Highness demanding to inspect the ship. Garvey made excuses and was able to put them off for days because he was too busy with parades, speeches, receptions, and the regal mass meetings he staged.

In the middle of this furious fund-raising, empire building, and organizing, Miller said, some delegates filed a complaint against Garvey with the U.S. Postal Service. Federal authorities said the Black Star Line did not exist, yet Garvey was selling stock for $5 a share in the company.

The federal government's Bureau of Investigation under the guidance of J. Edgar Hoover investigated Garvey. As a special assistant, Hoover had been watching Garvey's activities as early as 1919 when Hoover wrote the following memo:

"J. Edgar Hoover to Special Agent Ridgley
Washington, D.C., October 11, 1919
MEMORANDUM FOR MR. RIDGLEY

I am transmitting herewith a communication, which has come to my attention from the Panama Canal, Washington office, relative to the activities of Marcus Garvey. Garvey is a West Indian Negro and in addition to his activities in endeavoring to establish the Black Star Line Steamship Corporation he has also been particularly active among the radical elements in New York City in agitating the Negro movement. Unfortunately, however, he has not as yet violated any federal law whereby he could be proceeded against on the grounds of being an undesirable alien, from the point of view of deportation," it said. "It occurs to me, however, from the attached clipping that there might be some proceeding against him for fraud in connection with his Black Star Line propaganda and for this reason, I am transmitting the communication to you for your appropriate attention." The memo then summarized Garvey's activities.

"Subject a native of the West Indies and one of the most prominent Negro agitators in New York;

He is founder of the Universal Negro Improvement Association and African Communities League;

He is the promulgator of Black Star Line and is the managing editor of the Negro World;

He is an exceptionally fine orator, creating much excitement among the Negroes through his steamship proposition;

In his paper *Negro World* the Soviet Russian Rule is upheld and there is an open ad vocation of Bolshevism.

Respectfully,

J.E. Hoover."[14]

Hoover spent endless resources probing the UNIA activities in at least two dozen cities, according to the PBS series *American Experience* and the investigation involved at least seven government agencies.[15] "They were going to find some way of getting rid of Garvey because they feared his influence," historian Theodore Kornweibel says of Hoover and his government colleagues. "They feared the hundreds of thousands, the masses of blacks under his influence. Garvey rejected America, and they could no more agree to and accept a militant rejection of America by blacks than they could accept a militant demand for full inclusion by blacks." Hoover's determination led him to take extreme measures to counter Garvey's growing influence.

According to Kornweibel, "Hoover and the Justice Department were clearly hooked on a fixation on Garvey which would before long become a vendetta." Historian Winston James said, "Hoover placed spies in the U.N.I.A. They sabotaged the *Black Star Line*. The engines . . . of the ships were actually damaged by foreign matter being thrown into the fuel."

"Hoover also placed his agents closer to Garvey than anyone at the time could have imagined. As he and the U.N.I.A. increasingly came under attack from internal dissenters, black critics, and the federal government, one of the few people Garvey confided in was Herbert Boulin, owner of a Harlem-based black doll company. What Garvey didn't know is that Boulin was an informant for Hoover, known by the Bureau as Agent P-138," says Kornweibel.[16]

Whatever Hoover was looking for, federal agents said they found it and Garvey was indicted three years later in January 1922, for allegedly using the mails to defraud. He was released on $2,500 bail, funds raised by a group in Harlem that called itself Friends of Negro Freedom. It was a coalition of officials from the National Association for the Advancement of Colored People (NAACP), labor leaders, and ministers in the community. Garvey's followers organized large rallies in support of their leader and prosecutors were slow to move this case into court.

At the same time, opposition groups in Harlem launched a "Garvey Must Go Campaign." They lobbied the government to proceed against him, saying his program for black advancement was unsound and that Garvey himself "was a charlatan," according to stories aired in *The American Experience*, a public television broadcast series. "They believed that his plans for black progress ... were unrealistic and ill-advised; they considered the Universal Negro Improvement Association's grandiose titles and military regalia to be preposterous; and they thought Garvey ... to be little more than a self-aggrandizing buffoon," the broadcast declared. A. Philip Randolph had introduced Garvey to his first American audience on a Harlem street corner just a few years earlier. Now, he said Garvey had 'succeeded in making the Negro the laughingstock of the world."[17]

Garveyism was still the largest, single Black Nationalist Movement ever organized in twentieth-century America and this remains true today.

An accurate accounting of Universal Negro Improvement Association assets is difficult although several independent critiques of its soundness are available. These include investigations by political opponents and government agencies like the NAACP and the U.S. Justice Department. The Justice Department investigation started as early as 1917. It lasted for several years and contained thousands of pages of documents, including more than 1,400 pages on Garvey alone. There is ample folklore, newspaper, and magazine accounts of UNIA activities that help piece together a portrait of those years. While the accuracy of these sources needs to be scrutinized closely, all seem to share one significant fact: Garveyism had an unprecedented, large following of blacks around the world.

Numerically, the numbers of his following dwarfed the combined memberships of the most popular civil rights organizations formed by African Americans over the next 80 years, including the National Urban League, the National Association for the Advancement of Colored People, and the Nation of Islam combined.

Ironically, the Friends of Negro Freedom that first led the movement for Garvey after his arrest later became the group that was most opposed to Garvey. This change of heart apparently came after it was rumored that Garvey had held a secret meeting in June 1922 with Ku Klux Klan (KKK) leader Edward Young Clarke. At the time, Clarke was acting Imperial Wizard of the KKK and the two men met during a visit Garvey made to Atlanta. While details of the meeting or whether it had occurred at all seemed sketchy, speculation over it grew into multi-pronged offensives against Garvey and the UNIA. This meeting became Garvey's "most grievous error," according to Theodore Vincent, author of *Black Power and the Garvey Movement*.[18] Vincent said it energized a coalition against him in various cities, including New York and Chicago where publishers of influential black newspapers and magazines launched separate campaigns to get rid of Marcus Garvey.

Garvey later said he met Clarke to discuss their common goals. Garvey's back-to-Africa campaign would rid America of blacks, a goal that was heartily endorsed by Clarke and his followers.

"For his part," Vincent wrote, "Garvey saw this as a responsible . . . courageous act by the leader of a worldwide black movement whose members were exposed (daily) to the dangers of the robed and hooded Klan in the south and the blue uniformed and three-piece suited version in the north."

In public statements Garvey made to UNIA members one month later, he said the Klan was "really the invisible government of the United States of America" that represented "the spirit of nearly every well-thinking white American." In the strident way only a speaker like Garvey could, he declared the aims of the Klan to confirm the "purity of the white race" mirrored the UNIA goal of upholding the racial integrity of black people."[19]

Those words linked this black martyr to the most hated and feared white organization in America that every black in the country identified with decades of unpunished burnings, mob violence, and lynchings. Immediately, Garvey bound his enemies into "a solid, raucous, and unforgiving mass" against him, according to Pulitzer Prize-winning author David L. Lewis. He said volleys of personal attacks and threats of violence were hurled from both sides.

The Messenger, a socialist magazine published by A. Philip Randolph and his partner Chandler Owen in Harlem led the "Garvey Must Go Campaign" with a public attack in print.

"Marcus Garvey! The Black Imperial Wizard Becomes Messenger Boy of the White Ku Klux Keagle," the magazine declared.

William E.B. Du Bois, editor of *The Crisis*, joined the campaign to unseat Garvey. Du Bois labeled Garvey "A Lunatic or a Traitor" in a 1924 editorial in his magazine. "This open ally of the Ku Klux Klan should be locked up or sent home," the Du Bois editorial said.

In retaliation, Garveyites allegedly broke up "Garvey Must Go" meetings in Harlem and around the country. In this climate, Hoover was determined to get rid of Garvey's influence.

"They were going to find some way of getting rid of Garvey because they feared his influence," Kornweibel said. "They feared the hundreds of thousands, the masses of blacks under his influence. Garvey rejected America, and they could no more agree to and accept a militant rejection of America by blacks than they could accept a militant demand for full inclusion by blacks."[20]

Garvey still seemed unfazed and used the occasion of his arrest to hold additional fund-raising conventions at Liberty Hall. National delegates from states where Garveyites had organized as well as delegates from Africa, the West Indies, Central and South America, all converged on Harlem in support of their besieged leader. They carried gifts and thousands of dollars in individual donations to reorganize the Black Star Line, Claude McKay wrote in *Harlem: Negro Metropolis*.[21]

"It was during this time that a delegate from Central America drafted a new will bequeathing to Garvey's organization his estate, valued at over $300,000." Again, Garvey responded to these tributes in a manner appropriate for a grand potentate.

"The ribbons and braids of his gleaming satin robe were richer than ever, his plumes were as long as the leaves of the Guinea grass and as white as snow," McKay said. "Seated in his car as upon a throne, he received the ovations and salutes of Harlem."

His trial began in 1923 and lasted a month. According to McKay, the government's case against him seemed weak and failed to prove that Garvey had defrauded his followers or misused UNIA funds. "Everything seemed in Garvey's favor. The evidence for the prosecution was flimsy. There was no letter to prove that the Black Star Line had directly sold shares through the mails. The only physical evidence the government produced was an empty envelope, not its contents," McKay reported.

Always good for a colorful story, Garvey was a popular figure among the New York press corps. Knowing this, Garvey used his trial as an opportunity to further his causes even more in print during the proceedings. Early in the trial, Garvey dismissed his lawyer Henry Johnson and defended himself.

"For a month Garvey had a magnificent time in that federal courtroom. In his role as attorney for the defendant, he had such fun with the witnesses arrayed against him that he appeared to forget the gravity of the charge," McKay wrote.

Nevertheless, a jury found him guilty and he was sentenced to five years in federal prison. He appealed. While the appeals process dragged on for several years, Marcus Garvey's enemies grew. They wrote or signed petitions demanding that he be jailed, deported, or both. Many of his detractors were black like Randolph and included George W. Harris, a prominent politician and editor of a Harlem-based newspaper called the *New York News*; Robert S. Abbott at the *Chicago Defender*, and Chandler Owen, coeditor with Randolph on the *Messenger* magazine. Other prominent figures who petitioned the government against Garvey were realtor Williams Pickens and Robert W. Bagnall, both officials of the NAACP, the civil rights organization that had organized the Friends of Negro Freedom to defend Garvey shortly after he was arrested in 1922.

"Well, by June 1924, instead of perching majestically on his golden throne in some far away jungle clearing, being waited [upon] the erstwhile Black Napoleon and Provisional President of Africa, found himself sitting, disconsolate and alone, in a bare cell of the Tombs prison in Manhattan," UNIA member Milner said.[22] After a 27-day trial in U.S. District Court, the jury found Garvey guilty of attempting to defraud using the U.S. Postal Service.

"Loyal officers of the movement had a bail bondsman on hand, ready to secure the release of their idol" but an assistant U.S. Attorney "foiled this move by asking that Garvey be remanded to prison without bail." He allegedly claimed that Garvey's well-known personal army, the African Legion, "was well supplied with guns and ammunition and would probably help their chief to escape.

"And so, in the midst of heavily armed U.S. Marshals and a detachment of New York City policemen, the "Leader of the Negro Peoples of the World," was marched off to the Tombs. Later, he was transferred to a federal prison in Atlanta. "With him went his dreams of a great Black Empire, his visions of a final welding of all Negroes into one strong, powerful nation, with himself as dictator; his favorite supporters, elegant lords, princes, dukes and other personages of high-sounding title: like 'High Commissioner,' 'His Highness and Royal Potentate,' 'Minister of the African Legion,' 'The Right Honorable High Chancellor,' 'His Excellency, Prince of Uganda,' 'Lord of the Nile' and so on." Milner recalled.

Jail did not silence Marcus Garvey. It seemed to animate him, his countryman Claude McKay wrote, and he issued communiqués from his jail cell that appeared on the front page of his newspaper every week.

Legal wrangling between Garveyites and his detractors ensued. Petitions for a pardon were signed and sent to politicians, including President Calvin Coolidge. Jury members who had convicted Garvey, later signed a statement favoring his release. Media giants like the *New York Daily News*, the largest daily circulation newspaper in the world, demanded that Garvey be pardoned..

In the fall of 1927, the royal leader was freed and deported to Jamaica. He was transported to New Orleans where he boarded the *Saramacca* and sailed for Kingston. His dream of establishing a modern black empire in Africa sailed with him. "There was no evidence that he had ever set foot on that continent," his 1940 obituary in *The New York Times* read. "The Republic of Liberia was ... closed to him and his followers. He blamed the British and French Governments for that. His proposed hegira of black men and women back to the continent of their origin remained to the last simply a proposal." When UNIA founder left New Orleans bound for Kingston in 1927, he sailed into history as a clown, not as the martyr he had become to tens of thousands of black people around the world.

"Marcus Garvey's influence over Aframericans, native Africans and people of African descent everywhere was vast," Claude McKay wrote in *Harlem: Negro Metropolis*. "Whether that influence was positive or pervasive and indirect, Negroes of all classes were stirred to a finer feeling of racial consciousness. The intellectual Negro's hostility and criticism of Garvey were ... motivated by a spirit of resentment that the amazing energy and will to uplift awakened in the Negroes by Garvey were not harnessed" for more practical purposes. If Marcus Garvey did not originate the phrase, New Negro, he at least made it popular."[23]

Historians John Hope Franklin and Alfred A. Moss concurred in their comprehensive study *From Slavery to Freedom: A History of Negro Americans*.[24] Franklin and Moss wrote:

Although few black writers would concede it, there could be no denying that Marcus Garvey was one of the greatest energizers of the New Negro Movement by raising the consciousness of millions of black Americans, by outraging many of their articulate leaders such as W.E.B. Du Bois and James Weldon Johnson and by creating so much excitement in Harlem for black and white alike, Garvey stimulated a variety of forms of expression.

As unpalatable as Garveyism had been to the more conservative elements of the Negro intelligentsia, a group of well-educated men in this loosely formed group calling themselves New Negroes, created an unprecedented opportunity to advance their own political agenda. It began with the independent claims of orators like Hubert Harrison in the early 1920s and was repeated at a fancy dinner at a downtown club in 1924 where the first novel of a black woman, *There is Confusion* by Jessie Redmon Fauset, was introduced to white publishers. Led by Alain Locke from Howard University and joined by others, these New Negroes saw what Garvey and others in Harlem had accomplished as a rare opportunity for progressives, and they jumped at the chance.

It was like someone jumping at the sun, hoping to not be burned. Some said they succeeded, while others deemed the New Negro Movement a dismal failure. As an absolute, it is arguable either way.

CHAPTER SEVEN

Exit the New Negro

Many arrivals like Dorothy West, Richard Wright, Claude McKay, Charles S. Johnson, and many others only lived in Harlem for a few years. When they left, their reputations from those days in Harlem often faded too like the New Negroes who also came and went from Harlem over the years and were soon forgotten.

There was a declining artistic base in Harlem after the 1930s, but Harlem remained home to a booming, almost revolutionary political force with many facets whose imprint had a remarkable effect upon black and American culture. Some historians agree that the 1926 publication of *Fire!!!* was a significant watermark that saw the end of the short-lived, polite artistic movement first seen in Harlem and the beginning of a long and sustained period of black political and social activist movements in Harlem.

After *Fire!!!*, scholar Cheryl Wall, a professor at Rutgers University and a leading expert on the period said that the New Negro Movement no longer existed. Like the Negro himself, the New Negro was an abstraction, a rhetorical figure, not a flesh and blood individual.

"The literary movement that so many refer to as the 'Harlem Renaissance' remains contested terrain and the need to periodize and name the movement is ongoing," according to A. Yşmisi Jimoh.[1] "As the literary production of the New Negro era came to a close, participants in the literary movement such as Zora Neale Hurston, Sterling Brown, Wallace Thurman, James Weldon Johnson, Dorothy West, Arna Bontemps, Langston Hughes, Alain Locke, W. E. B. Du Bois, Charles S. Johnson and others gave different accounts of its value, its beginnings, and its end."

"Many students of the period regard the Harlem Renaissance as having ended ... in 1930," historian John Hope Franklin wrote, but "the Harlem Renaissance would not end in the foreseeable future. Black writers and artists would continue to claim the attention of an ever-increasing number of readers, listeners, and observers in many parts of the world. The twenties and thirties were quite special since they marked the emergence of the Afro-American artist who could say something significant, in so many different ways, about life in this country and ... transformed it into a powerful relevant statement that would greatly influence subsequent generations,"[2] Franklin said.

This idea installed during the 1920s elevating Harlem to the status of Mecca emerged from folk culture that was evident everywhere in Harlem. It became the center of plots in novels, short stories, and lines in poems about Harlem and life there. Wallace Thurman wrote a play called *Harlem*. Hughes wrote a famous poem many believe is called "A Raisin in the Sun" that was actually called *Harlem* too. The poem inspired a play and later a motion picture called *A Raisin in the Sun* by Lorraine Hansberry. The story was transported from Harlem to Chicago, but the upward mobile journey came from a spirit of achievement that was reeked of Harlem. In a story called *Cook* by Dorothy West under the name of Jane Isaac and published in her magazine, *Challenge* in 1934, we are invited into the Harlem residence and life of a prominent Harlem physician poised to open his own hospital. The story captured the mood and the state of mind that became well known during those years when West lived in Harlem. Over the years, that Harlem frame of mind moved beyond the borders of Harlem, New York, and later could be found across America in the piercing voices of gospel singers, the music people had started calling jazz and it spread as if the New Negroes had personally delivered this cultural message.

This frame of mind saw black activists and artists veer away from typical American artistic forms and social movements that had come before for black people; this attitude began the evolution of an indigenous, new American folk culture. Historian Norman Coombs said this is "to be understood as the African's emotional reaction to his American ordeal of slavery. Out of this environment along with its suffering and deprivation, has evolved an Afro-American culture. He added, "It was only with the emergence of the New Negro and the Negro Renaissance that this folk culture entered the mainstream of the art world. Previously, those Negroes who had gained enough education to participate in literary creations generally strove to join the American middle class, and tried to disavow all connections with their lower class background."[3]

This was the path taken before by numerous immigrant groups. In a growing circle of black writing, the need to assimilate had a chilling effect on the relationship these artists would have with the New Negroes who had initially embraced them.

"Alain Locke saw an opportunity and took it," wrote Andrew Cline in "Rhetoric of the New Negro," a scholarly paper. "For a moment, while he had the ear of the white literati, Locke spoke the words they wanted to hear. His purpose was honorable if misguided: He wished to see African-American writers published and further the goal of assimilation."[4] In the defining essays he published in *The New Negro*, Locke said what had to be said to make these things happen.[5] "To the ears of Du Bois's Talented Tenth, the words sounded like liberation," Cline said. To writers, musicians, artists, and politicians, he represented control, the one thing no real artists can tolerate as illustrated in the tone and substance of *Fire!!!*

The goal of the New Negro was more honorable, Cline notes. He said it was an attempt to create an image of a New Negro that could make stereotypical images of blacks like the Kingfish, Stepin Fetchit, and Jim Crow disappear from the American minds forever. Cline said it failed because the artists that Locke claimed to represent refused to "conform their art to a model of classic (white) beauty and their refusal to focus on the so-called best of their race."[6]

When bad economic times hit after 1929s and the New York Stock Exchange collapsed, Hughes said, it "sent Negroes, white folks, and all rolling down the hill towards the (federal welfare program called) Works Progress Administration."[7] By this time, many of the writers who had come to live in Harlem had already tapped into main arteries of Harlem culture. It led them straight to the soul of Harlem life as it was, not how it had been imagined by New Negroes. Historians and critics who said the period was doomed for failure, failed to realize that hundreds of thousands of blacks who flooded Harlem after the 1920s, came and never left.

Many notables lived on in Harlem for decades after the so-called Renaissance had been declared a failure. West stayed until an illness forced her to leave the city for Martha's Vineyard in 1940. Langston Hughes came in the 1920s and never left. Ralph Ellison lived on the Riverside Drive, a swanky boulevard on the fringe of Harlem, until he died in 1994. Director Orson Welles came to Harlem in 1936 to produce an all-black production of *Macbeth* at the Lafayette Theater. The largest African American Day parade was staged in 1969 in Harlem with Adam Clayton Powell Jr. as the grand marshal.

At last count, there were over 400 churches and synagogues operating in storefronts and grand cathedral-like buildings in Harlem representing major Christian and Jewish denominations. The National Black Theater set up shop in Harlem in 1968 and continues to mount productions there. There were many arrivals to Harlem. Hundreds of fraternal, cultural and social clubs, and political entities established residencies in Harlem and that foundation remains in the community today.

As these separate and singular movements took on life of their own, distinct from the racial and social politics of the communities where they occurred, this collective power unleashed what Gunter Lenz called "the subversion, revision, and transformation of their old forms of community and communal rituals."

Writing in the journal *Callaloo*, Lenz said the suspension of traditional, subservient behaviors among these Negro populations "opened up to the migrants from the South a new perspective on the validity and potential use of their folk culture and set free enormous energies for understanding, appropriating, and influencing a 'reality' that they at first could neither describe nor comprehend."[8]

It was expressed in music, dance crazes that eventually swept across America, in poetry, songs, novels, short stories in *Esquire* magazine and *Vanity Fair*, in politics and these stories rekindled old or existing social and political movements. It was thrilling, shocking and to many, a disturbing departure from the sometimes idyllic poetry, music, and literature being created to describe communities that were rapidly becoming poor ghettos while they were being called havens and heavens.

In "Harlem's America," an essay published in the fall of 1966 issue of *New Leader*, Ralph Ellison again tried to put this vast Negro Renaissance and American history into perspective.[9]

"It is a misunderstanding to assume that Negroes want to break out of Harlem. They want to transform Harlem, the Harlems of their country. These places are precious to them. These places are where they have dreamed, where they have lived, where they have loved, where they have worked out life as they could. All of these Harlems, Ellison said, contain important forms of social memory and literary invention of people with the power to reinvent themselves, places like Harlem and like Camelot," that imaginary realm where knights and the kings live forever. . . . Camelot . . . a city of shadowy palaces, is symbolic of the gradual growth of human beliefs and institutions, and of the spiritual development of man."[10]

In the minds of many, Harlem was Camelot—the realm of black kings and knights.

CHAPTER EIGHT

Mystic Knights

Harlem and what happened there had greater importance and impact than stories about rent parties, all-night drinking, and reviews of Cotton Club acts might have suggested. The Cotton Club was a segregated establishment owned by racist mobsters. The kind of frolicking captured in Carl Van Vechten's novel *Nigger Heaven* was an enticing slice of black life and became an indelible but scant sketch of the real Harlem.

Harlem had become home to the early literary works of a handful of writers. But these young artists were rebels who did not wish to join forces with an old guard of "race men" intent upon uplifting the images of the Negro in a nation that had long ago replaced slavery with brutal forms of indentured labor and widespread segregation. Race men and women raised families in another Harlem, who took refuge in this small section of New York; they reestablished churches, fellowship halls, and unions in this part of New York, which became their home.

"Old impressions, especially precious ones, die hard. Harlem was never Heaven. It was simply our home," poet Nikki Giovanni wrote. "The concept of a renaissance didn't need to include everyone or even most people. Do we really think the average Greek participated in the Golden Age? Do we really believe the average Egyptian reveled or prospered during the Age of the Pharaohs? Was the average Englishman aware of England ruling the waves? I don't think so. Most people simply tried to live their lives with whatever dignity was available to them," she said. "The same was true for the emancipated people who trekked North in search of freedom. They might not have found what they were looking for but neither did Pasteur, neither did Madam Curie neither did

Columbus but they found something that we all benefited from," she said.

"And so did Harlem," she explained. "It is to the credit of Black Americans that they anchored an age with a song; they built a foundation on a creed; they survived an unspeakable horror with a dream of tomorrow." Telling all of the stories that made Harlem come alive "brings the truth of ordinary folk back into the spotlight," she wrote. "How can the truth be controversial? How can we not celebrate the gifts that these wonderful people bring?"[1]

A black man called Kingfish was exalted ruler of a quirky fraternal order in Harlem. He became the most prominent black man in America in the winter of 1928, capturing the imagination of millions of radio listeners across the country. The uncanny arrival and popularity of this radio personality that March could not have come at a worse time for black leaders in the same community the fictitious Kingfish resided where the birth of a first generation of African Americans was evolving. There were political and social forces in Harlem moving to erase the many negative images of black folks as slaves, former slaves, descendants of slaves, and especially images of the obedient Negroes and transform these people into full-fledged Americans. This was a monumental task that had never happened before in America. A fast-talking con man named Kingfish was not a fitting representative for such lofty ideas.[2]

Nevertheless, a man called Kingfish, head of the fictional Mystic Knights Sea Lodge in Harlem, could be heard by millions of Americans across the country in a popular, nightly radio comedy show called *Amos 'n' Andy*. However, Harlem intellectuals who had arrived in New York in the same decade viewed this on-the-air phenomenon with great disdain. The Kingfish, the balding leader of a rag-tag bunch of janitors, cab drivers, and elevator operators, did not belong to their world.

As the exalted ruler of the Mystic Knights Sea Lodge, the Kingfish was a conniving conjure man whose money-grabbing conspiracies against his own brethren usually backfired. The radio show became as common in American households as war bonds. It debuted as a local program in March 1928 in Chicago. The sitcom was soon being heard in broadcasts throughout the country. On the radio, lodge brothers were in nightly slapstick antics.

The Kingfish, whose name on the show was George Stevens, repeatedly hatched plots to bilk his brothers. These cons were usually pulled on a gullible character named Andy and they almost always failed.

A well-spoken, intelligent cab driver named Amos was a minor character on the show and he made brief appearances. But one of the most notable characters in these episodes was a lazy, slow-talking janitor, Light'nin. Light'nin was a dupe like Andy who resembled racial stereotypes similar to the minstrel show character Jim Crow and Stepin Fetchit.

"Holy Mackerel, Andy!" the Kingfish always said, using this trademark phrase in every 15-minute episode after his cons failed. "We's got to stick together. Remember, we is brothers in the great fraternity, the Mystic Knights of the Sea," the Kingfish declared in a call for brotherly solidarity.

The show became the first syndicated radio program in broadcasting history and stayed on the air for the next three decades. *Amos 'n' Andy* captured a nightly audience of 40 million listeners, a figure that represented a one-third share of an audience of 120 million Americans.[3]

The exaggerated made-up plots accompanied by ignorant-sounding Southern dialects and the Kingfish's schemes touched off a flurry of praise and criticisms. Critics were appalled by the fact that two white men pretending to be black portrayed the Kingfish and Andy. Charles Correll and Freeman Gosden, the white creators, blackened their faces in publicity photos just like minstrel show actors, an act that added fuel to a raging debate over race in America. The framers of evolving civil rights organizations in Harlem were calling themselves black nationalists, socialists, communists, and others still saw themselves as New Negroes. They all viewed *Amos 'n' Andy* as a demeaning racial slur broadcast nightly into homes across a nation that had always ignored this community of African Americans.

Fans, however, praised the shows, saying the episodes captured the humor of a scheming rogue and a hapless patsy, not racial stereotypes. At the height of its popularity, *Amos 'n' Andy* aired 2,700 consecutive shows in four time zones every night at seven o'clock. It was the first situation comedy in radio about blacks to be broadcast over a major American network. *Amos 'n' Andy* also became one of the longest-running, regular features in the NBC radio and later its television lineup, airing a total of more than 4,000 radio episodes between the years 1928 and 1955. In 1951, the show was made into a half-hour television program that ran 78 episodes and featured an all-black cast. This too was a first in American television history.[4] A *New York Times* reviewer praised the TV show for having several good sight gags and said it reminded him of Negro actors in "the old medicine shows so common in the Midwest and South many years ago."[5]

However, when the broadcasts began, the images of blacks projected in them were seen as hurtful stereotypes by the leaders of a loosely connected group of different organizations in Harlem. The NAACP "accused Amos 'n Andy of portraying blacks as lazy, dumb and dishonest, or presenting every cast member as a clown or crook, depicting black doctors as quacks, of suggesting that black lawyers were ignorant and dishonest and of painting black women as cackling, screaming shrews."[6]

In reality, the 1920s had quietly become a turning point in both American and black history, although it isn't always framed in this way. The era marked the establishment of the largest African American community in a nation where black porters, scholars, socialists, communists, Black nationalists, doctors, maids, and gamblers had previously always lived in fringe, segregated parts of larger, mostly white communities elsewhere in the United States. In Harlem, these groups all lived together.

When black people gathered in Harlem, their numbers swelled. When the 28th annual Black Elks' convention was held in New York in 1927, the occasion was marked by a parade that marched up Fifth Avenue from 61st Street to 110th Street where it crossed west and headed up Lenox Avenue into Harlem. The parade was greeted by 40,000 spectators. While New York neighborhoods were often the sights of public displays of ethnic culture, a New York Times reporter said the crowds that gathered uptown had "a certain something to the sound of Harlem."[7]

"Self-consciousness about the political utility of sound did not preclude the enjoyment that noise could bring," the New York Times said. "When one local, Richard Bruce Nugent, recalled the Black Elks' parade, he too described it sonically. He said there was a unity in the noise these Harlem crowds made at parades and political rallies.[8]

Black people living in Harlem no longer saw themselves as the darkies, coloreds, or even as Negroes, all names they had been given since the time of slavery and accentuated in Amos 'n' Andy. On their way to the church, to the park, or the barbershop, they heard and saw black men give speeches and lead parades. In this community, preachers with even the ones with the most outlandish ideas could express themselves from a stepladder on Lenox Avenue and draw a lunchtime crowd of 500 faces. There were newcomers in the community from Africa, the Caribbean, and South America who began to sell books, newspapers, and magazines that had images and stories about all kinds of successful, educated black men and women all over the world, including some descended from real kings.

Although the chosen name at the time among some visionaries in Harlem was the New Negro, the question of what to call ourselves would remained an open debate for many decades. One thing was clear on the streets of Harlem in the 1920s, the descendants of Africans living in America no longer wanted to be coloreds and they would soon not be the same Negroes whose ancestors had been freed from slavery less than half a century earlier either. The idea of the African American had been born. Beginning in the seventeenth century when the first Africans were brought to America, their masters, overseers, and other whites called their captives slaves, or worse, chattel. In later centuries, blacks were called Negroes and Coloreds. They were called many derogatory names, including darkies and the most popular, nigger. But in the early decades of the twentieth century, intellectual blacks in Harlem, Washington, Philadelphia, and elsewhere quietly began searching for ways to stake their claim to the same rights afforded to all other Americans. At the same time, they were determined to erase old, painful images of them as singing, happy-go-lucky niggers in the fields of slavery. This growing feeling of self-esteem grew out of the emerging politics, art, and literature that collectively were being called the Harlem Renaissance in New York and later by others in the rest of America.

Like all communities, this new African American community of Harlem consisted of many different parts. Some called themselves Black Zionists, Black Nationalists, black writers, black poets, poets who were black. Baptist became Black Baptists; Methodist had become American Methodist Episcopal Zionist. They all flirted with various political parties and affiliations that included socialists, labor unions, and communists, all dangerous affiliations in a nation on the verge of hysteria over Communism. Some still called themselves New Negroes in the spiritual sense, an attitude that suggested the extinction of old views of African Americans as servants, maids, nannies, and the shuffling, grinning black fools who appeared in radio scripts like the very popular *Amos 'n' Andy*. This so-called Negro was intelligent, artistic, a strident American who spoke standard American English eloquently. These Negroes were ambitious, educated, and social engineers who championed labor issues and civil rights. In their leisure time, they had intellectual pursuits that uplifted the lives and images of blacks in America. *Amos 'n' Andy* fulfilled none of these goals.

In retrospect, of course, the *Amos 'n' Andy* show could be seen as the first radio and television shows set in a black community. Twenty years after those first radio programs, a variety show hosted by a black singer and called *The Nat King Cole Show*, aired in the early 1950s on prime time television. It was followed in the next decade by a popular comedy variety program, *The Flip Wilson Show*. In the 1980s, a program about an upper middle-class, black family in Brooklyn, *The Bill Cosby Show*, captured the imagination of American audiences in much the same way as *Amos 'n' Andy* had 50 years earlier. Projecting the family life of a successful black doctor and his lawyer wife, the show garnered a majority viewing audience for NBC during prime time too for most of the 1980s.

"Harlem was the heart of a black modernity in which blackness became an open signifier," says Paul Gilroy author of *The Black Atlantic: Modernity and Double Consciousness*.[9] Gilroy's statement marries two separate and simultaneous movements in American history. History always assumes that Modernism to be a European movement distinguished by writing, art, and politics with elements of primitivism, experimental forms, and alienation. Each of these elements aptly describes the nucleus of Garveyism, the socialist speeches of Hubert Harrison, the activism of union activists who agitated for change in thunderous speeches to throngs of black listeners in Harlem. It can also be seen easily in the works of Harlem artists such as Hughes, Ellison, Dorothy West, Zora Hurston, Frank Yerby, and many others.

"I teach American Modernism in culturally and racially diverse classrooms," says Adrienne Johnson Gosselin in *Beyond the Harlem Renaissance: The Case for Black Modernist Writers*. "Needless to say, I include black authors—not as Harlem Renaissance writers on the periphery of a larger, Euro-American movement, but as black Americans participating in the Modernist phenomenon." A significant watershed of black modernism was demonstrated in February 1919 celebrating the return of the all-black 369th Infantry who marched uptown to Harlem to the cheers of thousands. "The parade marks the beginning of the New Negro Movement ... while World War One left younger white intellectuals with the sense of disillusion that characters the works of Ernest Hemingway, the participation of 340,000 African American soldiers in the war to make the world safe for democracy was for black intellectuals irrefutable proof—logically, morally, and politically—of a racial claim as American." The march signified the Americanism of the 369th soldiers and their solidarity to the black crowds who cheered their march all the way uptown and into the waiting arms of the Harlem community.[10]

If Hemingway was the voice of white modernism, Dorothy West, Richard Wright, and Claude McKay became the voices of black modernism in Harlem, crucible of an emerging African American nation within the nation.

Nearly four years after the American Stock Exchange collapsed in 1929, Harlem intellectual and author of "Lift Every Voice and Sing," the black national anthem, James Weldon Johnson wrote:

> It is a good thing that [the editor] Dorothy West is doing in instituting a magazine [*Challenge*] through which the voices of younger Negro writers can be heard. The term "younger Negro writers" connotes a degree of disillusionment and disappointment for those who a decade ago hailed with loud huzzas the dawn of the Negro literary millennium. We expected much; perhaps, too much. I now judge that we ought to be thankful for the half-dozen younger writers who did emerge and make a place for themselves.[11]

While many say this was Johnson's homage to a failed renaissance, I speculate it just as easily could be seen as the noting of the continuum of a literary genre that thrived in later decades and carved its way into an American literary niche.

CHAPTER NINE

New York Frame of Mind

Social critics and the New Negroes in the early decades of the last century became the architects of a movement that would give birth to reimagined black life in America. In this new landscape, there would no longer be room for the comedy of white men in black face.

Harlem was now the staging area for the greatest civil, economic, literary, and social justice experiments ever staged in America. Eighty years later, in the early years of the twenty-first century, modern scholars would realize that these were actually simultaneous acts, not different ones that were called the Harlem Renaissance and the New Negro Movement, Modernism and Black Modernism. These theories were just the newest parts of a long chain of activist theory and activity in this community that had never been a homogeneous, single part of the one movement. Coupled with the ideas of agitators, organizers, writers, and black power advocates of an earlier time, Harlem of the 1920s and later decades became ripe as a breeding ground for the same kind of solidarity ironically that the Kingfish had pleaded for among his fraternal brothers on the radio.

Like the Harlem the radio Kingfish lived in, solidarity was often hard to find during the Harlem Renaissance years in the real New York community. The community had become the crossroads for many causes taken up a long time before anyone had named an era for all of this activity. The community was the vessel where a kind of alchemy of like and unlike elements came together as far back as the late nineteenth century when unlikely people, sophisticated, educated or not, shared common goals. Howard University poet and scholar Sterling Brown identified these as:

- The need to reclaim Africa as a source of racial pride.
- Reclaiming heroic episodes by blacks in American history.
- Voicing demands that black workers be treated equally and fairly.
- Using the propaganda of protest.
- Using the media to foster self-revelation and expression.[1]

To achieve these goals in segregated America had always been a monumental challenge. In communities throughout the country, blacks still could not vote, buy real estate, sleep in hotel rooms, eat in restaurants, or use other public accommodations like libraries, swimming pools, or public parks. Schools, neighborhoods, and other public facilities were segregated and had been since before the end of slavery.

These were all things that strong willed black men and woman were determined to change by doing what reconstruction after the Civil War had failed to accomplish. They were determined to claim citizenship on behalf of 20 million black people in a nation that had always ignored them. Harlemites had long made these demands in a series of cultural, political, and social movements that began as early as the 1890s. In a sense, what was first noticed in the 1920s and called the Harlem Renaissance may in fact had been a revival of political and social activism overshadowed or forgotten in favor of a more fanciful idea of an artistic Harlem community. These many and varied social ideals were vigorously expressed by the various organizations that had always been a vital part of Harlem.

"Harlem is a dream city pregnant with wide-awake realities," wrote Wallace Thurman, the Utah writer who was an early agitator and journalist in Harlem. "It is a masterpiece of contradictory elements and surprising types. There is no end to its versatile presentation of people, personalities and institutions. Harlem is a city of constant surprise, a city of ecstatic moments and diverting phenomena. It is an egregious ensemble, offering many surprise packets of persons, places, amusements, and occupations. It is a city in which anything might happen and everything does. Life there is not stable and monotonous. It is moving and colorful, and richly studded by contrasting elements and contradictory types," Thurman said.[2]

All of these forces churned together into a vibrant culture that transformed Harlem from just a place in the state of New York to a state of mind. Like some potent elixir, this was the essence of the Harlem

Renaissance, a self-conscious, willful, strident, and fearless movement that eventually became a driving force for change that slowly spread across the nation and lasted for decades longer than many believed. Each of the many real fraternities, groups, and organizations that were uptown, carved out cultural and political turf for themselves in the two square miles that made up Harlem. Their campaigns were deliberately planned and carried out by men and women who sometimes mimicked other successful political campaigns or structured their followers into subjects found in small European kingdoms.

"So you want me to tell you something about Negro Folklore well, here's a story about a strapping, jet-black Negro that will live as long as folk tales are handed down from generation to generation. To many, he was a clown; a jester who wanted to play at being king but, to hundreds of thousands of Negroes, he was a magnificent leader and martyr to a great cause; complete and unconditional social and economic freedom for Negroes everywhere. And, had it not been for one flaw in his plan of action, there would probably be no more than a handful us Negroes in America today. His name was Marcus Garvey,"[3] said UNIA member Wilbert J. Miller in an interview with WPA writer Vivian Morris on October 20, 1938.

Garvey was one of many who migrated to Harlem from all over the world. Their schemes sometimes did resemble those of the fictitious Kingfish. And like the Kingfish, they presided over entities and followers who believed their sometimes hypnotic rhetoric. Opponents saw them differently, calling them pretentious, contentious, and opportunists fighting the demons mainstream America who either did not see or care to see afflictions of black people. In some instances, these Harlem-based leaders pitted themselves against American idols that built railroads, the Ku Klux Klan and other homegrown terrorists, and against a federal government that drafted black soldiers into segregated forces but would not give them jobs when they came home from war wounded and broke.

Harlem was alive with all of this activity of black people calling themselves labor activists, socialist, communist agitators, political assassins, journalist, scholars, and intellectuals. These were the activities of the many dreamers who came to Harlem to hatch hard-to-win campaigns and many times lost causes. Still they came. Finding solidarity among these eclectic groups was not always easy, and it was often impossible.

They inhabited a Harlem where fishmongers, singers, and entrepreneurs were sometimes fraternal brothers in the same lodges or groups.

They embodied an intangible that no intellectual view of Harlem of the period, then or even now, has adequately captured or explained to my satisfaction.

In the 1925 Harlem edition of *Survey Graphic Magazine*, essayist Konrad Bercovici wrote that he found an emerging peasant culture flowing into Harlem that did not exist anywhere else in America.

"I listened to the preachers in the churches of Harlem. I understood the language," Bercovici declared, but he added something was left unsaid in sermons by ministers who seemed to be "fashioning another God for himself and for his congregation?"

In an essay called "The Rhythm of Harlem," Bercovici witnessed people using language he suspected had been lying dormant for a long time. It was in their souls, he said. "The color of the voice, the tone, the rhythm, the music of the phrase was something peculiarly their own. Beautiful? Yes, but different." While he did not always understand words he heard spoken uptown, he suspected there was another medium of communications, which he did not know.[4]

"I have heard Harlem men planning business, planning politics, speaking of life and death. And in all of this, though the surface was clear and understandable, there was another element under the surface, hardly hinted at in the spoken words," Bercovici wrote.[5]

Perhaps, Bercovici was talking about authentic neighborhood cultures, which Pulitzer Prize-winning writer Toni Morrison noticed too in her novel, *Jazz*. "When they fall in love with a city it is for forever. As though there never was a time when they didn't love it. The minute they arrive at the train station or get off the ferry and glimpse the wide streets and the wasteful lamps lighting them, they know they are born for it. There, in a city, they are not so much new as themselves, their stronger, riskier selves," is the language of Morrison's *Jazz*, a romantic language that black people know like they know their own music. And like Ralph Ellison before her, my brother and I in our time in the 1960s, Morrison admits in her novel, "I'm crazy about this city. A city like this one makes me dream tall and feel in on things. Hep."[6]

It was this kind of uplifting mood and a real passion for many unrequited dreams that flowed through the minds of the black, brown, and tan faces in a community like Harlem that had now become a citadel. Black people born in Florida arrived uptown and enrolled as students at City College or the prestigious Ivy League institutions they found uptown. The first time my grandfather took me to Harlem on the A Train, it was perhaps the most exhilarating ride of my life. We caught the train at the Nostrand Avenue stop in Brooklyn.

In Manhattan, the train stopped at 14th, 34th and 42nd Streets. Next came 59th Street, but when the doors closed at that station, everything changed. The A Train became an express, suddenly hurtling us uptown at wild speeds past station after station until it rolled into 125th Street, the first stop in Harlem. It was a rush I still cannot forget, all these decades later.

Others who came were in New York to become doctors, teachers, dentists, and clinical researchers earning degrees from Columbia University and other colleges just on the fringe of Harlem. Musicians like Edward Ellington left Washington, DC, to emerge in Harlem as a nationally known figure whose music was broadcasts from Harlem nightclubs to radio listeners everywhere. Everybody knows how they first got to Harlem, whether they actually took the A Train like me, or they arrived on the Westside by car on the Major Deegan, or made their way to New York by way of Grand Central Terminal. All of this was the frenetic pace of Harlem that Bercovici and Morrison recognized.

Bercovici said there had always been wildly passionate men and women leaders in Harlem. A journalist who covered Harlem, he they followers to their causes using God, sometime the promise of better jobs and sometimes they sought out leaders in an endless search black people have had for real freedom. Many used roaring speeches on the street or in editorials they ran in the many homegrown newspapers and magazines produced in Harlem.

"Night and day, life teemed along a twenty-block stretch of Seventh Avenue which some took to calling The Great Black Way," Bercovici noted. "The blocks on Seventh between 125th and 145th Streets, became a sea of unfamiliar faces that did not seem like strangers because they were all blacks. Every element of Harlem flowed through this wide promenade where sordid chaos on one block and mixed seamlessly with the "rhythmic splendor" of life on another.

"Majestic and well-kept, sandstone and brick apartment houses towered along Seventh Avenue. An array of ground floor barber shops sporting red and white leather chairs with chrome plated handles and foot rests, were nestled among glittering theaters with flashing marquees, noisy bars and pool halls," he said. "Honky-tonk blues and dance music blared everywhere, pouring out of the beauty parlors, second-floor dance halls and rent parties that were held on upper floors of these splendid buildings."

"There were many restaurants too. Some served West Indian concoctions made with Codfish, coconut and bananas. The aroma of home-cooked southern dishes like chitterlings, pork chops smothered in gravy or specialties from some part of Africa. Some of these eateries sported brightly colored, red, white or green awnings that reached from the main entrance to the curb across sidewalks that were wide enough to be roads themselves in a smaller city."[7]

He saw groups of well-dressed people in suits, broad brimmed hats, and other finery moving up and down Seventh Avenue. Depending upon the time of day, some were on their way to nearby churches, dance halls, or religious revivals," Bercovici reported. Some walked in a leisurely way while others seem to loiter with no particular place to go.

"Groups of boisterous men and boys, congregated on corners and in the middle of the blocks, making remarks about individuals in the passing parade," Wallace Thurman wrote. "Street speakers on every corner. A Hindu faker here, a loud-voiced Socialist there, medicine doctor ballyhooing, a corn doctor, a blind musician, serious people, gay [happy] people, philanderers and preachers," he added, characterizing these crowds.

Gatherings of all these divergent groups wandering Seventh Avenue, catching a subway train on Lenox, or attending a ball at the Savoy, are symbolic of Harlem of the 1920s, a crossroad of black culture, class, and creeds.[8]

Ellison once described the Negro as the nation's last, lost tribe. Families torn apart and scattered during hundreds of years of slavery and rebels who fled their surroundings after race riots or colonial disputes in the Caribbean regrouped in Harlem. Uptown, people just naturally found their own people again from Barbados, St. Helena Island in South Carolina, or someone from the same elementary school in Greenville, North Carolina. After finding each other now living in Harlem, they had resumed having annual reunions, dances, or lavish parties, but now they were held at the Savoy.

Harlem became a community of many varieties of academic, tribal artists, and regional cultures. In Harlem, these tribes of Negroes came together to preserve old traditions or to create new, and sometimes powerful political, labor, or social paradigms. They showed solidarity for each other sometimes in the most mundane activities. Each group would use the same beauty parlor or barber shop that catered only to Southerners from the same region or to West Indians from the same island community. These groups were numerous in Harlem and they transcended almost all religious, social, and economic borders.

Some of these groups had more formal names like the Independent Benevolent Protective Order of Elks of the World, the organization headed by numbers kingpin and gambling boss Casper Holstein. They were called the Commandment Keepers, a group of black Jews in Harlem. There was the Ancient Order of Free Gardeners, the Ancient Order of Mechanics, the Universal Negro Improvement Association, the Urban League, and the National Association for the Advancement of Colored People, all operating within a few blocks of each other.

While the *Amos 'n' Andy* radio program had been created by two unknown minstrel show actors, the show aptly mirrored a small but important uptown society in the 1920s. The Kingfish and his brothers made their way on to the stage of American and broadcast history. Groups in Harlem seeking to be identified by their geographic origins called themselves names like the Sons and Daughters of Barbados; the Dominica Benevolent Society or the Windward Islands Progressive League.

As like-minded groups arrived, they set up meeting places, fraternal orders, and self-help organizations much like the fraternity headed by radio personalities Kingfish and Andy.

The Prince Hall Masons, a branch of the North American Freemasonry founded by Prince Hall in the eighteenth century, had a Harlem chapter. The Independent Benevolent Protective Order of Elks of the World clustered new members in Harlem for monthly and annual events. These lodges began after membership of blacks was rejected by white lodges with same or similar names.

The inherent secrecy of these fraternal organizations made their lodges ideal places for meetings where prying eyes could not listen. This need for secrecy became useful when black railroad porters and maids tried to organize the first all-black union. Led by A. Philip Randolph, he gathered 500 sleeping car porters at the Elks Lodge #27 in Harlem in the fall of 1925. It was said to be the greatest labor mass meeting ever held by black working men, the *Amsterdam News* reported. It took a dozen years of organizing but in the 1930s, the Pullman Company gave the International Brotherhood of Sleeping Car Porters and Maids its first contract.[9]

The Commandment Keepers, the oldest and largest community of black Hebrews in the United States, was founded in Harlem in 1919. Though this congregation traces its origin to the activities of those who came to New York during the first waves of black migration and immigration, it was in the post-World War II years that the community took root, according to the New York Public Library Schomburg Center for Research in Black Culture. This congregation spawned six other synagogues in the Greater New York metropolitan area.

In a twist to the concept of the New Negro, the Commandment Keepers synagogue took the claim to new heights. "The Black Jews in the United States are a variant of a number of Negro groups whose members believe that the so-called Negro is misnamed, that they have recovered their true identity and religion that had been robbed from them by the slave masters, and that Christianity is the religion of the whites," Howard Brotz writes in an article titled "Negro Jews in the United States," *Phylon*, 1952.

"They have endowed themselves, a group of low social status, with honored descent from what is evaluated by them as an honored (non-white) group and in such terms that they not only have nullified the shame of slavery but feel superior ... to whites," he said. "In addition to the religious sects elaborating this theme, this a-political, self-indulgent nationalism that has also been the mainspring of several secular groups such as the Ethiopian World Federation and the Back-to-Africa movement of Marcus Garvey."[10]

Often referred to as The Royal Order of Aethiopian Hebrews and sometimes the Sons and Daughters of Culture, Inc., the Commandment Keepers Congregation was founded by the charismatic Rabbi Wentworth Arthur Matthew, a man with disputed origins. Some sources say he was born in Nigeria while others say he was a West Indian born on the island of St. Kitts in the Caribbean. In any event, Matthew fully adopted the idea of reinventing himself in Harlem just as many migrants and immigrants had also chosen to do. It was in vogue to reinvent oneself and Harlem was the perfect place to do it. Like many newcomers, Matthew was apparently not well liked by established men in Harlem like Du Bois, James Weldon Johnson, and others who viewed his sects as a cult. Nevertheless, they coexisted in Harlem for decades.

"Perhaps they instinctively felt the need of more local protection," Claude McKay wrote in *Harlem: Negro Metropolis*, speaking of the many lodges and organizations formed in Harlem. The first known group of black Democrats in New York called themselves the United Negro Democracy, according to McKay.[11] A man who called himself Chief Edward E. Lee organized that group. Lee's title came from the fact that he was a head bellman at a downtown hotel. Lee elicited political promises from leading figures in city hall, formerly known as Tammany Hall to appoint blacks to key posts in city agencies that served Harlem. However, white political leaders betrayed Lee's group of black Democrats when they appointed other whites to run the black voting districts.

"In Tammany politics as in the Republican Party, it was the same old chronic sickness of indirect representation, the eternal tapeworm in the belly of Negro life," McKay noted. He said this kind of political trickery did not go unnoticed by some of the more independent, out-spoken men uptown.[12]

CHAPTER TEN

Black Socrates

The solidarity Kingfish had pleaded for on the radio among the Mystic Knights, ironically, became the single-most sought-after commodity in the Harlem community. As people became increasingly aware of it and the political power it could exert collectively, the need for unity in the community also became evident for the first time as early as the 1890s, as many black political factions in New York and leaders began to vie for support of a wide array of causes and movements.

Communists, Socialists, separatists, religious cults, black nationalists and assimilationists and other groups, swarmed the streets of Harlem in search of converts. One of the most dramatic ways these men and women acquired a following was by giving stump speeches perched on top of wooden soap boxes or stepladders where they preached labor reform, tenant's rights, civil rights, politics, or the rights of workers to unionize.

One of the most exceptional men among these street orators was Hubert Harrison. In 1899, Harrison left his native St. Croix at 16 and worked his way to New York as a cabin boy. In the city, he worked routine jobs like a hotel hall boy running errands and the elevator for guests. At night, he took college courses and eventually became a foreign language clerk in the United States Post Office in Manhattan. Over the next four years, he studied anthropology, sociology, literature and drama, according to one biographer, and he joined the parade of Harlem street orators who took turns attracting crowds with speeches to crowds on Lenox Avenue.[1]

Using a stepladder to peer above crowd, he championed the causes of the underprivileged, the constitutional rights of blacks, Irish home rule, and independence in India and China from British rule. An avowed socialist,[2] Harrison founded the Liberty League in Harlem and published a newspaper called *The Voice*. Crowds flocked to his speeches by the thousands, according to accounts in *The New York Times*, which said Harrison drew diverse crowds in Harlem, at Columbus Circle, Ninety-Sixth Street, and Broadway or downtown on Wall Street.[3]

"Harrison roamed the city giving speeches to large crowds of whites and blacks in different parts of the city. Some of America's wealthiest men, attracted by his eloquence, would stop to hear his dissertations on philosophy, history, economics, and religion," according to *The Voice of Harlem Radicalism*.[4]

To earn a living, Harrison often sold books on the street to passersby, a common sight out-side of city subway stations. He was a successful vendor of books and allegedly sold hundreds of books on various scholarly subjects, including sociology and philosophy to black people, a group not well educated at the time and therefore not inclined to read.

Harrison's oratory came from his own writing. By the time he was 24, he was composing book reviews for the *New York Times* and articles for *The New Republic*, *The Nation*, the *New York Sun*, *Tribune*, the *World* and other metropolitan newspapers. As a practiced orator, Harrison did more than give speeches; he performed, bantered, and debated people in the crowds he attracted.

In public, he was said to be a fierce, hard-nosed debater. In private, friends said, Harrison was kindly and good natured, both among the common people and the broad-minded intellectuals he encountered. He was happiest and at his best on a soapbox surrounded by admiring listeners and a heckler or two to match him in a combat of wits. He would usually make short work of hecklers who entertained his audiences that drew outbursts of laughter from the crowds he gathered.

"It was a revelation to see Hubert Harrison mounted on the street corner ladder and surrounded by a crowd of several hundred Negroes discussing philosophy, psychology, economics, literature, astronomy or the drama, and holding his audience spellbound," according to blogger Andrew Wilson of Nassau, Bahamas.

"His achievements should prove an inspiration to many young Negroes, for despite the handicap of poverty, he became one of the most learned men of his day, and was able to teach the wide masses of his race how to appreciate and enjoy all the finer things of life, to glance back over the whole history of mankind, and to look forward as far as thought can reach," according to the *New York Times*. The newspaper said Harrison once drew a crowd of 11,000 listeners on September 11, 1922, in a speech he gave on the steps of the U.S. Treasury building across the street from the New York Stock Exchange. "Hubert Harrison, an eloquent and forceful speaker, broke all records at the Stock Exchange yesterday," *The Times* wrote.[5]

Often called the "Father of Harlem Radicalism," Hubert Harrison's legacy as a lightning rod for controversy was buried with him when he died suddenly in 1927 after appendicitis surgery. His sudden death less than 25 years after he arrived in Harlem and took center stage as an activist, agitator, and visionary, left his reputation unattended to and it soon withered before any historians of note could properly catalogue his contribution to Harlem history. Fortunately, that legacy was rescued and is now housed in papers at the rare book library of Columbia University awaiting further inquiry by scholars.[6]

Harrison's arrival in New York in 1900 was unremarkable except for the fact that just three years later he published a letter in *New York Times* expressing his interest in socialism, free thought, and radical independence for Negroes. He soon made his mark with huge crowds who gathered around his soapbox listening to fiery speeches covering almost everything that ailed Negroes, including race, class, politics, social justice, and a wide range of other subjects.

A prolific writer and founder of newspapers, magazines, and commentary in both local and national publications, Harrison quickly became well known in intellectual, social, and political circles in New York between the years of 1906 and when he died two decades later. His form and style ran counter to the voices of more conservative Negro leaders, choosing to taunt, challenge, and tangle with the most popular ideas and people of his time before he died. Unflinchingly direct, Harrison challenged some of the most powerful politicians and leaders in America, which helped him draw huge street crowds at the same time, and he became almost universally unpopular among his peers.[7]

Born in 1883 in Concordia, St. Croix, his oratory became legendary and was later copied by Marcus Garvey and decades later by Malcolm X. "Harrison's first publication ... a 1904 letter to the editor, took exception to a *New York Times* editorial claiming that a case of chicken stealing revealed a propensity to vice innate in the whole of the black race," wrote Mark Solomon in 2004.[8]

"The stereotypes and prejudices of Jim Crow America were not Harrison's only mark. Across time, Harrison elaborated a political and cultural outlook that challenged the nostrums of virtually every leading black figure of his day."[9]

Supporter of many causes, he jumped into the fray of the most controversial arguments of his time, notably criticizing Negro leader
Booker T. Washington's conservative view of racial justice, the views
of W.E.B Du Bois and many others.

He referred to Booker T. Washington, the conservative go-to-Negro
based at the Tuskegee Institute in Alabama as a "great leader, by the
grace of the white people who elected colored people's leaders for
them," he is quoted as saying according to Jeffrey B. Perry. He attacked
Du Bois for his tepid plea for Negro patients in demanding equal rights
during World War I.[10]

"The essence of the present situation lies in the fact that the people
whom our white masters have 'recognized' as our leaders (without
taking the trouble to consult us) and those who, by our own selection,
has actually attained to leadership among us are being revaluated and,
in most cases, rejected," Harrison wrote in *The Voice* on July 25,
1918. "The most striking instance from the latter class is Dr. W.E.B.
Du Bois, the editor of *The Crisis*. Du Bois's case is the more significant
because his former services to his race have been undoubtedly of a
high and courageous sort."[11]

Dr. Du Bois first sinned in his *Crisis* editorial, *Close Ranks*, "but
this offense lies in a single sentence: 'Let, us, while this war lasts, forget
our special grievances and close our ranks.' It is felt by all his critics
that Du Bois, of all Negroes, knows best that our 'special grievances,'
which the War Department Bulletin describes as justifiable, consists of
lynching, segregation and disfranchisement and that the Negroes of
America cannot preserve either their lives, their manhood or their vote
(which is their political lives and liberties) with these things in existence," Harrison wrote.[12]

If you add notables of the period like A. Philip Randolph, his partner Chandler Owen and black nationalist Marcus Garvey to
Harrison's targets in print, you begin to see that no prey was too large
or too mighty to escape Harrison's editorial ire.

In New York, he won the reputation for writing in a wide variety of
publications, including *The Call*, a socialist daily newspaper and *The
Truth Seeker*, a free thought publication with a national circulation.
When some of Garvey's tactics, particularly his public speaking are
compared to Harrison's brand of speaking, Harrison clearly influenced Garvey in form, if not in substance. Harrison's call for armed
self-defense not only anticipates Malcolm X making the same call in
many Harlem speeches decades later, his expression in speeches with

the phrase, "ballots, bullets or business" is especially notable for its similarity to Harrison's rhetoric.

As a founding member of the Liberty League, a rally at the Bethel African Methodist Episcopal Church on 132nd Street and Lenox drew a crowd of an estimated 2,000 people to the church to hear Harrison speak. The league was a scion of a growing New Negro Movement in Harlem. Harrison demanded in that speech that Congress make lynching a federal crime, according to press reports.[13]

Sporting a Liberty League flag flying the colors of black, brown, and yellow that were symbolic of people of color throughout the world then, Harrison said this New Negro Movement was breaking away from the old-time Negro leadership, a common thought among so-called New Negro leaders in Harlem at the time but Harrison was thought to offer a different point of view from most on the subject. One month later, the league launched the first edition of *The Voice*, a newspaper for the New Negro, edited by Harrison himself and published in 1924. A year later, *Survey Graphic* magazine published *Harlem Mecca of the New Negro* edited by Alain Locke and that issue made the phrase "New Negro" a populist cry that eventually became common in Harlem.

Strictly self-conscious about race, *The Voice* mainly wrote stories and articles demanding "political equity, social justice, civic opportunity and economic power," according to a biography of Harrison in the archives of Columbia University Rare Book Library where his papers are stored.[14] Attacking the conservatism of Booker T. Washington who preached tolerance and patience at the Tuskegee Institute, Harrison formed the Liberty Congress and staged the first black protests against U.S. involvement in World War I. Demanding democracy for blacks at home, he repeatedly called for the end of segregation. Most of his views were not championed by W.E.B. Du Bois and the NAACP, which preached patriotism despite the fact that U.S. troops lived in segregated quarters on bases in the United States and overseas. Harrison briefly edited the *New Negro* magazine, a publication owned and launched by Marcus Garvey.

"In the good old days white people derived their knowledge of what Negroes were doing from those Negroes who were nearest to them," Harrison wrote in *The New Race Consciousness* (1920), "generally their own selected exponents of Negro activity or of their white point of view.... Today the white world is vaguely, but disquietingly, aware that Negroes are awake, different, and perplexingly uncertain."[15]

Disquieting is a mild description of an angry race man like Harrison.

Joel Rogers, a close friend of Harrison said he gave speeches whenever an audience gathered around him. "He spoke wherever an audience could be had on subjects embracing general literature, sociology, Negro history, and the leading events of the day," Rogers wrote in 1972. "He wrote for such radical and antireligious periodicals as *The Call*, *The Truth Seeker*, and *The Modern Quarterly*, being perhaps the first Negro of ability to enter this field. His views on religion and birth control were often opposed by Catholics and Protestants alike, and at his open-air meetings he and his friends were obliged to defend themselves physically from mobs at times. But he fought back courageously, never hesitating to speak no matter how great the hostility of his opponents."[16]

Harrison's earned a place in this book about a renaissance in Harlem, if for no other reason than for the fact that he once said there had been no renaissance in Harlem.

"The phrase 'Harlem Renaissance' has captured the popular and scholarly imagination," Ernest J. Mitchell II wrote in the 2010. "Evoking a burst of black creativity in 1920s Manhattan the term enjoys almost unchallenged acceptance today," Mitchell writes.[17] "Yet the term did not originate in the era it claims to describe; 'Harlem Renaissance did not appear in print before 1940, and it only gained widespread appeal in the 1960s." Over the years between 1920 and 1940, the term *Negro Renaissance* was widely touted and criticized at the same time. As early as 1927, however, Harrison wrote a satirical critique about Harlem in a story, which ran in the *Pittsburgh Courier* under the headline "No Negro Literary Renaissance."[18]

"Seriously, the matter of a Negro literary renaissance is like that of the snakes of "Ireland—there isn't any," he said. "Those who think that there is are usually people who are blissfully ignorant of the stream of literary and artistic products which have flowed uninterrupted from Negro writers from 1850 to the present," Harrison wrote. "If you ask them about the historical works of Major Wilson, George Williams, William C. Neill, William Wells Brown, Rufus L. Perry, Atticus G. Haygood; the essays of T. Thomas Fortune, the fictional writings of Negroes from Frances E. Watkins to Pauline Hopkins, Dunbar and Chesnutt, they stammer and evade to cover up their confusion."

There was no renaissance, according to Harrison "precisely because there was never a hiatus of black literary product," Mitchell says.[19] Harrison was not alone in his criticism although his critique of the period was among the first and perhaps the boldest ever made contesting claims that a literary renaissance had flourished briefly in Harlem.

In December 1927, Harrison died suddenly, his only legacy at the time were his many articles and the thousands who attended his funeral. The Hubert H. Harrison Memorial Church was formed after his death but it no longer exists. "His radicalism on so many issues—race, class, religion, war, democracy, sexuality, literature and the arts—and the fact that he was a forthright critic of individuals, organizations, and ideas of influence" died with him and "were major reasons for his subsequent neglect," curators of his papers at Columbia speculate.[20]

Scholars have also ignored Harrison for decades with no full-scale biography of him available, according to Christopher Phelps from the Department of History at Ohio State University in a review of *A Hubert Harrison Reader* in 2004.

Jeffrey Perry, who edited *The Hubert Harrison Reader*, notes that Harrison was the consummate radical, railing against multiples of powerful leaders both black and white while he lived. In death, they ganged up on him in silence and collectively ignored his preaching.

"Harrison's crusty manner, acerbic style, and lack of calculation . . . led him to offer criticism that antagonized powerful leaders (black and white) and institutions who had no reason to regret his passing," Perry writes, "and that he left no institutional foundation for the perpetuation of his legacy and this may have sealed his fate."[21]

CHAPTER ELEVEN

The Last Leaf

Initially, all of the writers who came to Harlem were literary enigmas who had been porters, busboys and waiters, welfare examiners or students, when they were lured to New York with the promise of storybook success. Like the Renaissance itself, whose significance did not surface until decades after the luster of the period had long faded and was left to the handiwork of researchers and historians like me, some of these writers did become literary lions.

The writer's story I like best is that of Dorothy West because it is rarely told accurately. West was an obscure figure, like the other women of the period, because the spotlight was rarely shared by men with the women they knew. If the plight of white women was an issue of the 1920, the dilemma of black women is one still not fully realized. I studied Black Women and Their Fictions at Yale which was taught by Dr. Henry Louis Gates in the 1980s. The course had first been designed and taught by Toni Morrison when she was at Yale. West's two novels, *The Living Is Easy*[1] and later, *The Wedding*,[2] were not on the syllabus of either class. Among the most touted novels of the class was Hurston's *Their Eyes Were Watching God*,[3] but books and short stories by West were not taught at all, to my recollection.

When I first began my research into Harlem's past, West was generally associated with Hughes or Hurston but only tangentially. West had shared a second place short story prize awarded by *Opportunity Magazine* with Hurston. She was once romantically linked to Hughes by a librarian at the Beinecke Rare Book & Manuscript Library at Yale where I found correspondence between West and Hughes. The two had traveled to Russia together with a troupe of actors commissioned to participate in a play or film about Negroes in the United States that was never produced. Later, when Hughes was briefly in California, he wrote West a letter in which he suggested they have a child together when he returned to New York. This exchange was not clarified further. Generally, West was referred to as "the kid," the youngest member of Renaissance writers in Harlem. Later in her career, she became the writer who had left New York, who vanished after 1940, and had stopped writing altogether.

This was the battered, maligned, and ignored reputation West endured after having been a member of this elite group of well-off arrivals to Harlem in the mid-1920s. West had been recruited and brought to New York by the editors of *Opportunity* magazine when she won a literary prize for a short story called *The Typewriter*.[4] She lived and worked in Harlem between 1926 and 1940 as a welfare investigator and as a writer for the Federal Work Progress Administration when her mother's illness forced her to leave the city for Martha's Vineyard in 1940. She remained on the island until she died nearly 60 years later. When she left New York, her name and her reputation seemed to fade and disappear too. What seemed to be the end of a brief but promising career as a writer in no way represented the true nature of a career that began in her native Boston early in the twentieth century. That career was invigorated during her Harlem years and did not end as most histories about this writer suggest until almost the beginning of the next century when she died in her late 90s.

An aging West had been marooned on Martha's Vineyard in a literary wasteland off the coast of her native Massachusetts for decades until her reputation as a writer was rescued by a First Lady of the United States and one of the grand divas of televisions, Jacqueline Kennedy Onassis and Oprah Winfrey, before she died.

In the acclaimed autobiography of playwright Lillian Hellman, readers of *Pentimento*[5] were treated to an uneven but realistic journey through the life of a writer in the twentieth century that was sometimes fulfilling, usually exhausting, and occasionally cataclysmic. This choice to chronicle life as you see it as a writer has always been risky business for a woman whether she has the fortitude, the means, or the stamina to sustain herself.

Perhaps taking her cue from the career of another literary figure before her time, Dorothy West had staked out a room of her own early in her career where she could go to think and to write. This need to go off by herself to write is a recurring theme for West, who launched a career as a writer of short fiction as a teenager in her native Boston, a writing life that lasted for more than seven decades. That career continued even after her death in 1998; because I found a lost short story she wrote but never published. I found it in the archives of the Library of Congress in the Work Progress Administration files of the New York Writer's Project. It was called *My Baby*. It was about a boy who goes to live with a family in Boston where a little girl in the family unofficially adopts to shelter the boy. I published it in the *Connecticut Journal*, the literary magazine for the Connecticut State Universities system. Three years later in 2001, *My Baby*, was named among the "Best American Short Stories" edited by Barbara Kingsolver.[6] It marked the end of a long, literary adventure for its creator who was both an enigma of, and now a significant contributor to the landscape of twentieth-century American literature.

Dorothy West died in the summer of 1998 at age 91. I had been busy finding and collecting obscure essays and short fiction she had written at various times in her life, finally publishing them in a collection I called *The Last Leaf of Harlem*[7] published by St. Martin's Press. The title phrase was how West referred to herself when talking about her days in Harlem. She said that she was "the last leaf," or last living member of the artists and writers she knew in Harlem in the decades between 1920s and 1940.

The collection I published in 2008 is a literary rendering of her lost short fiction, some of it published, some nearly lost in library and newspaper libraries in New York, Boston and Washington where I found and compiled it just before her death. As a high school and later a college student in New York, I had never read or heard of West in my literature courses. As an adult, I found West was often mentioned in essays or articles about Harlem, but generally only in reference to literary luminaries like Richard Wright, Langston Hughes, or Ralph Ellison. These brief mentions of West, sparked my curiosity about her and I gradually discovered a prolific literary figure in West not evident in American or African American literary biographies. Over the years, I collected dozens of unpublished stories West had written before, during, and after she left Harlem. I had unwittingly joined a growing field of leading editors, producers, and media elites that included former First Lady Jacqueline Kennedy Onassis, the Feminist Press, and television network owner and film producer Oprah Winfrey in rediscovering Dorothy West. When *The Last Leaf of Harlem* was published, it was endorsed by Ivy League VIPs Dr. Henry Louis Gates at Harvard and Dr. Cornel West at Princeton.

An obscure figure in the latter decades of the twentieth century, West had stealthly made inroads into mainstream literary venues in

New York almost without notice or fanfare. She quietly wrote for the "Blue Ribbon Fiction" section of the *New York Daily News* under her own name without fanfare for more than 20 years between 1940 and the 1960s when newspapers still published fiction. Throughout her life, West had been a writer whose presence seldom invited comparisons to her contemporaries. She was an only child but was surrounded by close and distant relatives taken in by her family. She never married and used pseudonyms like Jane Isaac and Mary Christopher in her writing. This alone might have sealed her fate of self-imposed anonymity. The name Jane Isaac was used on a story called *Cook*, which appears in *The Last Leaf of Harlem*, but *Cook* was first published in a magazine called *Challenge*, financed and published by West herself. As a prolific writer in several genres, this pen name and others might have been used in other stories still undiscovered in West's papers stored at various universities after her death. One example cropped up while I was editing this book. There is apparently an unpublished novel or novella by West in the archives of Harvard University called *Where the Wild Grape Grows*.

Dorothy West lived the life of a writer, carving out her fiction from the days, nights, and experiences of her own life. Her writing life began with long, intimate pieces about family in Boston where she was born on June 2, 1907. She was the only child of Isaac West, a freed slave who became a successful businessman who sold produce in Boston markets. Her mother was Rachel Pease Benson, one of 22 children.

Her career was bookmarked by many essays about life in Boston, Harlem, and living on the island of Martha's Vineyard. Most of this work paints an idyllic portrait of life as West saw it. But her work portrayed racism and poverty too that she saw and experienced as a black woman writer in America. Contrary to the image of her as the soft-spoken voice of old-fashion ways and the gentle mores of the black middle class, Dorothy West was often a sharp social critic of them. She wrote short stories with the moral twists, human drama, and tragedy that marks most sustainable literature. Like her Russian mentor Fyodor Dostoyevsky, West aspired to create and recreate portraits of the human dilemma. In different ways and to different degrees, she succeeded but her work is rarely credited for having this kind of depth or critical edge.

West was largely a short story writer, but she wrote at least two novels that both chronicled and satirized black middle class and life on Martha's Vineyard. The stories, sketches, and remembrances in the Last Leaf of Harlem were found by me over a period of many years in widely scattered archives at colleges, universities, and newspaper morgues in Boston, New York, and Washington, DC. Her publishing credits began with the long short stories she published in Boston in the first two decades of the twentieth century. Her career ended at the end of the century with the writing of brief sketches she published in *The Vineyard Gazette*, the newspaper that published her work for more than 50 years.

One of the persistent criticisms of her work as a writer is the idea that she was not prolific, her work was spotty, and her career was marred by long, dark periods of inactivity.

This is perhaps the greatest fiction. Dorothy West is one of the apprentices of achievers like W.E.B. Du Bois and *Opportunity* magazine editor Charles S. Johnson. Johnson lured West to New York with a literary prize. Winners were selected by the most powerful editors in New York. It was through this kind of networking that Dorothy West broke through the ever-present color line and acquired the attention of New York literary agents such as Bertha Klausner and George T. Bye, both of whom also represented First Lady Eleanor Roosevelt. Klausner's client list included Cuban leader Fidel Castro, New York Rep. Adam Clayton Powell Jr., actor Basil Rathbone, and novelist Israel J. Singer. It was Bye who negotiated and won the long-standing literary contract for West at the *New York Daily News*, a deal that was not signed without some racial underpinnings that remained a secret for decades.

The bulk of Dorothy West's fiction was published in newspapers when fiction was common in large daily newspapers like the *Daily News*, the *New York Times*, and other major publications. Her first story may have been published as early as 1915 in the now defunct *Boston Post* and her last stories were published posthumously in the *Vineyard Gazette* and the *New York Daily News* in the late 1990s.

Her work belongs in the same canon along with thousands of unknowns who together created a widely popular genre of twentieth century literature called pulp fiction. The plots in pulp fiction are usually anchored in the daily lives of relatively ordinary people, much like the plots of opera and Shakespearean dramas.

No work is created in a vacuum, so the circumstances under which this work was created (for money, influenced by prevailing political winds, etc.) are factors that need consideration too. Although much of this work appeared in newspapers, it was fiction, not journalism. It is pulp fiction intended for the working-class readers who paid nickels or a dime to be entertained by their daily newspapers. It was not meant to be literature, no more than the pulp fiction of Dickens, Crane, or Hemingway was considered literary at the time it first appeared in newsprint. Dorothy West belongs to this literary club of writing giants.

Some of West's writing gives her membership in a subgenre of American literature. Although she was a black writer, West created characters that seemed to be raceless, not black or white. In other stories, her characters were presumed to be white. Venturing into this territory places West in an undefined, neither world of fiction.

Who gave Dorothy West permission to step out of her assigned role as a black woman writer? Charles S. Johnson, W.E.B. Du Bois, Richard Wright, or Langston Hughes, all friends and mentors West knew in Harlem? West was not mentored by the same folks who gave William Faulkner, George Gershwin, Dubose Heyward, William Brashler, and Joel Chandler, all white, who wrote about black folks and other cultures and not their own. Faulkner certainly knew and could write well about Southern blacks. Gershwin and Heyward successfully captured the character of Gullah culture down south in *Porgy and Bess*.[8] Brashler, a Chicago writer I knew in that city, was often criticized in the 1970s for trampling on the territory black writers saw as their own in his book *The Bingo Long Traveling All-Stars and Motor Kings*,[9] his novel about the Negro baseball leagues. Chandler, the Southern journalist from Atlanta, was the nineteenth-century chronicler of black folktales in the Uncle Remus stories. Dorothy West joins these folks in this sensitive, subgenre, seamlessly crossing the color line with the help of literary agents like Klausner and Bly and the powerful editors they did business with in New York.

West made no apologies for this. None is necessary. She almost never mentioned her *Daily News* contract in interviews over the years. This fact merely illustrates a more important idea, that Dorothy West was an innovator perhaps fearful of criticism in a time when America was still a segregated nation where blacks and whites did not intermingle anywhere in public and rarely in literary circles.

The collection of West's short fiction that I published spans decades between 1940 and the 1960s, years that were noticeably glossed over in some of the literary criticism I have read about West. Those same years and many more of her accomplishments were correctly noted in a general library reference work called *Contemporary Authors*. In it, I found a hint about the real legacy of Dorothy West, buried in between the lines of a small blurb about her career. "Critics and aficionados hope to read more of her creations, many of which remain unpublished," it said.

The sheer number of stories I have found so far refutes the widely held claim that she did not write during those years between two of her novels, 1948 and 1995. Dorothy West was rarely idle as a writer during her long life.

A graduate of the prestigious Latin Girls School in Boston, West grew up in black Boston as the daughter of a wealthy, former slave, Isaac West. She grew into a black woman writer who knew the sting of racism in America even though her work did not always reflect a direct awareness of it.

She wrote protest literature against racism, sexism, and all the other social ills that befell America after World War I, during the economic depression and the world war, which followed in the 1940s. Dorothy West was a social critic. But protest literature written by blacks in the early part of her century and in the succeeding decades did not sell when West was trying to establish herself as a writer. Protest literature would fail an aspiring black woman trying to sell short stories to white publishers.

The themes West chose to write about generally focused on social or moral issues. This does not mean she never wrote about race, but she was a pragmatist who used satire, subtle shadings, and outright sub-terfuge to deliver narratives that tackled difficult issues like race preju-dices or the oppression of women in America. Neither of these subjects were areas publishers were willing to pay a black woman or a woman of any color to explore. Yet, Dorothy West started a writing career in the early 1920s and sustained it for the next 70 years. This sometimes took courage and a great deal of cunning. Dorothy West had both.

Whether tending to the needs of the many relatives, who drifted in and out of her life as a girl in Boston or working as a welfare investiga-tor in Harlem, she was a writer first. When she joined a federal work project, the New York Writer's Project in the late 1930s, or later when she worked as a restaurant cashier on Martha's Vineyard, Dorothy West was still a writer in the act of gathering material for her next book or story.

Her fictions generally mirrored her surroundings and her stories are filled with the black and white people who were involved in her life. Hers was a life that seemed to always coexist with her stories, some-times making it difficult for an outsider like me to distinguish facts about her life from the fictions in it. Such is the life of a writer's writer. Dorothy West lived and worked inside of her muse, not side by side with it. The two were enmeshed into a kind of literary soup. This was a contemplation, which she began early in her life as a teenager that later made the fact and fictions of her life inseparable.

As self-styled, literary anthropologists, I first became acquainted with Dorothy West through a happy accident. In researching another collection of stories I was doing about the Harlem Renaissance, I knew that West had been in Harlem during the same period. Histories claim the Harlem Renaissance began in the mid-1920s when an unprecedented number of literary figures gathered in this all-black section of Manhattan and began to publish a wide assortment of novels, short stories, and essays. It was during this research in the early 1990s that I first found and began to admire her odd, sometimes old-fashion writing style. My interest in her work was later heightened when I found several unpublished stories she had written in the Manuscript Division at the Library of Congress in Washington, DC. These stories were mingled in among the works of other Harlem writers that included such well-known writers as Ralph Ellison, author of *Invisible Man*, and Zora Neale Hurston, author of *Their Eyes Were Watching God*, and Richard Wright, author of *Native Son*.

The first story I was impressed by was set in Harlem and called *Pluto*, a title taken from the dog character in the Walt Disney cartoon *Mickey Mouse*. In this first-person narrative, West is disturbed one morning while she was writing in her Harlem apartment by an unexpected knock on her door. What followed is precise and chilling social commentary about hunger and poverty during the Depression years. The piece is both subtle and piercing. It was so carefully crafted, it teeters on that precarious border where fact often meets fiction.

Pluto was written in the late 1930s when West worked as a $20-a-week-writer for the WPA of the Federal New York Writers' Project. It had never been published when I found it in the late 1990s. I immediately wondered why. To my amazement, there were at least a half dozen other stories by West in the same archive. The Work Progress Administration was a make-work federal project more commonly known as the WPA that was abruptly disbanded around 1940. When it closed down, thousands of manuscripts were shelved and forgotten for decades. These stories were part of a larger cache of narratives from the Federal Writer's Project.

Other work by West had been published in various ways throughout her career but much of it was lost too, but for different reasons. Many of the stories she wrote were buried in old newspaper archives that had never been indexed. Other work had been carefully indexed but hard to find because it was buried deep inside the literary collections of other writers like Langston Hughes, James Weldon Johnson in library collections at Yale, Boston University, and the Schomburg Center of Black Culture in Harlem. This is how I found pieces of her work in libraries up and down the Atlantic coast, each with similar stories but materially lost for decades.

In these hushed surroundings, I found manuscripts, old newspapers clippings, and pieces she wrote that were published under at least two different pen names. This work was certainly prized by the librarians who helped me locate the manuscripts I was collecting. But the ideas, sketches, and stories by the aging woman whose literary life I was stitching together had been obscured by years of neglect, time, and an array of unusual circumstances.

Ironically, Dorothy West was enjoying a renaissance of her own about the same time. Her name and reputation was being resurrected in wider literary circles and important literary scholars and popular critics were again feting her life and her work.

Time magazine, for example, said she was enjoying a second round of well-deserved fame with publication of her second novel, *The Wedding*, in 1995. Jacqueline Kennedy Onassis, the editor for Doubleday, had discovered West living on Martha's Vineyard. Onassis's decision to publish the first novel West had written in almost 50 years was cause for some celebration. Her first novel, *The Living Is Easy* (1948), had already been republished by The Feminist Press in 1982 and was still in print.

This renewed attention meant that Dorothy West had lived long enough to overcome stigmas about her life and career, becoming both famous and but still obscure at the same time in some ways because critics had still failed to fully critique her body of work.

Although she always saw herself as more of a short story writer than a novelist, she was most famous for the two novels she wrote five decades apart between 1948 and 1995.

In the limited circles of black Boston and in Harlem, Dorothy West had become famous by the end of the 1930s. By the start of the next decade, her work caught the attention of literary agent George T. Bye, a high-powered figure in New York. Bye represented First Lady Eleanor Roosevelt, Rebecca West, Katherine Anne Porter, and many other important writers of the period. In a lucrative deal, he negotiated for West to write regularly for the *New York Daily News*. She began a long-term relationship with the *News* to write short stories for the Blue Ribbon Fiction section of the paper. Laid out in the comic strip section, Blue Ribbon Fiction stories often ran on a page anchored by the popular *Terry and the Pirates* comic strip. For the next 20 years between 1940 and the early 1960s, this is where the name Dorothy West appeared over more than 40 short stories.

The first story depicted the life of a black couple in a Harlem tenement during the lean years of the Depression. It was called *Jack in the Pot*.

"They liked *Jack in the Pot*, the one and only black story (of mine) they printed," West said in an interview. She said her contract with the *News* was specifically contingent upon West not creating black characters in her fiction as she had in *Jack in the Pot*. That is why that story contained the first and only black characters she wrote for the *News* for the next 20 years. Her characters thereafter seems to be without race or any cultural traits that might imply that her stories were about black people or black communities.

"I wrote it for a contest (at a magazine). The magazine forwarded it to them for their Blue Ribbon Fiction," West said in an interview in 1978 for the Black Women Oral History Project at Radcliffe College. "I had to cut it. I learned a great deal at the News. I learned to cut," West said.

"All my friends were so contemptuous that I was writing for the News," she said. "It was keeping me eating. I got four hundred dollars." She said friends attributed the high fee she was paid to the fact that she had Bye as her literary agent.

"George Bye had me in his stable. He had Eleanor Roosevelt and a lot of famous people. I got him through Fannie Hurst. Zora Neale Hurston introduced me to Fannie Hurst," West said.[10]

Ironically, while West was represented by an agent whose clients were among the most famous people in the world, her fame and her work began to slip into obscurity even though she was now producing stories being read by millions of daily newspaper readers. After *Jack in the Pot* appeared, the stories she wrote over the next 20 years were distributed to hundreds other newspapers throughout the world by the News Syndicate, Inc., making Dorothy West one of the most widely read, obscure black writers in America at the time. Her characters weren't black, and she wasn't identified as a black writer.

This situation is ironic for several reasons. At a time when her fame and notoriety should have soared because of this relationship with Bye and the *News*, it plummeted. She fell from view of critics who either did not know she was now a regular contributor to the *News* or the fact that West, a black writer was regularly writing stories with an all-white cast, became a taboo subject. In any case, her career as a short story writer fell prey to rumors that she had retired. This claim remained a fixture in the literary biographies about her throughout most of the rest of her life.

So, while West was writing for a syndicate that distributed her fiction to hundreds of newspapers throughout the world, this became a shadowy time in her life.

This begins a significant chapter in West's literary career. Dorothy West became what author Robert A. Bone called an assimilationist.

She was not alone. West was developing as writer in the late 1920s when she met Zora Neale Hurston, Ralph Ellison, Richard Wright, Frank Yerby, and other fledgling artists in Harlem. In the early days of the Renaissance, these writers enjoyed being published in the mostly black, little magazines that sprang up solely to publish their work. In the years between 1920 and the late 1930s, the fiction of Harlem writers like West appeared in *The Crisis*, the NAACP magazine, *Opportunity*, the Urban League magazine, and in *Challenge* and later *New Challenge*, both financed and published by West. The plight of black life in America was regularly written about and covered in these magazines. But by 1940s, almost all of them except *The Crisis* had folded, leaving black writers like West with almost no place to publish their stories.

"A good index to the general temper of the period is the lack of any center of gravity for a specifically Negro art," Bone says in his book, *The Negro Novel in America*. "There are no little magazines in the forties and fifties to perform the function of *Fire!!!* and Harlem during the Renaissance, or of *Challenge* and *New Challenge* during the Depression." So, there was no cohesive movement in contemporary black literature, Bone said, which led writers like West, Frank Yerby, and even the acerbic Hurston to become what Bone called assimilationist writers. In those years, it was a pejorative word that usually meant the writer was a sell out. This is almost never talked about in literary circles today where Hurston's fiction is highly touted as being among the best of black women's fiction of the twentieth century. Today we would call them crossover artists whose work would appeal to both black and white audiences like singers Michael Jackson or the late singer, Prince.

"On the whole," Bone said in examining the period, "the young writers have preferred to seek non-racial outlets for their work. In doing so, these writers were abandoning the assertively racial fiction pioneered by Wright in novels like *Native Son*."[11]

Assimilationist turned to commercial fiction, which meant abandoning racial themes and in most cases, black characters and all-black communities altogether. In the years between 1945 and the early 1950s, some 33 novels by black authors were published. Thirteen, or more than a third of these, had predominantly or all-white characters.

Among the most notable writers of this genre were Frank Yerby, Hurston, and Ann Petry and West, by my reckoning. All knew West during their days in Harlem.

Yerby, who had first published his stories in *Challenge* too, had also worked with West and Ellison on the staff of the New York Writers' project of the WPA. According to Bone, Yerby had been a race conscious Southerner during his early years in New York. By the mid-1940s, he was still writing protest stories, but by the early 1950s, Yerby had moved to Spain and began to write wildly popular romantic, potboilers that featured mostly plots about white characters. This work carved out a new, crossover opportunity rarely afforded to black writers. Others followed this path too.

Chester Himes wrote *Cast the First Stone* in 1952. Willard Motley wrote *Knock on Any Door* in 1947 and *We Fished All Night* in 1951. All were novels with raceless characters. In 1948, Hurston wrote *Seraph on the Suwanee*, a novel set in the rural South. In it, Hurston's familiar black characters, communities, and themes have been abandoned for a whiter literary landscape. A year earlier, Connecticut-born writer Ann Petry, known for her protest Harlem novel, *The Street*, published *Country Place*. This story of dying values is set in New England, presumably patterned after Petry's mostly white hometown of Old Saybrook, Connecticut.

All of these writers became assimilationists and continued striving to break into the arena of mainstream publishing.

Dorothy West joined this group when she began writing for the *News*. She said the *News* did not want stories about black characters and this was a stipulation that was made implicit in her agreement with *News*' editors who agreed to publish her stories if she complied. Rather than showing us people with unusual character, who also happened to be black, West repeatedly delivered stories with ironic twists aimed at hearts and minds of readers who were mostly working-class whites. These characters sometimes lack the magnetic substances. These stories were syndicated by the News Syndicate, Inc. and were read by tens of millions of newspaper readers throughout the country and possibly the world.

West did seem like a fallen, literary figure of the Harlem Renaissance. Her creative flame did seem to flicker briefly in the 1920s, then go out 20 years later. This tragic story about the premature end of a promising literary career just seemed to be true if you only read widely believed folklore about her career. As romantic as this notions seemed, it was not true.

When she died, these same images about her fleeting fame and tragic end appeared in the many obituaries and eulogies published about her. They failed in almost every way to document the rich literary legacy Dorothy West actually left behind.

I came by this conclusion only gradually as I found more and more of her work after she died, including the possibility of a third, unpublished novel. The fact that this work existed and I was finding it was not the significance of my true discovery about Dorothy West

A librarian at the Schomburg Center for Research in Black Culture in Harlem clarified that significance by reminding me that her work had never been thoroughly indexed, making it difficult to compile into a comprehensive collection that could be reviewed properly.

Ironically, the community that had once made West somewhat famous during the 1920s, seemed to suffer the same fate of obscurity as her career over time. Harlem and the giant intellects, orators, the best black legal minds in America and community organizers, who flocked there in the 1920s that made Harlem trendy, all slipped into a historic fog by the turn of the century and Harlem, like Ralph Ellison's *Invisible Man*, became invisible, a no-man's land when worsening economic conditions in the 1930s and later dried up the trendy, progressive life, which had once brought white tourists uptown to Harlem in droves. That's when standard history books say the Harlem Renaissance abruptly ended despite the fact that West, Ellison, and Zora Neale Hurston all published landmark novels years later.

Like the unnamed character in Ralph Ellison's novel, Dorothy West had gone underground and remained there until Dr. Henry Louis "Skip" Gates from Harvard and Jackie Onassis and Oprah all found her again living quietly on Martha's Vineyard. But as West told an interviewer for *Ms.* magazine in 1995, just because "I had left New York ... didn't mean I had stopped writing."

CHAPTER TWELVE

Legal Defense

In 1938, a young lawyer named Thurgood Marshall traveled from Baltimore to Harlem and checked into the 135th Street YMCA. It was where his old college friend, Langston Hughes, had suggested he stay. The Y was often a first stop for new arrivals to Harlem. It was where Hughes had stayed. There he met a young writer named Ralph Ellison, who waited tables at the Y when he first came to New York.

But Thurgood Marshall was not new to Harlem, having lived there as a boy while his mother went to Columbia University. Hughes and Marshall had gone to Lincoln University together. Marshall and his wife, Vivien "Buster" Marshall, would later move up to 409 Edgecombe Avenue, a large apartment building in the Sugar Hill section of Harlem where well knowns like Crisis editor W.E.B. Du Bois, painter Aaron Douglas, writer Zora Neale Hurston, band leaders Duke Ellington, Count Basie, and musician Miles Davis had also lived. But Marshall did not return to Harlem to hobnob with notables. He had been summoned to Harlem by a mentor from Howard University where Marshall earned his law degree to help build what would become the greatest civil rights legal strategy ever devised. It was designed to topple one of the pillars of legal segregation.[1]

About the same time, Doctors Kenneth and Mamie Clark also arrived in Harlem that same year as the Marshalls. The Clarks first came to New York to study at Columbia University and later to open what would become a landmark nonprofit, the Northside Center for Child Development. Although the Marshalls and the Clarks did not know each other in those early days, their work in child psychology and Marshall's legal work would eventually cross paths in landmark arguments Marshall's legal team would bring to make before the U.S. Supreme Court.[2]

Research the Clarks did at Northside would become a linchpin for a landmark case the young lawyer would eventually argue before the U.S. Supreme Court 25 years after the two couples came to Harlem.

Three years before Marshall came to Harlem to work in the 135th Street offices of the National Association for the Advancement of Colored People, his mentor at the Howard University law school, Charles Hamilton Houston, had mounted a legal argument against segregation in *Murray v. Pearson* case against the University of Maryland Law School. Ironically, the school had refused Marshall's application years earlier because he was black. Instead, Marshall went to Howard where he first met Houston. Now, Houston had recruited Marshall to argue against the Maryland position in *Murray V. Pearson* under Houston's guidance.[3]

The university's lawyers claimed Maryland had met existing "separate but equal" law requirements that allowed Maryland to refuse to admit black students as long as the state had provided adequate facilities for non-white students. Marshall represented Donald Murray.[4] The school had argued it had granted qualified blacks students scholarships to out-of-state schools instead of admission to the University of Maryland. The state court rejected the argument, saying alternative opportunities in the state were not equal under the law and ordered Maryland to admit qualified black students. It was an omen that would later revisit Marshall in his tenure as founder and head of the NAACP Legal and Defense and Education Fund,[5] which in 1940 set out to defend black defendants in a wide variety of jurisdictions and cases throughout the United States.

Marshall became a well-known figure in Harlem, known throughout the community as "The Lawyer," a nickname he heard whether he was getting a haircut, walking home to Sugar Hill from the subway, or enjoying a night out with his wife at the Savoy Ballroom.

Marshall was recruited by Houston to come to Harlem where he would lead a team of black lawyers over the next two decades whose work would garner the attention and accolades in the law community everywhere. They were shrewd legal strategists, particularly in civil rights cases despite a checkered record of victories and losses.[6] Marshall was seen as astute in selecting cases that attacked segregationist in the South, where he often challenged discriminatory real estate covenants and other racially charged actions against black, Jews, and other minorities.

Behind Marshall's legal strategies, engineered and overseen by Charles Houston, there was always a long-term goal attached to the case these Harlem lawyers took on. This long view was derived from the work and goals of Houston, who had been vice dean at Howard Law when Marshall had earned his law degree there.

In an ironic twist, segregation at the top law schools in the country had created a talent vacuum that funneled nearly a quarter of all black lawyers in the United States at the time to Howard University where they all came under the watchful eye of Houston.[7] This elite cadre of legal minds included Thurgood Marshall. You might say that Houston was the spitting image of the Talented Tenth persona touted by Du Bois. The son of a prominent Washington, DC, lawyer, Houston went to Amherst College in 1911, attended Harvard Law, graduated cum laude, and was a member of the prestigious *Harvard Law Review*.

In 1935, Houston left Howard for Harlem to become special counsel for the NAACP. He recruited Marshall to join him. For the next five years, he conceived and hatched legal strategies largely carried out by Marshall and others aimed at killing legal segregation in public schools. To do this, Houston sought to overturn a long-standing sacred cow of legal segregation. White southerners and others had enshrined segregation under an 1896 Supreme Court law, *Plessy v. Ferguson*, which held that racially "separate but equal" facilities qualified as legal under the "equal protection" standard of the Fourteenth Amendment of the Constitution. Over the next 20 years, NAACP lawyers took on a wide variety of cases throughout the country. Their lawyers took on murder cases where the defendants were black, they filed wrongful death charges in lynching cases with black victims. But, they were always on the lookout for segregation cases they hoped would eventually overturn the *Plessy* case, the foundation for legal segregation[8] by winning an array of segregation cases.

Houston's strategy for knocking down *Plessy* would require building a preponderance of legal evidence and they decided to do it by accumulating wins in segregation cases in various jurisdictions over time around the country. As a part time lawyer for the NAACP, Marshall worked with Houston in winning *Murray v. Pearson*. During this time, Houston announced he would return to private practice. Privately, he had paved the way for Marshall to replace him, knowing the NAACP could not afford to pay two full-time attorneys. Houston returned to Washington where his father, William L. Houston, had a successful practice that could accommodate his son, according to the *American*

Bar Association Journal.[9] "This fight for equality of educational opportunity (was) not an isolated struggle," Houston said. "All our struggles must tie in together and support one another ... We must remain on the alert and push the struggle farther with all our might."[10]

In Washington, the younger Houston regularly held legal tutorials in an old dining hall at Howard and later in the basement of Founder's Library to continue his plan of attack upon *Plessy*, the journal wrote. "Houston assembled some of the country's finest black legal talent on a moment's notice to discuss pending cases, hold dry runs of oral arguments, and to rewrite briefs. Marshall would hop the Washington bound 'Congressional train' in New York, arriving at Howard Law School within hours. Other well-known faculty and alumni of Howard Law would converge for Houston's brainstorming sessions too," the journal said. "The cases handled by Houston and his understudies in the '40s amount to the footprint of the American civil rights movement."[11]

In covering Marshall's arguments in various cases, a reporter for United Press International said that Marshall was ... an outstanding tactician with exceptional attention to detail, a tenacious ability to focus on a goal—a deep voice that often was the loudest in the room. He possessed a charm so extraordinary that even the most intransigent Southern segregationist sheriff could not resist his stories and jokes," the wire service said.

Although these strategies were born in Harlem, their deliveries were generally made in hostile, Southern jurisdictions where most juries and judges had never encountered a black lawyer before. In *Lyons v. Oklahoma*, Marshall was one of the trial lawyers for W. D. Lyons, arrested for the 1939 New Year's Eve murder of Elmer Rogers, his wife, and their four-year-old son in Choctaw County, Oklahoma. Lyons confessed to the crime twice before his trial, presumably after being beaten and threatened by the county prosecutor's office.[12] Marshall's belief that Lyons was innocent was bolstered by the fact the prosecutor delayed his trial for more than a year, contrary to what typically occurred when blacks were charged with murdering whites in Oklahoma, according to the *Virginia Law Review*. Marshall traveled to Oklahoma for the trial in January, 1941.[13]

"When Marshall entered the courtroom, word spread that a nigger lawyer from New York was on the case," according to news reports. "The court personnel were very nice and explained that this was their first experience in seeing a Negro lawyer try a case, the first time they had seen such an animal."[14]

Marshall conducted the cross-examination of the police witnesses because "we figured they would resent being questioned by a Negro and would get angry and this would help us," Marshall later said. "It worked perfectly. They all became angry at the idea of a Negro pushing them into tight corners and making their lies obvious," he said. "Boy did I like that and did the Negroes in the courtroom like it. You can't imagine what it means to those people down there who have been pushed around for years to know there is an organization that will help them," he said in a letter to Walter White, then the national director of the NAACP in Harlem.[15] Despite Marshall's defense and another confession, the jury found Lyons guilty but refused a plea by the prosecutor for the death penalty, rendering a life sentence instead. While Marshall's team lost, the mere fact that a legal defense team had traveled to Oklahoma from New York in the case was part of a trendsetting strategy. The NAACP Education and Legal Defense could act on behalf of otherwise defenseless black defendants anywhere.

The battle over school segregation everywhere in the United States came to a head in the 1950s when Marshall and his Howard lawyers were finally able to attack legal segregation in the *Brown v. Topeka, Kansas Board of Education* case before the U.S. Supreme Court.[16] According to an article in the *New American* magazine, "The stakes were higher when NAACP lawyers shifted the focal point of their efforts from universities to the segregated public schools that educated many of the nation's children. There were actually five cases from three states that were combined into the court docket as *Brown v. Board of Education of Topeka, Kansas*. In arguing the Kansas case, the lawyers brought in evidence from previous cases from South Carolina, Virginia, Delaware and the District of Columbia."[17]

One key argument came with the testimony of City College of New York psychologist Kenneth Clark, founder of Northside Center for Child Development in Harlem who said segregation was harmful to the mental health of minority children.[18]

Testifying for Marshall's team, Dr. Clark offered results from a series of tests conducted on black elementary school children using black and white dolls. When asked which dolls the children preferred, children between the ages of three to seven repeatedly chose white dolls. When asked which dolls were nice and which looked bad, they chose the white dolls as good and black dolls are bad. Clark said these choices were the direct result of school segregation that instilled a sense of inferiority in the children tested.[19]

The cases were argued in 1952 with some states attorneys conceding that facilities in black schools in their states were not equal to facilities in white schools. They assured the court those disparities would be remedied in time and lower courts had agreed to give states time to equalize facilities in black schools.

The cases were argued at the Supreme Court in December 1952 and reargued again in December 1953. While various questions were argued, Thurgood Marshall's stubborn insistence repeatedly urged the court to assume authority over the equal protection under the Fourteenth Amendment that would bar state-authorized segregation.

"Arguing the case for South Carolina was John W. Davis, a former U.S. solicitor general and ambassador to the United Kingdom, and Democratic candidate for president in 1924. Though semi-retired at 80, he was still widely regarded as one of the nation's most formidable lawyers," the *New American* article said.

"Davis cited a lack of evidence that the 14th Amendment was intended to empower the federal government to outlaw segregation in the schools. During Reconstruction, he said, the Freedmen's Bureau, established by Congress, set up segregated schools throughout the South. During that same time, the District of Columbia, under congressional rule, continued to run segregated schools," the magazine said.[20]

"Marshall, in rebuttal, insisted the issue was one of fundamental rights and equality before the law. The only way for the court to uphold the practice of school segregation," he said, was to "find that for some reason, Negroes are inferior to all other human beings."[21]

In writing the opinion of the court, Chief Justice Earl Warren said the court could not turn the clock back to 1896 when *Plessy v. Ferguson* was written, but he said, "We must consider public education in the light of its full development and its present place in American life throughout the Nation." On that basis the court would determine that racially segregated schools, "even though the physical facilities and other 'tangible' factors may be equal, nevertheless deprived minority children of equal educational opportunities." The court specifically noted Dr. Clark's "doll test" results saying segregation in schools did have "a detrimental effect upon the colored children, by instilling a sense of inferiority [that] affects the motivation of a child to learn. . . . Any language in Plessy v. Ferguson contrary to this finding is rejected."[22]

The unanimous decision of the court was issued on May 17, 1954, legally ending segregation in public schools everywhere.

In succeeding years, Marshall continued to find his place in the federal judicial system after his *Brown vs. Board of Education* victory. He resigned his position with the NAACP in 1961 when he was nominated by President John F. Kennedy to become the second African American to sit on the U.S. Court of Appeals for the Second Circuit, which heard cases filed in New York, Connecticut, and Vermont. In 1965, Marshall was appointed solicitor general of the United States, which meant he would argue on behalf of the federal government in cases before the U.S. Supreme Court.

Notably, he made his first arguments as solicitor general in an iconic civil rights case involving the murders of three activists, James Chaney, Andrew Goodman, and Michael Schwerner. The three victims, who had been registering black voters in Nashoba County, Mississippi, were killed in 1964, by racist conspirators. The Mississippi state courts had refused to convict the murderers, but Marshall persuaded the Supreme Court to order a trial on federal civil rights charges. Seven of 18 defendants were convicted and received relatively minor sentences for the murders.

In 1967, Marshall was nominated by President Lyndon Johnson to sit on the Supreme Court and his nomination was confirmed in the fall of that year, making him the first African American to sit on the high court. Marshall served on the court until 1991 when he retired. He died in 1993.

CHAPTER THIRTEEN

The Gospel of Powell

The benefits of an afterlife is the mainstay of most Christian theology, black people who had fled traditional, rural life in the South, needed and sought faiths that tended to more urgent needs such as safety, food, shelter, and a religion that built upward mobility and self-esteem. There was no better place on earth where this kind of worship was more present than in Harlem at the dawn of the twentieth century.

Many self-styled men and women of faith anointed themselves with titles like pastor or bishop and they concocted complicated rituals that incorporated tribal customs from Africa along with more familiar sacramental customs found in the Catholic or Episcopal religions. One such deity was known in Harlem as Daddy Grace or Sweet Daddy Grace. His contemporaries included pastors like Father Divine, Noble Drew Ali, Ernest Holmes, and Adam Clayton Powell, Sr.[1]

Daddy Grace had been born Marcelino Manuel Da Graca or Charles Manuel, depending on your source material. It was rumored that he came from Cape Verde, the island off the coast of West Africa. A traveling man, Daddy Grace set up shop in various places throughout the United States, including West Wareham, Massachusetts, where he built the first House of Prayer in 1919, but he also assembled worshipers throughout the South in the 1920s and 1930s who flocked to his revivals.[2]

"From those flamboyant beginnings, guided by that message of economic self-reliance, Daddy Grace's church, the United House of Prayer for All People, has grown into an unusually prosperous religious organization," according to the *New York Times*. "A church that started out selling toothpaste and shoe polish now has extensive, and growing, real estate holdings in cities across the country."

"An examination of court and property records shows that the House of Prayer is a major real estate power in many cities, with tens of millions of dollars worth of church buildings and residential and commercial space. It plans to spend more than $200 million on new development around the country," the newspaper reported.[3]

Some said Grace was a scoundrel but most stories about Daddy Grace always had traces of legend in them. His empire, estimated to have been worth hundreds of millions, was also one of the most talked about among several legendary preachers who establish churches in Harlem. Hawking everything from God's salvation to hair straighteners, cold creams and Daddy Grace toothpaste, and *Grace Magazine*, there is little doubt that Grace was a hustler above all else.[4]

Some of the pastors who came to Harlem, came peddling various brands of religion derived from progressive, fierce ministries like the New Thought Movement of Father Divine, who became one of Harlem's biggest landlords.[5] The gospel of Divine believed in acquiring wealth through other businesses, including restaurants and grocery stores. Moving his church from the South to Harlem in 1915, Divine, whose real name was George Baker, grew the church beyond its Harlem borders as an enlightened movement that took on many civil rights causes.

Like Marcus Garvey, Father Divine created a "kingdom" in a rented three story headquarters on 115th Street until it was sold to rival Bishop Daddy Grace for $18,000 who claimed to have over 100 churches with between 100,000 and 300,000 worshipers.

An eyewitness account of the religious followings of Father Divine can be found in the archives of the Library of Congress where I found the work of Frank Byrd, a New York writer working for a federal project.

In a 1938 narrative written for the Work Progress Administration's (WPA) Federal Writers' Project called "The Kingdom Banquets," Byrd said Father Divine held frequent banquets that became legendary in Harlem. Byrd said Father Divine began his cult-like church in Sayville, L.I." "Not until recently, however, has this writer availed himself of the opportunity to sit through the numerous courses of one of these colorful, gargantuan feasts. It was, to say the least, an unusual experience.[6]

"About nine o'clock in the evening the official feasting begins. Gathered about the Father are his legal satellites, staff members, personal attendants, followers and sympathizers. The table is modeled somewhat after the accepted seating arrangement of Christ and his disciples at the Last Supper, with the exception of the fact that where Christ seated twelve Father Divine seats hundreds. Interested outsiders are segregated to side tables. They may eat at the huge banquet table only when they become members of the movement or come as invited guests of the Father or his followers," Byrd said.

"The table is heavily loaded with fresh fruits of every description, whole hams, chickens, suckling pigs, legs of lamb, pig knuckles, pork chops, baked breast of lamb, beef stew, corn, cabbage, kale, spinach, potatoes, rice, celery, sliced tomatoes, large bowls of chopped lettuce and green peppers, cakes, pies, pitchers of coffee and milk. It is a gourmands dream, a hobo's heaven. When the meal is well under way, Father Divine rises, beams (as only Father Divine can beam) and says in that crisp, energetic way: 'Peace, everyone! Righteousness, Justice and Truth, Good Health, with Good Manners and Good Behavior for you! By so doing and so being, we will have a righteous government in which to live. Is everybody happy?' Judging by the almost uniformly beatic [pleasant] expressions on the faces of the angels, everybody was more than happy. And if there was any further doubt of it, the tremendous volume of answers in the affirmative was enough to dispel any possible lingering doubt. Not that there seemed to be any doubt in Father Divine's mind. He seemed quite sure of what the answer would be. In fact, while the 'Thank you Fathers', 'We're so happy' 'Yes Father, you're so sweet' and so on were still filling the air, the good Father appeared impatient and not a little annoyed at not being able to go on with his piece," Byrd wrote.

"After all is quiet and serene again and the angels have resumed such mundane activities as polishing off an unfinished pork chop bone, or sopping up some fine, brown spare rib gravy, Father takes up where he left off and, apparently inspired by his own voice, warms up to his message with all the fire and enthusiasm of a seasoned politician. Scribbling frantically at his elbow are a battery of alert stenographers who are busy recording, verbatim, every word of their leader for the subsequent edification of followers who were unable to be present, and, of course, for posterity," Byrd said.

"Well, this goes on for one, two and well into three hours. I ask if this is the usual procedure. The answer is yes. 'Maybe longer' I am informed of course the speaking does not go on uninterrupted for all this time. Speeches, as most speeches should be, were occasionally interrupted with sudden outbursts of song. Two of the most popular were: 'Father Divine Is the Light of the World' and 'Fathers Got Me in the Palm of His Hand'."[7]

Byrd said many of his followers brought musical instruments to make additional gestures of worship for their leader. New converts filled with the spirit or full of gratitude, get up during these services and make open confessions of their sins before they were taken under the protective influence of the Divine parish, according to observers.

Some stories about the church have raised eyebrows while others are typical religious tales of worship. In one instance, Byrd said, a well-educated white woman from Californian and member of the Divine movement for over three years sang Father Divine's praises to the highest during one service. She said that a perpetual craving for alcohol had almost robbed her of her reasoning. She quit her job and came to join Father Divine and she said joining the church gave her peace of mind she could not find anywhere else.[8]

"'You appear to be quite normal," Byrd asked the woman. "How do you find this business of sexual abstinence?"

"It doesn't worry me at all anymore," she declared. "Of course, I'll admit that when I first came here, it bothered me a little, but with the help of Father, I've mastered it completely. Now, all men seem like brothers to me. I don't think of them in a physical way at all."

"She seemed quite earnest and sincere and continued to explain to me how happy she was in the work of the Kingdom and in being a servant of 'God' ".

"All I want in life," she said, "is to continue doing his will."

"During these spasmodic testimonials, the angels, whenever they feel the spirit, break into song, speak in unknown tongues, shout 'Thank You, Father,' declare 'It's wonderful' extoll the sweetness of life and each other and vow undying love for and servitude to Father Divine. Even when they feel the urge to express themselves, they offer further proof of being only 'His' children. They raise their hands, like children in a school-room, wave them frantically and, if they are recognized, rise and speak. If not, they remain dutifully quiet and politely yield preference to some other brother or sister. They may all sing at once but only one at a time attempts to talk," the public domain WPA history said.

Often during these worships, people take the floor and express emotions that are filled with religious spirit. Sometimes they sing, sometimes they pray loudly and testify. Music is played spontaneously and the tune is recognized by others who join in and the hall is soon filled with throbbing music. Those with instruments improvise on the straight melody or often come in with only a soft chord or melody. This may happen 20 or 30 times before the meal officially comes to a close.

"Father Divine modestly accepts credit as composer of some of the Kingdom songs but in other cases, lyrics are made up by different angels to suit well-known Negro spirituals, operatic arias, or just plain [Broadway] Tin-Pan Alley tunes. In all of them, however, Father Divine is the theme. They apparently never tire of singing their lord and master's praises," Byrd said.

Harlem also played hosts to scores of more traditional religious houses, with congregations ranging from several dozens in storefront locations to mega churches with congregations spiraling into the tens of thousands by the mid-twentieth century. One of these was the social gospel ministry of Adam Clayton Powell Sr., leader of Abyssinian Baptist Church.

"At the turn of the century, less than 740,000 African Americans lived outside of the south, a mere 8% of the total African American population of the United States," according to Jonathan Walton, writing in the *Journal of African American Studies* in 2011.[9] "By 1970, 10.6 million, 47% of the total African American population, lived outside of the south. ... The dramatic population shifts of the migration eras are important when giving an account of the development of densely populated African American communities in major cities ... The mass influx of migrants led to exponential membership growth among previously established churches," Walton said. "African American congregational life in New York City provides an instructive example. By 1930, there were at least seven churches in the city whose membership totals exceeded 2,500. In almost every case this growth was characterized by great celerity. Between 1914 and 1920 alone, the Metropolitan Baptist Church in Harlem grew from 300 to 3,500. Metropolitan blended its spiritual mission with social concerns. The congregation ran a grocery, hardware store, and operated properties in Harlem to provide affordable housing for church members. Metropolitan's neighboring church, Abyssinian Baptist, undertook similar efforts," according to Walton. Originally located downtown, Adam Clayton Powell reestablished the church in Harlem in 1923 and "Abyssinian became one of the most vibrant and vital social institutions in black New York," according to the journal.[10]

"Though church membership was comprised of many 'well-to-do Negroes,' in reaching out to migrants with a comprehensive social ministry that included a community house for the homeless and soup kitchen for the hungry, the church sought to disrupt class lines and economic barriers. By the time Adam Clayton Powell, Jr. a well-known community activist who was later elected to Congress, took over the congregation from his father in 1937, Abyssinian's membership exceeded 10,000," according to this source. Other sources estimate the congregation had surpassed that number by the time the younger Powell ran the church.[11]

These years when the church was headed first by the senior Powell and later his son, were known as the Powell era.

It began as wave after wave of migrants flowed into Harlem, seemingly on the tides of a social gospel movement, "which began among white Protestants in the north around 1880," according to Jon Michael Spencer, writing in the *African American Review* in the fall of 1996.[12] Spencer said this movement spread to elite black churches around 1895 and is aptly characterized in the 1923 poem *The New Negro* by Reverdy Ransom, the 48th bishop of the African Methodist Episcopal (AME) Church.

Echoing a recurring theme of duality made popular by W.E.B. Du Bois in his book, *The Souls of Black Folk*, Ransom's poem characterized the New Negro as both new and "as old as the forests primeval." Ransom rhapsodizes this emerging Negro as being as naked in New York of 1923 as his ancestors were centuries before running in the jungles of Africa until they were caught and enslaved, lynched, emerging in the twentieth century as a polished man of strength and power. It was a stunning portrait of the New Negro Harlem leaders were proselytizing.

In 1926, this new progressive element that could be found in a wide array of Harlem institutions and they were noted by a philanthropic award created by William E. Harmon, the Harmon Award. It was established to honor African American achievement in different fields that included literature, music, religion, fine arts, business, and industry. The award was first won by writer James Weldon Johnson in literature in 1928, the same year that two New York ministers also won for efforts to develop the church into an entity of social and community service, according to Spencer. "Two years later, in 1930, a Harmon award was given to other intellectuals in the arts and letters, and Adam Clayton Powell, Sr. won the coveted prize for religious service."[13]

In a biography of the senior Powell, Judith Newman characterized this towering 190 pound man as "a bum, a drunkard, a gambler, a gun-toting juvenile delinquent with brass knuckles ... who walked away from it all" to lead one of America's largest churches for nearly 30 years.[14]

The stepson of a former slave, the fair-skinned, blue-eyed Powell looked like mulatto ancestors from the Piedmont section of Virginia. A light-skinned southerner seemed like an unlikely character to lead a mega black church in New York City. It was even more unlikely given the size and influence this church family he led had acquired, not just in New York, but across international boundaries.

Abyssinian Baptist Church ... is widely regarded as the most influential of all African American churches today. "In fact, some contend that it is America's most prominent church, period," wrote Alan L. Hayes in a 2008 edition of *Anglican and Episcopal History*, on the bicentennial anniversary of the church. "It played a vital role in the Harlem Renaissance of the 1920s, when that section of New York became (as many believe) the cultural and spiritual center of black America," Hayes said. "Its campaigns against segregation in New York during the Great Depression laid a foundation for the Civil Rights Movements in the American South two decades later. It has been identified as the first mega-church; by 1937 it was reportedly the country's largest Protestant church, with a membership of 14,000."[15]

In the traditions of New York abolitionists like Frederick Douglass, Harriet Tubman, and Sojourner Truth of the previous century, Powell was a powerful, enigmatic speaker by almost all accounts of his life. A reckless gambler in his late teens, Powell claimed to have had a religious conversion through unspecified circumstances. He exchanged card playing for revival meetings and wound up at the Wayland Seminary and College in Washington, DC, where he earned a degree in 1892. He became pastor of Ebenezer Baptist Church in Philadelphia in 1893, growing that congregation from a mere 25 to 600 members. In 1908, he became pastor of Abyssinian Baptist, which he eventually moved from Lower Manhattan to Harlem in 1922 and the new sanctuary was completed around 1923.[16]

During the same period alone, Powell began a community House for various activities and started the Highways and Hedges Society to care for abandoned children in Harlem. He also established a link between the church's nursing education program to the Nursing and Education Departments at nearby Columbia University. Around the same time, the church launched four Boy's Clubs and six Girl's Clubs chapters for children in Harlem. While still building his own church, Powell allegedly also raised money for every church building fund in Harlem, church history claims. Significantly, around this same time, the Abyssinian elders with Powell's leadership, build a medical center that later became Harlem Hospital.[17]

Consolidating a passion for civil activism, the elder Powell's often thunderous influence from the pulpit was combined with his leadership in the National Urban League and the National Association for the Advancement of Colored People, both headquartered in Harlem. His influence through his church and his leadership roles as a member of two of the most powerful civil rights organizations in U.S. history extended Powell's reach and influence well beyond the boundaries of his church, Harlem or New York.

"On July 28, 1917, Powell co-organized with other religious leaders and civil rights activists a 'silent protest parade' in protest of the East St. Louis, Illinois, massacre of blacks by a white mob on July 2, 1917, as well as other recent anti-black mob violence in Memphis, Tennessee, and Waco, Texas," by one account remembered by his son Adam Clayton Powell Jr. as told to Charles Hamilton in *The Political Biography of an American Dilemma*.[18]

By many accounts, membership in this church generally involved building and participating in many activities aimed at educating and helping other church members establish upward economic mobility.

"Under his leadership, the new Abyssinian became more than a house of worship, more than a social center for the Harlem community, more than the largest black church in America," Judith Newman wrote in a *Scholastic* profile of Powell. "Powell's church symbolized what he called the social gospel, a message that urged his followers not to wait for reward in the afterlife, but to work aggressively to improve their own lives and their community's social conditions."

That message was infectious and reflected the spiritual and social side to Powell's mission, Newman said. "I want to establish the kingdom of social justice," she wrote, quoting Powell's vision for building the world's largest religious, social, and educational institution. Embodied in this idea were extensive Bible classes, a school of education to train general education teachers, literacy classes, dressmaking, nursing curriculum, and business courses. "The church opened a home for retired people who could no longer support themselves," Newman wrote.[19]

In a colorful observation of church organizing activities, a Federal Writers' Project observer submitted the following account to the Woodrum Committee's hearings on Religious Beliefs and Customs to the Congress in 1939. It was a public domain document written by Harlem Writer's Project worker, Vivian Morris, who visited the Abyssinian Baptist Unemployed Section and Adult Education to interview church members.

"Reverend Powell might be a Baptist preacher, but he sho don't believe only in preachin bout God," one church member was quoted as saying "He preached the government right into givin' us all these teachers to teach us all the things we didn't have a chance to learn when we were young. This was the community house, but now it's a school, better for the community," the unnamed member said.

Powell's enthusiasm and religious fervor, he said, were easily transferrable to parish members through what he called "Emotionalism."

It is the electric current in the organized Christian Church, he said. Confine it to batteries, and this wild and frightful something could run our trains, drive our automobiles, and bring New York and South Africa within whispering distance of each other.[20]

Religious scholars, both formal and informal, have characterized Powell as Jesus-like, embodying the often-used phrase, what would Jesus do? One who not only questions this claim, German theologian Dietrich Bonhoeffer came to Harlem to observe it firsthand. Bonhoeffer arrived in New York in 1930 to attend Union Theological Seminary in Manhattan. Like Powell, Bonhoeffer was concerned with Christianity's role in secular life and Powell's church came under Bonhoeffer's microscope for this reason.

The black Baptist experience not only introduced him to an entirely new form of Christianity but provided the possibility for balancing the probable tensions in his own life and central European Christianity between emotion and reason, between thought and action, between individual and group needs, Ruth Zerner writes in a 1976 issue of *Union Seminary Quarterly Review*. During his time as a seminary fellow in New York, Bonhoeffer simultaneously studied Powell's methods and would naturally apply them to his staunch resistance to the rising threat of the Nazi and Hitler back at home.

"The life-affirming leitmotifs of black Christianity resound with an emphasis upon the centrality of Jesus Christ and the supportive experience of community solidarity,"[21] Zerner said. "The themes of Christ and community were familiar to Bonhoeffer, but novel was the unique, passionate exuberance with which they were expressed" by Powell. "Unforgettable for Bonhoeffer was the joyful, emotional liberation of Black Baptist worship, particularly in its music and audience participation. The action-oriented program of Abyssinian Baptist Church also could not have escaped Bonhoeffer's attention. Under Nazi influence, diversity was at first shameful in Nazi Germany and later criminal during and after Bonhoeffer's visit to Harlem. It also could not have escaped his notice that Powell's church was inter-racial at a time when all of America was segregated, especially in churches on Sunday's.[22]

"Powell ... worked to include white people into the life of the church," writes Louis Porter II *in Crosscurrents*, published by the Association for Religion and Intellectual Life. "His goal was to help 'all races understand each other better that they may love each other more,' Porter writes, quoting Powell himself."[23]

Although little has been written about Bonhoeffer's time with Powell in Harlem, what leaks through in reading about this period is the sloganeering that had become commonplace among Harlem leaders of the period during the birth of the so-called New Negro.

Bonhoeffer's analysis implied that the church is in a particularly strategic position to help heal America's racial tensions, writes Mark Ellingsen in the *Journal of Church and State*. "The church, like all communities, can be a place in which we become who we are meant to be. And in our largely fragmented contemporary situation, it is the one community that, at least in principle, can cut across racial lines and so provide opportunities for nurturing whole human beings who know and interact with each as beloved Thous."[24] It would not be difficult to imagine being under Powell's influence and find it easy for an old Negro to reimaging themselves as New Negroes.

After three attempts to retire were rejected by the parish, Adam Clayton Powell was finally allowed to step down in 1937, succeeded by his son Adam Clayton Powell Jr. but not without dissent and some rancor. Church politics abound among Baptist congregations and this church was no exception. Like his father, the younger Powell was an unlikely candidate to replace his father in this influential pulpit.

Significantly, "the Powells were at the helm of the church during some of the most significant moments in American history, including the two World Wars, the Great Depression, the Great Migration, and the Civil Rights movement," according to a history of the church, *Witness*.[25]

As the elder Powell led his "Social Gospel" into the community and grew it until his retirement, historians writing in *Witness*, credited the younger Powell with transforming his father's model church into a modern church. Powell, Jr. nearly eclipses his father in significance to the history of Abyssinian. With a personality that was "larger than life and a flamboyant lifestyle to match."[26]

It was this flashy lifestyle that caused elder's in the church to baulk at his rise to his father's very powerful bully pulpit.

According to various biographers, it would have not surprised many of the church elders if the young Powell grew up to live an unremarkable life. When Garvey left Harlem, if Harlem had to choose a royal family, the Powells would have been it. Adam was waited on by servants as a child and doted upon by parents who spoiled him. The young Powell acquired a deserved reputation as a hell-raising teen. When he grew older he could be seen spending as much time in nightclubs as his father's church. In 1926, Powell left Harlem for Colgate University in central New York where few blacks attended. Rather than suffering abrupt culture shock, by all accounts the fair-skinned, wavy haired Powell easily pretended to be white and generally got away with it. His deception was discovered when he pledged for a fraternity that conducted a background check and discovered his real background. He was ostracized on campus by both blacks and whites, this embarrassment many said became a turning point in his life.[27] Never again would Adam Clayton Powell deny who he was."[28]

According several accounts, Powell's awakening upstate soon became evident when he returned to Harlem of the 1930s where the economic depression had devastated the community. Attending divinity school, it was also evident that the younger Powell was now seriously being groomed as heir to his father's pulpit. What began to happen next seemed unlikely to his conservative detractors in the church.

Powell quickly threw his energy into organizing food and clothing drives, elders noted. This was a time when jobs were scarce ... and people who had to contend with the added barrier of racial discrimination had no chance at all of landing one. So Powell organized picket lines against Harlem merchants who were willing to take money from black customers but refused to employ black staffers. This was a long-standing, festering problem. In moves that would later be repeated by national civil rights leaders in other parts of the country, Powell led a movement to integrate the bus companies, telephone and electric utilities serving Harlem, employing these boycotting techniques fully two decades before the world's attention was focused on the anti-segregation lunch counter sit-ins in North Carolina, and now famous boycotts of Birmingham and Selma, Alabama.[29]

Again running against the grain of the political mood of the city in 1941, Powell ran and won a seat on the New York City Council as a member of the Communist Party. Immediately, City Councilman Adam Clayton Powell Jr. began haranguing Mayor Fiorello LaGuardia about discrimination in city hiring and substandard healthcare at Harlem Hospital, now a city-run facility founded by Powell's father. While serving the church as his father's replacement and a councilman, Powell ran for the U.S. Congress and became the first black congressman from New York. "Under his leadership the church became a center for significant social protest," the authors of *Witness* said. "He became one of the city's most controversial ministers and there was, in the twentieth century, perhaps no religious or political figure more controversial and complicated than Adam Clayton Powell, Jr."[30]

The young Powell was not merely the mirror image of his father in deed or in action. On his first day in Congress (as a Democrat), legend has it that Powell desegregated the House in several ways.[31]

Soon after his arrival in Washington, Powell challenged the informal regulations forbidding black representatives from using capitol facilities reserved for members. Following the lead of Oscar De Priest, Powell often took black constituents to the whites-only House restaurant and ordered his staff to eat there. Always looking for ways to advance racial equality, Powell also successfully campaigned to desegregate the press galleries. Powell's aggressive stance on discrimination within Congress led to numerous confrontations with John E. Rankin, a Democrat from Mississippi and one of the chamber's most notorious segregationists. Even before Powell's election to Congress, Rankin disparaged attempts to integrate the Capitol.[32]

"That gang of communistic Jews and Negroes ... tried to storm the House Restaurant and went around here arm in arm with each other" was Rankin's inflammatory response to a 1943 protest and characteristic of his stance on civil rights. When Rankin made known his intention to avoid sitting near an African American member, Powell responded to the slight by sitting close to the southern politician whenever possible. Also, Powell retorted, "I am happy that Rankin will not sit by me because that makes it mutual. The only people with whom he is qualified to sit are Hitler and Mussolini."[33]

In 1958, Powell made headlines when he was indicted by a federal grand jury for income tax evasion. His trial ended in 1960 with a hung jury. Like Garvey, Powell thrived on publicity and did not withdraw from his often flamboyant lifestyle because of it. While his antics often got him in trouble in Washington, at home in Harlem his actions were seen as bold and rebellious.

Weary of Powell's legal problems and his unpredictable antics, the House Democratic Caucus stripped the New York Representative of a committee chairmanship on January 9, 1967. The full House refused to seat him until the Judiciary Committee completed an investigation. The following month, the committee recommended that Powell be censured, fined, and deprived of seniority, but on March 1, 1967, the House rejected these proposals and voted—307 to 116—to exclude him from the 90th Congress (1967–1969).[34]

It would take years of reelections before the junior congressman from Harlem would gradually assume powerful leadership positions in Washington through seniority. Battling congressional opponents, surviving death threats for decades, Powell also successfully fought off a bold attempt to unseat him, something that had not happened in 150 years of congressional history. He was reelected again and again by New York voters during this siege. The Supreme Court eventually ruled that Powell's expulsion from the House had been illegal. The fight had cost him his seniority. The 1968 victory of Richard Nixon saw an ailing Adam Clayton Powell retreating from national politics. He was unseated by Harlem Democratic Charles Rangel in 1970 and Powell died almost two years later of cancer.

In a speech before the House on February 11, 1997, Rangel praised his predecessor, saying, "Thirty years ago this month, the House of Representatives was preparing to take one of its most infamous actions. On March 1, 1967, the House voted to exclude from the 90th Congress Representative Adam Clayton Powell, Jr."

Two years later, that action was overturned by the Supreme Court as unconstitutional, and Representative Powell returned to his seat, stripped of 22 years seniority. "Today, as we prepare for the challenges of the 21st century while reappraising the gains of the civil rights movement, we find that we are riding the shoulders of those great leaders, such as Powell, who came before us. Through their efforts, we have overcome the legal segregation and discrimination that dehumanized us as a people. Through their efforts, a viable black middle-class of successful professionals, homeowners, and college graduates has emerged." This was the legacy of the Powell years in Harlem, an indelible stamp on an emerging culture of African Americans.

CHAPTER FOURTEEN

The Crisis

Although Harlem did not become predominately black until the early decades of the twentieth century, New York was home to the first black-owned newspaper in the nation, half dozen widely read black newspapers and the first nationally circulated newspapers and magazines owned and published for black readers.

While many once powerful, influential national publications launched by publishers based in Harlem are now defunct, these journals always played a pivotal role in leading many battles against lynching, widespread discrimination in housing, school desegregation, labor, and segregated public accommodations that marginalized blacks throughout the country. Behind each of these publications that sprang up and flourished early in the century, there usually sat a charismatic radical or progressive leader at the helm to champion these causes from a desk somewhere in Harlem.

These publishers generally shared common traits with others in American publishing. "Great magazines are made by great editors . . . great magazines . . . express the personalities of the men who edit them," Theodore Peterson said in an editorial seminar on the American Press in 1966.[1]

In writing his Ph.D. dissertation at the University of Texas at Austin, Marvin G. Kimbrough described the role of W.E.B. Du Bois as founding editor of *The Crisis: A Record of the Darker Races*, one of the longest, continually published black magazines in U.S. history, as the personal opinion vehicle for Du Bois, not a news magazine as the subtitle suggests. Today, the magazine is still in print and the title has been modernized to *The Crisis*. Founded and launched by Du Bois in Harlem one year after the National Association for the

Advancement of Colored People was founded in 1910, Du Bois held the reigns of *The Crisis* for nearly a quarter of a century, resigning in 1934 due to creative differences with NAACP leadership. Although seen as the editorial voice of the NAACP throughout most of its life, Du Bois himself said, "Personally, my interest in the NAACP has been centered in this (publishing) branch of the work. It has been my life work," Kimbrough quotes Du Bois as saying. Black publishers like Du Bois in nineteenth- and twentieth-century America were leaders who had and expressed the audacity to champion Negro causes when no other media dared cover black issues.

As a writer and reporter of Time Inc. and *The Crisis*, I could still feel the powerful legacy of *Time* magazine left behind by founder Henry R. Luce, 30 years after Luce had left the 50th Street building in Manhattan. When I wrote commissioned articles for *The Crisis* in the 1980s, the editors assigned articles that were clearly aimed at the civil rights advocates of the era. While many thought *The Crisis* was primarily launched to cover black issues, a closer reading of the magazine shows that Du Bois used a firm hand in accepting and rejecting editorial content he supported or rejected.

It is commonly believed that Luce created the most popular news magazine in modern times, a view that was no more accurate than the idea that Du Bois merely echoed the opinion of the NAACP board members in *The Crisis*. Luce, a staunch anti-Communist, said he created *Time* magazine to lead readers away from the dangers of Communism.

"The Crisis magazine was more of a reflection of Du Bois's personality, thinking and concerns than that of the organization.[2]" Du Bois made his editor's desk a podium for his own changing ideas.... The concept that an editor's ideology often reflects itself in his magazine was voiced not only by friendly and unfriendly critics of Du Bois; it was also shared by Du Bois himself. "If ... *The Crisis* had not been in a sense a personal organ and the expression of myself, it could not possibly have attained its popularity and effectiveness," Kimbrough writes in his 1974 paper.[3]

Launched with the declared mission "to set forth those facts and arguments which show the danger of race prejudice, particularly as manifested today toward colored people," Du Bois edited *The Crisis* with the firm hand of founder and editor-in-charge with a mission not unlike Luce's. The magazine "takes its name from the fact that the editors believe that this is a critical time in the history of the advancement of men.... Finally, its editorial page will stand for the rights of men, irrespective of color or race, for the highest ideals of American democracy, and for reasonable but earnest and persistent attempts to gain these rights and realize these ideals," the magazine said in 1910. But Du Bois was no loyal rank-and-file NAACP member or an employee of the civil rights organization who took direction without comment. Case in point, although the organization paid the bills and supported the widespread circulation of the magazine throughout the United States, *The Crisis* often published scathing editorials written by Du Bois, which the NAACP leadership either disagreed with or knew nothing about until they read them in the magazine. In later years, Du Bois quietly made no bones about his sometimes floundering loyalties to the organization that paid the magazine's bills, writing in his book *Dusk of Dawn*[4] in 1940 that he had always intended for *The Crisis* to voice his personal opinions on a wide variety of issues affecting the lives of African Americans.

"I determine to make the opinion of the Crisis a personal opinion; because, as I argued, no organization can express definite and clear cut opinions ... the Crisis would state openly the opinion of its editor, so long, of course, as that opinion was in general agreement with that of the organization," he claimed, ignoring the fact that many of his opinions clashed with the organization's more conservative views and tactics throughout his 24-year tenure with the magazine.[5]

In the early years of *The Crisis*, the magazine courted and published the work of many black writers who would later become well-known pioneers of African American literature. These included Langston Hughes, Zora Neale Hurston, James Weldon Johnson, Arna Bontemps, and many others who became the "Who's Who" of the Harlem Renaissance. This editorial strength of the magazine is largely credited to fiction editor Jessie Fauset, who published a wide range of poetry, prose, short stories, essays, and plays in *The Crisis* during time there.

After Fauset's departure in 1926, Du Bois took the literary helm of the magazine as well and his choices in what to publish or not to publish, veered sharply from the choices Fauset had made for the magazine. In my reading of the magazine during those years, I believe Du Bois at first obeyed the political correctness of praising creative expression, saying things like "The Crisis could bring beauty into the home," while his opinion that "all art is propaganda and ever must be" was at the crux of his decision over what made it into the pages of *The Crisis* and what did not. The commentary and Du Bois's opinions could be seen throughout the magazine, particularly in the political cartoons, illustrations, and graphic photographs of crimes committed against African Americans, especially lynching. If shock and awe worked, Du Bois employed it whenever it suited his purposes to drive home some editorial impressions he wanted to make.

An analysis of *The Crisis* during Du Bois's tenure shows he held the editorial reins of the magazine's editorial policy tightly until he resigned as editor in 1934. His views and that of the NAACP board were split when Du Bois advocated black separatism from America while the NAACP board took a softer approach to social reform and made appeals for racial justice without taking a radical stance as Du Bois often did. All along, Du Bois was the loudest radical voice in a conservative organization that believed in asking for change, not dismantling or abandoning America to achieve it. To truly understand the challenge Du Bois faced as editor of this publication at the time, readers must understand the time and climate under which his radical words were published.

A Harvard scholar, Dr. Du Bois was always a contrarian with varied opinions in about many causes. Du Bois clearly used the wildly touted power of the press to disseminate his ideas about the racial divide in his time between blacks and whites and he rarely, if ever, apologized for his opinions. His voice is easily found in any of the five magazines in his lifetime, *The Crisis*, *The Moon*, *Horizon*, *Brownies Book*, and *Phylon*. *The Crisis* and *Phylon* are still in print and published by the NAACP and by Atlanta University respectively. Du Bois's toil in the storefront offices of the NAACP in the early years when he edited *The Crisis* in Harlem were formative years for black leadership in Harlem when the New Negroes were in the throes of a growing self-awareness. The idea that a self-aware, new Negro could participate in reimagining the Negro triggered a raging debate that required the same fearlessness future President Barack Obama would later exhibit in a successful campaign in 2008 that landed him in the White House as the first black president of the United States. In 1910, the win or lose stakes involved halting the widespread lynching of blacks, many unsolved murders of Negro men, women, and numerous other injustices.

"I count you among the chief American writers of your day and trust that some of your books will be read in years to come, as a statement of conditions in a critical time for the Negro race, you are an extremist—and so was (abolitionist) William Lloyd Garrison," Albert Bushnell Hart writes in a letter to Du Bois. The Harvard historian goes on to quote Langston Hughes as saying it was widely known and respected that Du Bois's views were so controversial "he was the center of disagreements as a teacher, as an NAACP executive, as a political partisan, that his close association with black journalism is submerged."[6]

Du Bois, Garvey, and labor leader A. Philip Randolph pioneered an unprecedented brand of advocacy journalism in this era from their positions in a city with an exploding population of migrating blacks in Harlem. Their examples spawned a robust, militant black press, and investigative journalism that certainly was carried on in Harlem by *The Crisis*, *The Messenger*, *Negro World*, *The Amsterdam News*, *The New York Age*, and *The People's Voice* in later decades of the twentieth century.

A simple survey of the names chosen for some of the other magazines and newspapers published in Harlem beginning in the early decades of the century echoed the tone and temper of their radical editorial tone. There was *The Crusader*, *The Emancipator*, *The Crisis*, *The Messenger*, *The Voice*, *Challenge*, *Opportunity*, *New Challenge*, and others. While many of these publications were new, many of the older more conservative newspapers, also began to show their tempers too, particularly when they wrote about race, equity, and a lack of equal justice.

"The vitriolic utterances drew the notice of the government and caused agents of the Department of Justice to take steps to suppress them," Roi Ottley and William Weatherby wrote in their book, *The Negro in New York*. "Under the caption, Radicalism and Sedition among the Negroes as Reflected in Their Publications, these organs were cited in a 1919 Department of Justice report highlighting the radical nature of Harlem publishing. Clearly alarmed by the tone and timbre of these Harlem newspapers and magazines, the sitting attorney general at the time, Mitchell Palmer, said it would be a mistake to believe the articles and columns contained in their publications were not the ignorant vaporing of untrained minds. He said the publications were edited by more than fifty men of education, who wrote in fine, pure English, with a background of scholarship and were defiantly assertive of [the Negro's] equality.

"The number of restrained and conservative publications is relatively negligible, even some of these . . . have indulged in most intemperate utterances, though it would be unfair not to state that certain papers" that are exceptions. "I can think of no magazine—that maintains an attitude of well-balanced sanity," the attorney wrote.[7]

One neglected example of crusading journalism nurtured and widely practiced in Harlem can be seen in the career of writer Marvel Cooke.

Du Bois hired Cooke as an assistant at *The Crisis* in 1926 where she wrote critiques of writers like Langston Hughes, Zora Neale Hurston, and other Harlem celebrities. She later wrote for *The Amsterdam News* and founded the first chapter of the New York Newspaper Guild. From 1940 to 1947, Cooke worked for *The People's Voice*, the weekly owned by Adam Clayton Powell Jr. until she was hired by *The Daily Compass*, becoming the first woman and black journalist in New York to be hired by a mainstream publication.

Living at 409 Edgecombe Avenue in the Sugar Hill section of Harlem where Thurgood Marshall and other notables lived, Cooke made a name for herself shortly after Du Bois resigned as editor of *The Crisis* with a story that carried the headline, "The Bronx Slave Market," an exposé about the exploitation of black domestic workers. Cooke's investigative reporting is chronicled in the *Journal for the Study of Radicalism*, Fall 2012.[8] Cooke teamed up with reporter Ella Baker in a 1935 story they wrote for *The Crisis* about exploited domestic workers in Bronx.

Desperate and impoverished, black domestics worked for the highest white bidder for daily work on the corner of 167th Street and Jerome Avenue at Simpson and Westchester Avenues in the Bronx. The Cooke and Baker team joined what they called the "paper bag brigade," named after the women brought a change of clothes, toothbrushes, combs, and whatever they might need in paper bags in case they landed an overnight, sleep-in job. The women who gathered on this corner daily, waited in front of "Woolworth's (department store) for housewives to buy their strength and energy for an hour, two hours, or even over night work for a day at the rate of between fifteen, twenty, twenty-five ... cents an hour." The Bronx Slave Market (story) was shaped by the authors' concern with the exploitation of working poor African American women, the Radicalism journal reported.[9]

Their reporting prompted Federal Writers' Project worker Vivian Morris to also pose as a domestic worker and write her own version of the Bronx Slave Market story.[10] The story was not published until I discovered it in the archives of the Library of Congress and published it in a collection of stories in *A Renaissance in Harlem* in 2001.[11] Cooke's coauthor, Ella Baker, went on to become a prominent civil rights worker in the 1950s, according to LaShawn Harris, writing in a Michigan State University journal. Historian Howard Zinn called Baker "the most tireless, the most modest, and wisest activist I know in the struggle for human struggle."[12]

"Cooke's ability to unravel and depict New Yorkers' everyday politics was made possible by her unique style of collecting and gathering information. Like Zora Neale Hurston, African American writers and cultural anthropologists, Cooke immersed herself in the lives of her subjects and embraced radical methods of producing social knowledge," Harris wrote. "Cooke traversed class and respectable lines, and embodied a style of performance that was unusual for many African-American middle-class women. . . . Cooke became an authority on her subjects and provided her readership with first-hand knowledge of New York City's burgeoning under-class," Harris says.[13]

Much like President Barack Obama in his early years as a state senator in Illinois, Cooke joined an unknown, yet significant political action group of black women. While Obama operated as a crusading Democratic Party community organizer from Hyde Park, Illinois, Cooke joined a small cadre of black women who were attracted to and joined the Communist Party during the first half of the twentieth century, according to Harris. "Black female communists were effective community mobilizers and national leaders, wrote for and distributed radical left wing publications such as The Daily Worker, served as Communist Party (CP) representatives at national and international conferences, ran for political office under the Communist ticket, and . . . became fiery street corner orators," Harris noted, much like Garvey, Randolph, Harrison, and later Malcolm X on the streets of Harlem.

Like the varied and multiple brands of New Negroes striving to gain a toehold in the broader American landscape as whole Americans, Cooke joined black women reformers "to create a set of guidelines and behavioral patterns that demonstrated a moral, well-mannered, and culturally advanced race," Harris contends.[14] This was a general creed of the New Negro, although the idea was expressed differently by various leaders who had all adopted this new aesthetic view.

"Black female middle-class up lifters also argued that radical and confrontational forms of protests were counterproductive to solving the Negro Problem" as it was outlined in Du Bois's classic *Souls of Black Folk*.[15] "While Cooke and other African American Communist Party women subscribed to some aspects of respectable politics, they maintained, largely through their activism and political writings, an outward public decorum that was not a precondition toward achieving civil rights," Harris observed. "For these emerging activists, respectability was about asserting and demanding race, gender, and class equality and citizenship rights through public confrontation and direct action protest."[16]

Prophetically, Cooke and her Communist colleagues in Harlem of the 1930s were mimicking the oratory and organizing tactics that had been pioneered on Lenox Avenue by new Negroes like Garvey, Hubert Harrison, and Randolph decades earlier and later used by Obama in national speeches that propelled him into the leadership of the Democratic Party and eventually into the White House where he led the nation for two terms.

Harris has chided scholars for ignoring Cooke's career as a journalist and her activism like her mentor, Du Bois, although their politics and civil disobedience tactics differed almost until the end of Du Bois's life when he too became an open Communist. . . . Like the thesis of this book, her career as an investigative journalist was "overshadowed by more commonly studied New York topics and civic leaders made famous because of their participation in Harlem's brief literary and the New Negro Movements.

Scholar Jacob S. Dorman contends that the history of black Harlem during the Progressive Era (1890s–1920s) has become largely dominated by stories about the community of poets, artists, religious eccentrics and exclusive clubs and cabarets, not about political activists like Cooke. Unfortunately, he said, Cooke's "reform style remains outside of intellectual discourses and categories on African Americans and women."[17] There were many other women like Cooke who came to Harlem to establish themselves. They too had mentors like Du Bois.

Du Bois was no anomaly in New York publishing. His self-styled, single-minded editorial posture reflected a general rule in magazine publishing rather than an exception to it. He resembled publisher, Luce, the fearless Republican opposed to Communism who founded the *Time* magazine. Luce clearly intended to shape American opinion and sway readers when he launched *Time-Life* using aggressive, subjective journalism. Shortly after I began writing for a Time Inc. magazine, it was immediately clear to me that there was no place in the building where an objective idea could survive the Luce legacy. Luce and Du Bois's brand of publishing was no different than publishing had been in 1827 when *Freedom's Journal* was first in New York. As the first black-owned newspaper in the United States, it was a national magazine that was banned in many communities so it had to be smuggled into some black communities, particularly in Southern states. Started by Samuel Cornish and John Brown Russwurm, founder of the New

Demeter Street Presbyterian Church, Cornish's parish was also the first black Presbyterian Church in New York City. Russwurm, senior editor of the *Freedom Journal*, arrived in New York the year the abolitionist newspaper was launched. A proponent of American blacks colonizing African communities like Garvey later proposed, Russwurm's advocacy journalism encouraging black readers to leave America, made him a controversial figure of his time, just as it did in Garvey's. Much like Du Bois and later Garvey, Russwurm's views whipped up storms of disagreement around the newspaper. He resigned and left New York for Liberia in 1829, one of the colonies set up by the American Colonization Society to repatriate blacks back to Africa. In 1836, he became governor of another small colony of American blacks in Africa, Maryland, set up by Maryland State Colonization Society. This kind of idea was routinely ridiculed by Du Bois in *The Crisis*. Ironically, Du Bois in his later years renounced his American citizenship and he too fled America for Accra, Ghana, where he died in 1963 as a self-imposed exile and Communist Party member at the age of 95.[18]

CHAPTER FIFTEEN

The Messenger

In order to understand the significance of attempts by black leaders like Garvey, Hubert, Fortune, Powell, Randolph, or Du Bois, to debate the ways and means of overcoming the many difficulties of the so-called Negro in America, the period must be viewed through the lens of observers of those times. It is only from this perspective that we can now try to understand the importance of their triumphs and their failures.

By the 1920s, Harlem had become the unofficial black capitol of America. It was in Harlem that some of the greatest social engineers, civil rights architects, legal minds, and activist found themselves and each other. They were not friends, colleagues, or even kindred spirits sometimes. In more cases than not, they were rivals, tasked with the enormous duty of carving out a path toward citizenship for disenfranchised Negroes. This was an achievement the Emancipation Proclamation, a Civil War and a period of reconstruction, had promised 12 million Negroes but was never delivered. It was this goal that was debated night and day in the salons, parish houses, and dance halls of Harlem in the 1920s and decades beyond this benchmark year.

Negroes throughout most of the United States did not attempt to use predominantly white, mainstream restaurants, universities, or other public facilities in their communities because they often faced rejection, violence, arrest, or worse if they did. Segregation was generally practiced everywhere in some form throughout the country, even in northern and western cities like Boston, Philadelphia, or California, where segregation was not officially sanctioned but still widely practiced. America was two countries: one white, the other black and marginalized. This is unimaginable today, particularly among millennials, sometimes called Generation Y, the generation of Americans born between the years 1980 and the 1990s when Barack Obama was the sitting black president of the United States.

During the Progressive Era and later, black leaders were tasked with dismantling what conservatively can be called American apartheid, systemic discrimination that relegated blacks to decaying ghettos in cities or isolated neighborhoods where only blacks lived. The many movements Negro leaders in Harlem formed, in the simplest form, had at least two prongs. First, Negroes had to abandon their own acceptance of the widespread discrimination they faced. Second, it was hoped, their leaders could implant the idea in all Americans that black people had the right to be full-fledged citizens, not just the disenfranchised descendants of former slaves banished to the back of buses, the balconies of movie theaters, isolated neighborhoods, and barred from enrolling in public universities because they were black. In *The Negro Faces America*, Herbert J. Seligmann, formerly a writer for the *New Republic*, spells out these difficulties.[1]

Politically, he said, Negroes "had all but accepted the belief current in the southern states that their government was not and would not be a democracy," Seligmann said in the 1920 book published by Harper Brothers. Although still in print, Seligmann's work is now in the public domain and can be found in many academic libraries and general interest databases. "As individuals, fiercely though their resentment might blaze at brutalities and indignities visited upon men and women of color and at the universal discrimination in industry, they had to acquiesce in the treatment meted out to them." Theories and tactics to overcome these problems abounded at the time and varied from the very conservative approaches of Negro leadership like Booker T. Washington of the Tuskegee Institute in Alabama to the militant, widely debated views of men like W.E.B. Du Bois, editor of *The Crisis*. He was the chief critic of Washington's conciliatory views on civil rights. Du Bois bluntly demanded civil freedoms for blacks. Then there were the more radical views of socialist like A. Philip Randolph and Chandler Owen, editors of *The Messenger* who preached self-defense, organizing, self-reliance and socialism, not democracy.

"Many a Negro hoped to achieve peace by conformity; therefore conservatism became a sort of norm for colored people in the United States," Seligmann wrote. Washington said the path to citizenship was economic and he touted the learning of trades for black workers seeking to escape discriminations. Washington's strategy was compelling at the time "but Negroes in the United States found the attempt at economic progress alone insufficient," Seligmann said. "As early as 1910 . . . groups of colored people and their white friends realized that the white man's political power could be used to nullify the Negro's economic progress. . . . Add to political and civil disabilities social discrimination directed especially against the successful individual of color, and Booker Washington's avenue to freedom became perilously insecure." Intellectuals like Du Bois, grassroots organizers like Garvey, Randolph, and Hubert Harrison, began their campaigns for the establishment of the "New Negro" as their moniker although each might define it differently. "It will be seen that in all but name the 'new Negro' was already in existence, a far cry from the humble servitor, the 'good old darky,' the mythical personality compounded of servility, vice, and gratitude. If between the evolved and educated Negro citizen and the drifting roustabout of the far south yawns the interval between the primitive and the civilized, that same gap is observable among white men in New York City," Seligmann noted.[2]

The "New Negro," then, is a name not so much for a being brought into existence during the world war as it was a label or what might be called a "brand" today for people becoming more self-aware and finding solutions to their most immediate problems.

"Certain colored men, notably (Randolph and Owen, Garvey, Charles S. Johnson, Alain Locke, and others in Harlem), gave the term their own special significance in that they applied it to the class-conscious, progressive, revolutionary, or sometimes socialist aims they in part represented, but mainly [it became] that something they hoped to evoke. . . . This was the left wing of the Harlem community representing the farthest swing away from the accommodating optimism of Booker Washington and others like him who were also in the community. It repudiated even Du Bois and *The Crisis*, who sometimes wavered and baulked at more radical ideas, together with all reform movements for the advancement of the Negro under the capitalist system, Seligmann said.

In its own emancipation proclamation in *The Messenger*, Randolph and Owen outlined the task that lay before all black leaders of their time, saying, "Booker T. Washington is no more, and with him has passed the old me-too-boss, hat-in-hand, good nigger which you and your ilk so dearly love." This assault on Washington in *The Messenger* had begun with a similar commentary started by Du Bois in *The Crisis*. "In a sense they carried on Doctor Du Bois's insurgence from the Booker Washington leadership," Seligmann said. "Like Doctor Du Bois, they set out to create new habits of thought among American Negroes, and, like him, they represented an attitude which had grown ripe for expression."[3]

In any serious survey of scholarship surrounding the Harlem Renaissance that is not a clone, or a rehash of claims about a sudden "flowering" of literary outpourings during the period, several names from the period emerge that require further scholarship. These include but are not limited to Timothy T. Fortune, Adam Clayton Powell Sr., Adam Clayton Powell Jr., Hubert Harrison, Garvey, and two names that are prominent in almost every history of the period, Du Bois and Randolph.

Among the excellent scholarship that should be noted about the period are David Levering Lewis's two volume, Pulitzer Prize biographies of Du Bois, *W.E.B. Du Bois: Biography of a Race, 1868–1919*, (Owl Books 1994), winner of the 1994 Pulitzer Prize for Biography and also winner of the Bancroft and Parkman prizes; and *W.E.B. Du Bois: The Fight for Equality and the American Century 1919–1963* (Owl Books 2001), winner of the 2001 Pulitzer Prize for Biography and the Anisfield-Wolf Book Award. Together, these biographies more than adequately cover Du Bois's lifelong struggle with the race question that ended ironically in 1961 with his exile to Accra.

There are numerous biographies of Randolph, including the most recent, *A. Philip Randolph, Pioneer of the Civil Rights Movement* by Paula Pfeffer, Louisiana State University Press, 1990, 1996.

Du Bois was born in Great Barrington, Massachusetts, and educated at Harvard, a rarity in 1888.

Randolph was raised in the South by a stern African Methodist Episcopalian, a faith at the center of black radical politics reaching back to the eighteenth century. It was this brand of black radicalism that Randolph brought with him when he arrived in Harlem from Florida in 1911 as a hired hand aboard a steamship. He came to New York secretly hoping to launch an acting career. The political and social conditions he encountered as a black man, derailed those plans and transformed this 22-year-old minister's son into a lifelong political activist. He became a formidable strategist.

A graduate of the Cookman Institute, a Crescent City, Florida, high school established by Methodists after the Civil War, Randolph hired himself out as a hand aboard a steamship going to New York City. Working odd jobs as a dishwasher and waiter, he enrolled in City College of New York whose campus bordered Harlem. There he met campus socialists who advocated for working class people, like the domestic workers of his father's parish back in Florida. Randolph joined raucous debates on campus and became a vocal street orator whose views on the rights of workers became well known.

This young, headstrong socialist sauntered into a party one night at a lavish mansion on 136th Street where he met an attractive widow named Lucille Green. The party was given by Madame C. J. Walker, the hair pomade and beauty culture millionaire. Lucille was a beauty shop owner and a graduate of a beauty culture school owned by Walker that made her the first black woman millionaire in America. After a brief courtship, Lucille Green married Randolph.

At the same party, he also met the president of a restaurant waiter's union in the city. Chandler Owen asked Randolph to edit a hotel waiter's magazine called *Hotel Messenger*. Randolph accepted but was fired a short time later when an editorial he wrote favoring young waiters over senior waiters angered other union leaders. Owen and Randolph both departed *Hotel Messenger* after the incident. In 1916, they joined the Socialist Party and a year later launched *The Messenger*, a magazine they claimed would become "the first voice of radical revolutionary economic and political action among Negroes in America."[4]

The tactics Randolph and Owen pioneered in the 1940s would drive a difficult labor movement leader for two decades into strategies that could be later forged into meaningful strides for civil rights.

Garvey, Du Bois, and Randolph had all been firebrands in the Harlem community, intellectuals, and streetwise organizers whose politics differed in fundamental ways. Each commanded a large followings in Harlem, a distinction that targeted each leader as ripe targets for federal scrutiny. Garvey's rapid rise to power in Harlem had come to the attention of federal authorities through J. Edgar Hoover who became a special assistant to U.S. Attorney General A. Mitchell Palmer and later the first director of the Federal Bureau of Investigation. Du Bois and Randolph were both prime targets for federal investigators then and throughout the rest of their lives.

"He (Hoover) stayed up all night reading the radical pamphlets and literature," according to Theodore Kornweibel, and "quickly became the Justice Department expert on radicalism." The targets of Hoover's hunt were suspected political enemies of the American government, particularly Communists and Socialist radicals like A. Philip Randolph. Reading Hoover's files on Randolph, the attorney general quickly labeled him "the most dangerous man in America."[5]

The aggressive grassroots political activity in Harlem at that time made many activists there prime targets for federal inquiries, not just

Randolph and Du Bois. These probes looked at the activities of Randolph, Du Bois, and writer and editor James Weldon Johnson among many. Federal authorities targeted black celebrities who lived in or visited Harlem frequently. These included the coming and goings of the flamboyant boxer Jack Johnson who came to Harlem often with white women always in his entourage.

Hoover and his agents relied heavily on the public statements made by the black radicals they targeted. It was not difficult. Extensive files were kept on black publications like *The Crisis*, the *Chicago Defender*, the *Baltimore-Afro-American*, and *The Messenger* and many other black publications. *The Messenger* openly challenged the conservative politics of NAACP leaders like Du Bois and writer James Weldon Johnson and the radical politics of Garvey, especially after Garvey blundered once and briefly aligned himself with the Ku Klux Klan.

"When Randolph arrived in Harlem in 1911, the lack of self-reliance and independence from white control among African-Americans frustrated him," writes Beth Tompkins Bates, who authored *Pullman Porters and the Rise of Protest Politics in Black America*. "He criticized black leaders who were part of what he called the Old Crowd, subsidized by the Old Crowd of white Americans—a group which viciously opposes every demand made by organized labor for an opportunity to live a better life."[6]

Significantly, Bates notes that Randolph campaigned for new leadership in Harlem and the ouster of black politicians who did not serve the needs of the black people they claimed to represent. Jumping into New York State and city politics, Randolph made an unsuccessful bid for the office of secretary of state in New York on the Socialist ticket in 1921.

The Crisis, Garvey's *Negro World*, Randolph's *The Messenger* and other publications that sprang up in the first two decades of the twentieth century became the voices of a multicultural community of black people from Africa, the Caribbean, and the South, a new cultural phenomenon in America at that time. Each magazine and newspaper offered readers a wide variety of poems, essays, editorials, and journalism that exposed more than the myths about the freedom for blacks in America. *The Messenger*, for example, radicalized working-class readers who were being exploited by employers who hired them as maids and bellhops at hotels across the nation. Railroad porters read about their low wages and long working hours in the pages of this Harlem-based magazine and they organized against this oppression. Other workers could learn of unionizing activities by reading articles and advertisements calling for them to join mass protests covered regularly in *The Messenger*.

In September 1919, a poem written by railroad porter Claude McKay appeared in *The Messenger*. It was called *If We Must Die*, a call to action, protest poem for young black Americans who faced daily segregation and the humiliation of widespread discrimination and violence by white mobs. In her introduction to a collection of stories originally published in *The Messenger*, Sandra Wilson wrote, "These writings resonate with the new type of black militancy *The Messenger* helped to produce. *The Messenger* called for a brand of socialism that would emancipate the workers of America."[7]

Like Garvey and many others during this period, *The Messenger* also announced the arrival of a New Negro. But this Negro, it said, would be more strident than any of the others, and no longer be willing to turn the other cheek. In his attempt to organize the Brotherhood of Sleeping Car Porters, Randolph's newspaper made clear what the greatest handicap to organizing them would be in 1925:

"The handicap under which the porters are now laboring are due to the fact that there are too many Uncle Toms in the service. With their slave psychology they bow and kowtow and lick the boots of the company officials, who either pity or despise them. The company uses these me-too-boss, hat-in-hand porters to spy on the independent manly men. They are always afraid that somebody will rock the boat that the good white folks will get mad. They are always singing to let well enough alone, even though they be kicked and spat upon; that the time isn't ripe for the porters to stand up like men. The officials know this, the white employees on the railroad know this and the public knows it. This sort of porters who have a *wishbone* where a backbone ought to be, must be brushed aside and made to understand that their day has passed, never to return.

It is reported that Frank Walsh, Chairman of the Industrial Relations Committee, indicated that it was obvious upon cross-examining the Pullman porters during the Congressional investigation of the Pullman Company, that the porters had been coached. And naturally, because their transportation had been given them by the Company, they testified in favor of the Company and against themselves and their fellow workers. Happily, however, this type of porter is gradually losing his influence."[8]

This same kind of strident declaration came even earlier during racial upheavals in Washington and Chicago in 1919 that turned into violent riots. In editorials and articles noticing this turmoil, *The Messenger* declared this "new style Negro was determined to make this nation safe for black people." Under the influence of socialism, this "new style Negro" would not be subdued with political spoils and patronage into a false sense of security. Black men must fight back," the magazine declared. This was a call to arms in a segregated society that was seen as a dangerous act of treason and Randolph rose to the top of a secret FBI Most Wanted list.

Garvey, Randolph, and his partner Chandler Owen, were all steeped in the street oratory of Hubert Harrison. Garvey was a separatist, Randolph and Owen were Socialists and Harrison, who also edited Garvey's *Negro World*, was a leading political voice in Harlem who urged street blacks in Harlem to seize their rights to life, liberty, and the pursuit of happiness on the same streets of Harlem. Howard scholar Alain Locke and W.E.B. Du Bois urged Negroes to work within the framework of American society using education, politics, and achievement to win gain opportunities to which they were entitled. Radicals rejected these as a tepid response to the long-standing, homegrown terrorism against blacks.

Although all of these leaders belonged to different factions, they unwittingly belonged to a growing brotherhood of self-proclaimed New Negroes. Together and separately, they represented dangerous black symbols to authorities. "The New Negro Movement, whose leaders included Randolph, Chandler ... Hubert Harrison, and many others, showed that they had little fear of reprisals and 'the time for cringing is over," wrote Beth Tompkins Bates, a scholar writing for the University of North Carolina Press.

This radical view was not only feared by federal investigators but it was also seen as dangerous rhetoric by more conservative leaders in Harlem. This was particularly true when it came to the NAACP.[9]

This brand of black political radicalism was fueled by a significant metamorphosis that began to occur in the black labor and civil rights movements in America. While most other newspapers and magazines in the early 1920s were heralding the brief flowering of Negro arts and letters in Harlem, *The Messenger*, *The New York Age*, and *The Amsterdam News* covered beats extolling the plight of black Americans coping with the ills of a thoroughly segregated, racist society. Unfortunately, *The Messenger* was published sporadically over an 11-year run because of financial difficulties and it folded in 1928. By this time, Randolph had been recruited to lead a group of railroad porters and maids struggling to unionize almost 10 years later, *The Messenger* had ceased to exist.

Decades after the Great Migration (exodus) had gotten underway, Southern migrants who had settled in Detroit, Chicago, Cleveland, New York, and other major urban cities in the northeast sadly discovered they had merely replaced one kind of oppression in the South for the urban equivalent. This was particularly true in employment where black workers still could not join 24 national labor unions, nearly half of these affiliated with the American Federation of Labor. Together, these unions made up the backbone of the powerful American labor movement. These unions were organized by craft, not by industry. There were also many nonunion jobs reserved for blacks like those filled by thousands of porters and maids who worked on the railroads that crossed the nation in 1920. They made beds, cooked meals, and carried bags for sleeping car train passengers, all service jobs that had once been done by ex-slaves after emancipation.

Even 100 years after slavery in 1963, America remained a segregated society. The ideals of freedom, justice, and equity were still just the rhetoric of the post-Civil War and Reconstruction era for black Americans. "Barriers also restricted where blacks in the Promised Land could live, walk, and play," Beth Tompkins Bates wrote. "Racially restrictive covenants limited space allocated for black residents even as the urban black population mushroomed," she said.[10]

Restrictions on European immigration during World War I, however, created job vacancies in many northern industries. At meat packing plants in Chicago, for example, Bates said some 12,000 blacks workers were able to find work in an industry controlled by sometimes fierce union politics. "Despite discriminatory policies, of labor unions and employers, which kept black workers in so-called 'Negro Jobs', they made significant inroads in manufacturing industries," Bates wrote. "Tension between black workers and white unionists were rooted in the exclusion practiced by the predominately white labor movement."[11] Black workers, barred from every major union in America too kept their distance from union organizing activity. Without the same protections as other workers, black stockyard workers could be exploited by management and attacked by unionized white workers fearful of losing their jobs to blacks who worked for lower, nonunion wages, Bates said.

Luxury sleeping rail cars were the invention of George Pullman, owner of the Pullman Company that he created shortly after the

Civil War. Pullman hired only black men and women as porters and maids to work in sleeping cars. The cars were equipped with sleeping and restaurant accommodations and by 1925, were a common part of every long distance train route in America. They belonged to pseudo-unions set up and run by the Pullman Company. One was called the Employee Representation Plan, or ERP, and another the Pullman Porters and Maids Protective Association.

"These men, always present with a ready smile and an open palm" responded to "the seemingly incessant call of 'George,' an appellation used regardless of their own names," according to document archived at the Chicago Historical Society. "Such smiles masked a deep resentment among the porters" to being all called George by businessmen and tourists, according to "Miles of Smiles," a Public Broadcasting Service documentary about Pullman porters.[12] The open palm was a polite way of summoning tips, according to Rosina Tucker, who narrated the documentary. That open palm was a constant reminder of the low wages that porters were paid, said Rosina Tucker, the wife of a male porter with the unusual name for a man, Berthesa Tucker.

The Pullman Company was the largest, single employer of black men in the nation by 1925, employing 12,000 black men and women. In 1915, porters and maids worked 400 hours a month, averaging 14 hours a day. They earned a base pay of $27.50 a month while white conductors earned $150 a month. By 1920, porters and maids were making $60 a month and 60 cents for each additional 100 miles they traveled after they had logged in 400 hours of work.

In return for these wages, porters paid for their own meals, equipment, and uniforms. They had to report to work five hours before train departure time and were required to reimburse the company for lost linen, according to Pullman records.

"It wasn't only the pay and the hours that were bad," Tucker said in a story released in 1996 by a U.S. Department of State in honor of Black History Month. "Pullman porters were all black. They were all called George and could be fired just for not smiling frequently and not looking happy," said Tucker.

Porters tried to organize themselves into an independent union, making at least five unsuccessful attempts, according to company records kept by the Chicago Historical society. The Pullman Company was ruthless when it came to quashing this kind of activity. The company fired hundreds of porters for union activities, according to railroad and union records in Chicago.

In 1911, a porter in St. Paul, Minnesota, named Frank Boyd tried to rally support for a proposed wage hike from $25 a month to $50. To quash this activity, the company offered porters an immediate raise of $2.50 a month and rank and file members refused to holdout for higher wages, according to Boyd. Boyd was born in Kansas City in 1881. He worked various jobs in the Midwest, including one as a porter for a barbershop until he joined the Pullman Company, starting on a run aboard Northern Pacific Railroad trains. Boyd had attempted to organize porters into the Railroad Men's Industrial Association and failed. Boyd was fired and he appealed this action to the company under provisions of the company union, the Pullman Porter's Protective Association and lost. Boyd, whose statue now stands in a St. Paul, Minnesota, park honoring his unionizing, said he filed the appeal only to dramatize the fact that the association was merely a company-controlled organization, not a worker's union.

Benjamin Mays, a graduate student from South Carolina who later became president of Morehouse College in Atlanta, met the same fate. In 1917, Mays was enrolled at Bates College in Maine and he worked as a Pullman porter during the summer. After a brief attempt to unionize porters, Mays was fired. Realizing these efforts would continue to be futile for insider organizers, porters like Mays sought the help of an outsider in Harlem in 1925. A. Philip Randolph was invited to a meeting of porters in New York where he was asked to lead a campaign to organize the 12,000 porters and maids into a national union. It was a task that would take more than 12 years.

Randolph formed the Brotherhood of Sleeping Car Porters, asking the membership to name him president of the union. The Pullman Company responded by forming a wide network of spies who began to systematically inform on the activities of porters. Hired enforcers, according to union records, assaulted union organizers who began to quickly form locals in states across the country. Organizing porters against this company was a formidable task. By 1925, the Pullman Company was the largest, single employer of blacks in America. The company insinuated itself into community affairs in towns and cities all across the nation, donating money to black organizations, especially black churches. In many ways, the Pullman Company was seen as a caring employer. This image of the company's benevolence paid off as black ministers and other well-placed spokesmen countered what union organizers and African American newspapers editorialized against the company. Despite their low wages, porters had steady jobs, which enabled them to buy homes, automobiles and Pullman porters were considered middle-income wage earners. Union organizers would refer to company sympathizers as Uncle Toms, remarks that made organizing efforts even more difficult.

When the company fired hundreds of porters for participating with Randolph in setting up union locals, it had the desired chilling effect on union organizing. Civic organization accused union organizers of biting the hand that was feeding the families of thousands of porters and maids.

In the first three years of the union's life, numerous confrontations with management and with black community leaders, forced the Brotherhood of Sleeping Car Porters to ironically become a clandestine, underground railroad-type organization. Randolph devised pledges, held covert meetings, and members used secret code words and signals to thwart spies employed by Pullman to report on unionizing activities. They often met secretly in fraternal halls or church basements where their meetings could not be compromised.

In issuing a secret password for members only, Randolph told Chicago union leader Milton P. Webster that "it is of the utmost necessity that each brother understand the importance and significance of the password in order that they will get real meaning of the word and become Brotherhood men in deed and in spirit. The password was "solidarity." Each union member took an oath, saying "I do" to the nine points it contained, after which they repeated the phrase, "so help me God."

"Then give him the pass word with your right hand and his clasped in the act of shaking," a Randolph memo instructed. "Your left hand and his should extend straight downward by your sides clenched, fist-like."[13] Recruits were thus given a speech:

> Today you have been given the password of the Brotherhood of Sleeping Car Porters, the largest Negro trade union in the world. It is more than a union; it represents the most significant effort ever made by our race to advance. It holds out to the Negro boys and girls of the future their brightest hope for man's chance in the struggle to live.
>
> The word Solidarity is one of the few words in the English language that is inextricably bound up with the history of the human race ... Also, when man first began to enslave his fellow man, the one word that those who were enslaved needed to know the meaning of and practice was Solidarity. It is also the word

that the rulers and oppressors of men have feared, and still fear, because they know that if the oppressed and enslaved peoples understood the meaning of Solidarity and practiced it, the end of their rule-ship would follow.

In choosing Solidarity, we have a word that is of tremendous significance to us both as Pullman porters and as Negroes. Guard this word and practice its meaning and no power on earth can defeat us.[14]

This kind of secrecy and stealth was reminiscent of the covert plans used by escaping slaves who traveled along a covert route north to freedom that was paradoxically called the Underground Railroad. The route Randolph began plotting in 1925 in the struggle to unionize these workers was rife with difficulty. The first three years were marked by noisy mass meetings disrupted by company plants and these activities were criticized in news stories and letters to editors denouncing Randolph's unionizing.

C. L. Dellums who organized a union local in Oakland, California, and was a vice president of the Brotherhood's Pacific Coast region was fired in 1928 by a superintendent who told him, "All we're doing is providing you with transportation all over the country to spread this Randolph Bolshevik propaganda."

In the same year, union plans to call a nationwide strike were launched, organizers believing that a porter's strike would cripple the passenger rail industry. Although there were 12,000 porters and maids, the union still struggled to enroll a majority of them in the still fledgling union. During the first 12 years of the union's struggle for official recognition, fewer than half of those employed belonged to the union. The fear of reprisals was strong. Despite the conditions union leaders campaigned against, the prospect of steady work, undeclared tips, and extensive travel made these jobs more desirable than the usual kind of work reserved for black men during this period.

It was obvious that Pullman could replace striking union workers immediately. Knowing this, Randolph attempted to lure support for his cause among influential outsiders. He hoped they could convince federal authorities to intervene because a Pullman strike could threaten the railroad industry. But an official for the National Mediation Board wrote to James Weldon Johnson, an officer of the NAACP, saying every porter employed by Pullman could walk off the job immediately and essential rail service would be unaffected.

Knowing a strike would fail, Randolph called it off, causing dissension in the union among insiders including Milton Webster, one of his most trusted and toughest advisors. This decision to use restraint and compromise would become a useful tool in negotiation tactics Randolph would later put to greater use.

He knew a strike under the wrong circumstances would have failed. An unsuccessful strike at that time could have diluted the union's already waning strength. A year later, the American stock exchange crashed and the nation plunged into the economic depression of 1929. "Their situation became particularly troubling because, with the onset of the Great Depression, porters who had jobs were increasingly glad to have them," according to a survey of union records done by William Harris, the president of Texas Southern University. "Those who had once braved the company's opposition and joined the Brotherhood of Sleeping Car Porters, now deserted the union in droves," Harris added.[15]

In Harlem, Randolph struggled to devise new strategies to bolster union organizing activity. While porters could be fired for unionizing on the job, Randolph pressed their wives into service as organizers. Conservative ministers and publishers of newspapers like the *New York Age* continued to deliver sermons and editorials against Randolph's efforts, and customers of his wife Lucille's beauty shop began to boycott her business.

The Depression years brought New Deal politics to the nation under the Democratic administration of Franklin D. Roosevelt. While Pullman had thwarted any vigorous organizing of the black union, conductors, engineers, and other railroad workers had the protection of all-white union representation. In 1934 and 1935, after years of frustration under Republican administrations, the major railway unions convinced Congress to pass two important pieces of legislation. The Amended Railway Labor Act and the Wagner-Connery Act specifically outlawed company unions like the one Pullman had controlled for porters.

"Without question, the act covered porters only because of the major effort that Randolph and Webster had expended lobbying for their inclusion," Harris wrote. "On the basis of this new protection, Randolph requested the National Mediation Board to certify the union as the official representative of the porters and order the Pullman Company to negotiate a contract."[16]

The board ordered a rank and file election to determine jurisdiction and certified the Brotherhood of Sleeping Car Porters on June 1, 1935, as the official representative of railroad porters and maids at the company. That same year, Randolph affiliated his union with the powerful American Federation of Labor, which had refused their application a decade earlier. Two years later, the union and the Pullman Company signed a contract.

A. Philip Randolph had not only started the first black union in American history, he provided it with a seat under the powerful umbrella of American labor where he could fight against the widespread discrimination of blacks in all unions. This experience negotiating union contracts where the art of compromise can be a weapon, proved to be a useful tool a few years before the start of World War II.

CHAPTER SIXTEEN

Going Home

The growth of African American study courses in universities, web-sites, and other scholarly resources, has begun to fill a gap in black history. One of the glaring omissions is the story of long-standing, widespread, homegrown terrorism black Americans everywhere faced at the end of the nineteenth and well into the twentieth century. Black lives did not matter in a nation where lynching, wrongful prosecution by law enforcement and racist juries reigned terror on blacks without fear of judicial punishment.

The real fear of being hauled off the street, thrown in jail, beaten, raped, lynched, or murdered were real problems in the lives of African Americans. Unsolved murders of black men, women, and children were commonplace and laws against this kind of violence against blacks were seldom enforced.[1]

As a boy, I remember stories about blacks being accosted by local sheriffs or white men down South. I heard these stories from the parents of my friends in New York and Connecticut where I lived. I overheard men and women telling stories about trips they made down South, especially in the summer when many families returned to the South to visit family in the Carolinas, Louisiana, Florida, Georgia, or Mississippi in a famous song recorded in those years by activist singer Nina Simone, "Mississippi Goddam." It was a song about the wide-spread discrimination throughout American, taking aim at the state where the abuses were the most flagrant. Even as a boy, I understood it was a protest song, a commonplace, popular genre in America for my generation. There was always a clandestine, secret nature to these family trips down South that usually began under the cover of darkness.

None of the black families I knew up North ever traveled South on buses, trains, or planes. Despite being poor, driving was the most common form of transportation in the 1950s for these families. Most traveled by large, older modeled, four-door sedans like the boxy Oldsmobile, Mercury, or Chevrolets brands. I understand why now. Large cars were needed to transport large families South safely. All public transportation in the South at the time was segregated. Blacks had to sit in all-black sections of trains and in the back of buses if they traveled on public transportation. Blacks did not travel or mingle anywhere with white passengers anywhere South of the state of Delaware where the South and North were officially separated by a surveyed line separating the North from the South. That line is called the Mason-Dixon Line, the traditional North and South border. It is the most traditional border between North and South. Surveyed by Charles Mason and Jeremiah Dixon between 1763 and 1767 to resolve a border dispute involving Maryland, Pennsylvania, and Delaware, it marks Maryland as the beginning of the American south.

When a family went South, these trips were carefully planned. Fathers checked the tires, the engine oil, windshield wipers, and other mechanical parts to ward off any unexpected breakdowns or repairs that might have to be handled on the road. Faulty parts were always replaced before these long trips. In the 1950s, there were few interstate highways anywhere in the United States so the entire trip, often covering thousands of miles, round trip, had to be driven on local roads from town to town, state to state. It generally took days of driving from our homes in New York in the summer, driving from mildly warm weather in the North into brutally hot, often humid Southern climates in a time when air conditioning in automobiles was rare.

While the fathers of my friends made sure their cars were roadworthy, the mother, grandmother, or older sisters of the family prepared shoebox lunches and dinners for the trip. They filled the trunk of the car and the floor of the back seat with jugs of water and ice tea for these long trips every summer.

Our neighbors, Al and Hazel Harris, made this trip every summer to New Orleans. The Harris's were an elegant couple with no children. Al wore dashing, tailor-made suits and Hazel wore frilly summer dresses and fancy hairstyles few women I knew could afford in those days. Al was sort of a businessman who owned one of the most popular bars for black men in the neighborhood. Women seldom went to bars. The Harris's did not drive used Olds or Chevys. They bought the latest, high-end black Cadillac sedans, new ones almost every year.

Their cars were always black and always clean because they paid me to wash and polish their car on weekends. I also walked their poodle dog afternoons after school and washed their Caddy every Saturday or Sunday morning. On one of those mornings, I arrived to wash the Caddy and found Al sitting on the passenger's side of the car with the door open. When I got closer, I greeted him, saying good morning, and watch him quickly shove something into the glove compartment and snap the small door shut. He jumped out of the car, slammed the door, and went into his house. I thought nothing of the incident at the time but I later realized what I might have seen. Al, like all families who ventured South during those summers, carried a loaded pistol in the glove box. I always knew Al was different from the other men in my neighborhood. Like my dad, most men were factory workers and never wore suits except to funerals or to church on Sundays. Not Al. Al wore suits everyday. He wore shined, new shoes and shirts washed and starched by the Chinese laundry around the corner. When I got older, I learned that Al ran a gambling business from his home. He owned the bar and ran an illegal numbers lottery game similar to the state lotteries that would become popular decades later in every state. It was called "the numbers," a game actually banked by mobsters who used local racetrack results to generate a random three digit daily number, based on the track numbers of the winning houses in the first three races. People bet nickels, dimes, or dollars on numbers they hoped would win this daily lottery that paid off before dinner was on the table in most houses. Al had underworld, mob connections, particularly with a gangster named Vic who would often visit Al in his bar late at night. Vic, like Al, always wore a suit and drove a big black Caddy too.

As I got older and met other men like Al, I realized that Al was different from these other men in our neighborhood because of the way he earned a living. Al Harris, had migrated North from New Orleans. Al and Hazel were more urbane and stylish than most people in the neighborhood. But Al was like the other Southern men I knew in our community in one respect. I learned they all carried pistols in the glove boxes of their cars when they left New York or New England to go South on vacation or for funerals to protect themselves and their families on the road.

This memory returned to me years later when I was in the Navy and was stationed on a ship headquartered in Norfolk, Virginia. One weekend, I went further South with shipmates heading for Charlotte, North Carolina where my girlfriend at the time was going to college.

I rode with three other sailors early that morning, traveling South before daybreak. We were all heading to different places in the South, but Charlotte was the first stop. Unfortunately, we got a flat tire about 30 miles north of Charlotte. We all got out of the car and helped the driver jack the car up and change the tire. Before we could get back on the road, a police cruiser rolled up behind us and parked with his parking lights on. The driver did not get out. He just sat there quietly in his car, his police lights flashing in the predawn morning light which made me nervous. There were no other cars on the road that morning. When we had changed the tire and were about to get back into our car, the lanky cop got out of his cruiser sauntered over to us.

"You boys should probably follow me," he said.

The driver, who was white and was from South Carolina said something like "That might not be necessary?"

"Now son, we don't want no sass talk outta you here, this early in the morning, do we?"

"I'm not sassing you, sir," he said, "but we're all in the service and heading for a little R & R," he said.

"Now that might be, but ya'll should probably just follow me anyway," he said.

"Yes, sir," the driver said and got back in the car.

Two of us were black, one was Latino, and the driver was white. The cruiser pulled out in front of us and we followed him off the highway onto local roads leading to a small town. The driver spoke first, saying this was not right. We all agreed but had no idea what we were in for until the cruiser drove into the town and parked in front of a one car garage. He came over to the car and told us to follow him inside a side door to the garage. The cop led us to a door, stepped inside, and flicked on a light. In front of us was an overturned, wooden shipping crate with a large piece of plywood nailed to the overturned bottom. On what seemed like a makeshift desk was a hammer. In front of this rigged desk were old wooden movie seats. As my eyes focused to the new light, the room resembled a courtroom. The cop gestured us toward the seats and we filed in, one by one, and sat down. He stood quietly by the door without speaking to us further.

In a short period of time, a white man entered the garage, nodded to the police officer by the door and made his way to the bench before us and it occurred to me then that this was some kind of local court for sure. The man who had just entered walked behind the crate, grabbed the hammer, slammed its head down hard on the plywood surface and said, "This court is now in session!"

My mind raced back to those days when I washed and polished Al's caddy. I remembered that morning just before he was planning to drive back to New Orleans, and the image of a pearl-handled pistol flashed in my mind's eye, not really knowing what kind of pistol Al might have had in his car, if he really carried a pistol or not.

We had been charged with obstructing a public highway although we had pulled over on the wide shoulder of the road and were at least one car length off the highway.

"I object," our white companion yelled out. I cringed and I could tell my car mates were cringing inside too.

I elbowed my shipmate who had spoken up for the group. "Naw," he stammered, "this ain't right. It's a speed trap!"

"What'd you say, boy," the cop yelled, taking off sunglasses he wore, despite the fact the sun had now come up and it was daylight outside.

"Your honor, that boy sassed me when I stopped them too," the cop added.

"Alright, heard enough. I find ya'll guilty of obstructing a public thoroughfare and fine you $200," the judge said.

We looked at each other without speaking. "Can ya'll pony up your share?" the driver asked. We nodded and began counting out twenties, tens, and fives until it totaled $200. The driver took the money and walked it up to the bench.

The judge took it, counted it out and said, "Naw, $200 a piece or it's the county jail."

I just had $250 in cash, planning to be on leave for seven days before I had to return to my ship. I just prayed the others had their share too. The Spanish sailor needed $30. I gave it to him. Like me, the others were on leave, and had the cash too. We all paid. We got in our car but instead of continuing our trip South, we drove back up North to the naval base, broke but grateful we got out of that town alive. Anything could have happened to a bunch of sailors in civilian clothes on that highway in the middle of some unnamed county deep, somewhere in North Carolina. I did not have to imagine this horror. I had read about lynching, men spirited away to chain gangs and worse made up entirely of black prisoners. What I imagined paled to the reality of being black anywhere in the South in those days, a reality Al Harris and those migrant black men in my neighborhood, but originally from the south, did not have to image.

It was still the feudal South in the 1950s, and America was thoroughly segregated. It was the very thing my neighbors from the

South had fled but could never forget. Years later, when I heard that a childhood friend from the North had been arrested in Georgia and sentenced to do time of a chain gang, I shuddered to think what minor infraction had landed him in this kind of real Southern hell.

What I imagined had been a pearl-handled pistol in Al Harris's glove compartment might just as well had been something more useful, a small green book thousands of black travellers carried with them whenever they were traveling down South.

It was called *The Negro Motorist Green Book*. Published in Harlem by Victor H. Green, a Harlem publisher who printed the annual travel guide for black travelers in the United States when open and legally sanction discrimination against non-whites and Jews was widespread throughout the country.

"In order to travel in the United States today, American Negroes annually purchase 15,000 copies of The Green Book so that they may know where they can get a room in which to sleep, and where they can find a barber shop in which to get a haircut. ... Congress should outlaw Jim Crowism on all types of interstate carriers. The past failure of Congress to act in this respect has actually encouraged the states to adopt Jim Crow regulations, which constitute an unwarranted burden on interstate commerce," Carey McWilliams said in "The Color of America," an essay he wrote in the winter of 1941.[2]

"To appreciate the necessity for federal legislation, it should be kept in mind that local Jim Crow regulations have been constantly increasing, not decreasing—in severity. In Virginia, for example, a Negro was formerly defined as a person who had one-fourth or more Negro blood. In 1910, this definition was changed to one-sixteenth and in 1930 it was changed to apply to any person in which there is any ascertainable quantum of Negro blood. Coupled with this new definition, Virginia also passed in 1930 a race registration act. Most other southern states have followed the same trend."

"In most southern states today the races are separated by legislative enactment, in telephone directories; in places of employment; in schools. Statutes provide for separate toilets; separate pool halls; separate busses and bus drivers; separate teachers and separate schools; separate playgrounds and separate libraries; and separate hospitals, asylums; reformatories, prisons, and orphanages. Even separate Bibles are provided in court, for each race must swear to the same God on a separate copy of the identical text."[3]

The NAACP and other Negro advocates cautioned Negroes against using public transportation during this time, generally known as the

Jim Crow era, a derogatory term named after a minstrel character that mimicked blacks because of the widespread segregation. Despite the expense, these advocates encouraged blacks to buy cars to avoid unequal treatment on the road. "All Negroes who can do so should purchase an automobile as soon as possible in order to be free of discomfort, discrimination, segregation and insult," NAACP writer George Schuyler wrote in 1930. In 1936, Green published the first edition of *The Green Book*.

The book was useful for a wide variety of obvious reasons. White-owned businesses refused to serve traveling blacks food, gasoline, accommodations, and other services. Threats of physical danger lurked everywhere, particularly in whites-only municipalities, known in the *Green Book* as "sundown towns." It was a term meant to warn travelers to get through specific towns before sundown. Green said he published his booklet "to give the Negro traveler information that will keep him from running into difficulties, embarrassments and to make his trip more enjoyable."

Green, a U.S. Postal worker, was as much of a visionary as any other publisher in Harlem of the 1930s.

"Would a Negro like to pursue a little happiness at a theater, a beach, pool, hotel, restaurant, on a train, plane, or ship, a golf course, summer or winter resort?" an editorial in *The Crisis* said. "Would he like to stop overnight at a tourist camp while he motors about his native land 'Seeing America First'? Well, just let him try."[4] There were laws on the books that prohibited discrimination against Negroes like the Civil Rights Act of 1875 that said it was illegal to discriminate against Negroes at public accommodations and transportation, law that was never enforced. Backlash to the act prompted the U.S. Supreme Court to declare it unconstitutional and states forced interstate railroads to enforce state segregation laws, citing the 1896 *Plessy v. Ferguson* that upheld "separate but equal" accommodations laws.

Negroes who had migrated from farms in the South to northern cities like my own neighborhood, could find work in factories, as domestics and railroad porters, and other occupations, prospered up North and now could afford middle-class luxuries like an automobile.

U.S. Congressman John Lewis recalled the preparation his family made one year for a trip through the South:

"There would be no restaurant for us to stop at until we were well out of the south, so we took our restaurant right in the car with us," Gavin Wright says, quoting Lewis in his Harvard University Press book, *Sharing the Prize*. "Stopping for gas and to use the bathroom took careful planning. Uncle Otis had made this trip before, and he knew which places along the way offered 'colored' bathrooms and which were better to pass on by. Our map was marked and our trip was planned that way, by the distances between service stations where it would be safe for us to stop."

These conditions were not limited to the South. According to James Loewen, author of *Sundown Towns*,[5] there were at least 10,000 sundown towns across the United States, including large suburbs like Glendale, California; Levittown, New York; and Warren, Michigan. Loewen said over half of the incorporated communities in Illinois were sundown towns and in one, Anna, Illinois, which had expelled all Negroes in 1909 and "the unofficial slogan was "Ain't No Niggers Allowed."[6]

Even the most cautious traveler could easily run afoul of local laws and racial customs without a Green travel guide. Subtle mistakes sometimes involving driving etiquette in some parts of the country that were dictated by racism. "In the Mississippi Delta region, local custom prohibited blacks from overtaking whites in their cars to prevent their raising dust from the unpaved roads to cover white-owned cars," writes Mark Foster in *The Journal of Negro History*. The article was called "In the Face of 'Jim Crow': Prosperous Blacks and Vacations, Travel and Outdoor Leisure, 1890–1945."[7]

"Racist local laws, discriminatory social codes, segregated commercial facilities, racial profiling by police, and sundown towns made road journeys a minefield of constant uncertainty and risk," writes Kate Kelly, quoting from *The Green Book*.[8] Courtland Milloy, writing in a *Washington Post* article from 1987 with the headline "Black Highways: Thirty Years Ago. We Didn't Dare Stop," says he grew up hearing the stories of "so many black travelers . . . just not making it to their destinations."[9]

Like my neighbors, John A. Williams said it took more than nerve and courage for any black man to drive coast to coast in America during the first half of the twentieth century. He said it took "nerve, courage, and a great deal of luck," aided by "a rifle, and shotgun," he writes in his 1965 book, *This Is My Country Too*.[10]

Although the dangers of traveling South was never openly discussed by neighborhood men around children where I grew up, *The Green Book* and a loaded pistol were both necessary for black travelers. America was a haven for white terrorist, not just in the South but in New England too where a grand wizard of the Ku Klux Klan once lived in Meriden, Connecticut. While agents of J. Edgar Hoover's

Bureau of Investigation had feared a Negro insurrection for decades due to Marxist agitation, the bureau, which later became the FBI, failed to recognize or chose to ignore roving bands of white terrorist in almost every state who regularly threatened and killed black citizens without fear of reprisals from local or federal law enforcement. There have always been terrorist groups in the United States. A little green book published in Harlem and widely distributed throughout America helped save black lives well into the 1960s, when there was finally federal laws enacted to prevent racially motivated domestic terrorism.

According to a report published by the NAACP in 1919 titled "Thirty Years of Lynching in the United States: 1889–1918," 2,522 black Americans were lynched—hanged, burned alive, or hacked to death—between those years. Lynching was the most violent form of discrimination. Offenses the victims were accused of were usually minor, such as stealing a cow, attempting to register to vote, or speaking out. There were often allegations of sexual assaults against white woman or simply talking back to a white person. Rather than receiving a fair trial, blacks were often lynched by white mobs. Of course, many victims were innocent. Lynching was a major means used to control blacks during this period.[11]

In the early decades of its existence, the NAACP sought broad solutions to widespread discrimination problems. By the 1930s, lynching had been a long-standing threat to black Americans throughout the decades of the twentieth century, the NAACP tried to get J. Edgar Hoover and the Bureau of Investigation to intervene and prosecute lynch mobs with little success. One tactic involved legislation that gave the bureau jurisdiction in cases involving kidnapping crimes during which victims were transported across state lines. It was called the Lindbergh Law, named after pilot Charles Lindbergh, whose son was kidnapped and transported across state lines in 1932.

In the fall of 1934, Claude Neal, a 23-year-old black peanut farm worker, was arrested in Greenwood, Florida, for the murder of a 20-year-old white woman named Lola Cannidy and transported to Alabama.

"The facts in this case were never in doubt," Kenneth O'Reilly writes in a 1960 edition of *Phylon*. Neal was moved from jail to jail in different parts of Florida, according to news reports and was eventually moved across state lines to Alabama. "Abducted in October 1934 from a jail in Brewton, Ala., Neal was driven into Florida and lynched," O'Reilly said. "The murder was advertised in local newspapers and radio broadcasts and thousands of spectators turned out to watch." NAACP leader Walter White told the membership in Harlem days after the murder that Neal had become the 45th lynching victim since FDR took office in 1933.

"At a press conference a few days after the Neal lynching, President Franklin Roosevelt was asked if he would recommend passage of a pending lynching bill," O'Reilly said in the *Phylon* article he wrote for the Clark Atlanta University-based magazine founded by Du Bois. "The president ducked the question by asking for some time 'to check up and see what I did last year.' Roy Wilkins, who had become managing editor of *The Crisis*, also founded by Du Bois, called Roosevelt a coward.[12]

Walter White, Roy Wilkins, A. Philip Randolph, and a loose knit coalition of other Harlem leaders decided formally and informally to make a variety of civil rights demands to Roosevelt on the heels of the U.S. Justice Department establishing a Civil Liberties Unit as part of the Criminal Division a few years later in 1939. By 1941, the Bureau of Investigation had become the FBI. The new Civil Liberties Unit was investigating more cases where blacks were victimized, but "its efforts during the war years were neither enthusiastic or effective. In the civil rights field, the FBI was invisible."[13] O'Reilly said.

"In February, 1942, following the lynching of Cleo Wright in Sikeston, Missouri, Attorney General Francis Biddle ordered FBI agents and Civil Rights section attorneys into the case," O'Reilly said. "In contrast to the other 3,842 recording lynching between 1889–1941 ... Wright's brutal murder drew the United States Department of Justice into that area of civil rights for the first time."[14]

The loosely organized brotherhood of black men—the New Negroes from Harlem—had finally raised the awareness of the Negro, both in the black community and beyond by successfully insisting upon federal intervention in lynching. By the 1940s, these same men had begun to devise a civil rights strategy that would eventually result in one of the greatest compromises ever made in the history of the most segregated nation in the world outside of South Africa. These race men from Harlem had also unwittingly laid corner stones for the greatest assembly of civil rights marchers to ever gather in America.

CHAPTER SEVENTEEN

March on Washington I

While Asa Philip Randolph had become a household name in Harlem and on passenger trains throughout the nation where members of his Brotherhood of Sleeping Car Porters worked,, his success in forming the first all-black union against the powerful Pullman Company was about to blossom his notoriety even more by 1937. The union became the sanctioned representative of the 12,000 member porter's union and was also allowed to become an international member of the powerful American Federation of Labor that year. This extended Randolph's reach and influence nationally beyond Harlem and a confluence of events, including a speech he gave to porters at a convention in Madison Square Garden, hurled him to the summit of his career as a labor organizer.

Germany declared war on the United States in December 1941. It sparked a natural boom in the defense industry that fueled a spike in jobs for white defense contractor workers but not for blacks. This obvious disparity caught Randolph's attention. Upon further investigation, he learned that government instituted training programs to meet this growing demand for defense products but the program excluded blacks "with the assumption that such training would be wasted on them; even blacks with training were not considered for skilled positions," according to White House documents.[1]

"The general manager of North American Aviation said that 'Negroes will be considered only as janitors,' and in Kansas City, Standard Steel informed the Harlem-based Urban League 'We have not had a Negro working in 25 years and do not plan to start now,'" the White House documents said.. The government said more than 250,000 new defense jobs were closed to blacks. In the aircraft industry, for example, only 240 of the 107,000 workers were black. In construction, there were labor shortages, but contractors ignored experienced black painters, plasterers, and bricklayers and hired all-white workers. At the same time, blacks in the military were victims of similar discriminatory practices at a time when large numbers of black recruits were conscripted to fight the wars in Europe and later in the Pacific. These ironies were not lost on black leaders. At the same time they were begging the federal government to intervene to protect and legislate on behalf of blacks to shield them from the same kinds of discrimination in the private sector while government contractors were openly discriminating against black workers without consequence.

In a Madison Garden speech in 1940, Randolph declared discrimination by federal contractors and the military would be priorities of the labor organizations that he now headed. First Lady Eleanor Roosevelt heard that speech and when she queried her husband, he noted that his secretary had been approached to schedule a meeting with black leaders from New York but the meeting was never scheduled.

By late in September, a meeting was finally scheduled with Roosevelt, members of his cabinet, and a contingent of Harlem leaders that included Randolph, Walter White, head of the NAACP, and T. Arnold Hill, an administrator of the National Urban League.

It was a rocky, tense encounter. Armed with the facts about widespread racial discrimination in both the military and by defense contactors, Randolph bluntly demanded access for blacks to all-skilled trade union jobs and an end to segregation in the Armed Forces. Cabinet members argued that integrating the military during a war would be disruptive in war time. When asked about integrating the Navy, Navy Secretary Frank Knox said it would be impossible. "We have a factor in the Navy that is not so in the Army," he said, "and that is that these men live aboard ship. And in our history we don't take Negroes into a ship's company."

"Without realizing the stereotyping inherent in the statement, Roosevelt suggested putting Negro bands on white ships so the white sailors could get accustomed to blacks on ships."[2] Despite this and other rebuffs during the meeting, the president thanked Randolph and the others for the meeting and promised he would call the civil rights leaders for a follow-up discussion or a meeting soon. The leaders left Washington saying they were pleased with the outcome at the time.

Behind closed doors, however, the president's men opposed all changes both inside and outside of the military/industrial complex, and they were especially opposed to any issues involving defense, according to historian Doris Goodwin.

"There is no time for critical experiments which could have a highly destructive effect on morale," Army Chief of Staff George Marshal said.[3]

The Randolph contingent never heard from the president but word about the White House debate among cabinet leaders came in a press briefing held by FDR's press secretary, Stephen Early. Sharing a draft for reporters, Early said the War Department would not intermingle colored and white enlisted personnel in the same regiments. In language used in the briefing, Early suggested that all who attended the meeting with Roosevelt had agreed this stance would be best for the country for the time being. Randolph and the others were infuriated that the White House had feigned their approval by suggesting quietly that the decision was not a subtle snub. The Harlem contingent made their displeasure public, still they were ignored by Roosevelt and the White House. It was clearly a second snub, one that incited the Randolph contingent to mobilize for action against the government.

Back in New York, Randolph conferred with NAACP head Walter White on how the group should proceed. Conferring with the government had failed. Instead, Randolph met with White, Hill, and trusted advisors of the Brotherhood of Sleeping Car Porters and together they devised a plan that would launch the first national protest network. He formed the March on Washington movement and told advisors "I think we ought to get 10,000 Negroes and march down Pennsylvania Avenue asking for jobs in defense plants and integration of the armed forces. It would shake up Washington," conceiving of the march as a show of black mass power.[4] Washington, DC, is located below the Mason Dixon line and considered the South. Like the rest of America, it was a segregated city and the White House in particular had a distinct hand in cementing discrimination in the nation's capital.

During his term in office, President Woodrow "Wilson permitted segregation in federal offices soon after becoming president, treating it, he said, not as an instrument of humiliation, but as a means to ease racial tensions," according to documents in his presidential library in Staunton, Virginia. The move enraged black leaders immediately and "Du Bois and likeminded thinkers disagreed heartily with Wilson's choice, petitioning repeatedly for the suspension of the practice. Wilson refused." This was in the 1920s. Now 20 years later, the whole city of Washington was a southern, segregated city.

"Segregation in Washington, D.C., was a glaring example of the contradictions in American society," according to documents in the Smithsonian National Museum of American History. "In the 1950s the city's government, including schools, was under the control of Congress. Its members proudly portrayed the city as the capital of the free world, where democracy and personal freedoms were defended against the threat of communist totalitarianism. Yet, most of the city's public facilities, schools, and housing were segregated by law or practice."

Randolph knew the White House was in the South. He hatched a plan to muster support for a mass movement against discrimination throughout the country in speeches he gave in 1940 and 1941. In these addresses, he issued a precise, damning manifesto that demanded jobs in national defense and an end to Jim Crowism in the armed forces.

"While billions of taxpayers' money are being spent for war weapons, Negro workers are being turned away from the gates of factories, mines and mills—being flatly told, 'Nothing Doing.' Some employers refuse to give Negroes jobs when they are without union cards and some unions refuse Negro workers union cards," he said. "Negroes can kill the deadly serpent of race hatred in the Army, Navy, Air and Marine Corps, and smash through and blast the government, business and labor-union red tape to win the right to equal opportunity in vocational training and re-training in defense employment."[5] Randolph's army of 12,000 Sleeping car porters fanned out across the nation, summoning support for the March on Washington movement by soliciting already established local organizations wherever they traveled. Union members attended outdoor meetings, put up posters, and sold buttons supporting the march. The porters' union financed the movement with union dues. The march was the talk of Harlem in beauty parlors, bars, and barbershops. The porters' union office in Chicago drew upon local contacts to organize participants in that city to pledge to take part in the march. One local network was the Chicago Congress of Negro Organizations, which said it was prepared to join the protest in Washington late in March 1941. In Alabama, the head of the local porters' union and president of the NAACP local chapter organized transportation to get an Alabama contingent to join the march in Washington. When the organizing peaked, nearly 40 chapters of the March on Washington movement had been formed around the country by the spring of 1941. The black press in at least 18 cities covered local and national stories about the march. By May, the plan was set and announced in a flood of propaganda issued in the "Call to Negro America to March on Washington for Jobs and Equal Participation in National Defense on July 1st, 1941."[6] By mid-May the national office of the NAACP in Harlem produced funds to support the march and advised all branches of the organization throughout the country to also support local march on Washington groups in their cities.

By June, it became clear that tens of thousands of Negroes would descend on Washington and they would demand that President Roosevelt issue an executive order ending discrimination among defense contractors and abolish Jim Crow treatment of Negroes in the military. This pressure was applied directly to the president and his advisors, a bold move using direct, public confrontation, a new tactic that had never been tried before on such a broad, public stage.

"Although alerted in January that Randolph had suggested a black march on the Capital, the White House had been ignoring the march all spring and denying repeated requests from Walter White to discuss the exclusion of black workers from employment." according to the Global Nonviolent Action Database. "However, it could no longer deny the threat of a mass march, especially since Randolph had sent letters to President Roosevelt and other high government officials requesting them to address the marchers at the Lincoln Monument following the March." A protest that had hoped to assemble at least 10,000 participants, had projections that grew beyond 100,000 by June. In a segregated city like Washington, this flood of Negro protesters became a frightening prospect that bordered on being revolutionary.

"The idea that masses of blacks would be brought into one of the most segregated cities in the country shocked and frightened the white community," according to the Global Nonviolent Action Database.[7]

"The president understood that there was gathering momentum for the march. Roosevelt was in a quandary: while he feared the effects of a march, he also worried about not antagonizing southerners in Congress who already opposed him on many other issues. Either choice would result in some serious political fallout, according to reporter David Brinkley, author of *Washington Goes to War*.

"When Eleanor Roosevelt demanded to know how Randolph proposed to feed and house his black marchers, Randolph answered they would register in hotels and order dinner in restaurants." He never revised his statement but privately, his organization asked the March on Washington committee to request the support of black churches and schools in the capital to help feed and house the marchers, according to a White House website. The image of a black invasion of lily-white hotels and restaurants in the capitol city was enough to send shock waves throughout that pristine little southern town, according to Randolph biographer Paul Pfeffer.

Some feared the march would trigger a race war on the streets of the nation's capital. Already a target of a long-standing Justice Department surveillance, Randolph was called "the most dangerous Negro in America," according to Nebraska Rep. Arthur Miller.[8] The president had enlisted his wife Eleanor and a close friend of Randolph's, New York Mayor Fiorello LaGuardia, to convince Randolph to call off the march.

The First Lady met with Randolph and LaGuardia in New York, then she returned to Washington where she told her husband the only hope of preventing the march was a face-to-face meeting with Randolph. It was arranged and for June 18, 1941 when Randolph and NAACP leader Walter White again met with Roosevelt at the White House. In her book, *No Ordinary Time*, Doris Kearns Goodwin notes that Roosevelt tried to keep the meeting light with political anecdotes. Randolph, in no mood for banter after repeatedly being snubbed by the White House, told the president, "Time is running out. We want something concrete, something tangible, positive and affirmative," Randolph insisted, and proceeded to make his goal even clearer. He wanted a signed executive order desegregating the defense industry.[9]

The president insisted that nothing could be done until the threat of the march was removed. Randolph flatly refused.

Goodwin describes this decisive exchange in her book:

"How many people do you plan to bring?"

"One hundred thousand, Mr. President."

The figure was staggering, Washington overrun by 100,000 angry, marauding blacks.

It was possible that Randolph and White were bluffing but the president had no real way of knowing.

Turning to White, Roosevelt asked, "Walter, how many people will really march?" White did not blink when he said "One hundred thousand, Mr. President."

What took place next was unprecedented in black history.

Randolph said the idea for the March on Washington movement came to him during an organizing and speaking tour of the South for the porters' union. In a way, he launched the idea almost immediately, proposing the idea of the marches in cities he visited all over America. In his wake, union organizer T. D. McNeal stayed behind in each city to "work up negroes to come to Washington for this demonstration."[10]

The idea reached far beyond the demands Randolph and company were making of the president.

Even though the March on Washington movement's most active chapters were in northern and midwestern urban centers, the spirit and consciousness of the upstart protest organization quickly spread nation-wide. The number of small branches that were launched throughout the country demonstrates MOWM's national appeal, but the most active chapters were in major urban areas with sizeable African American populations like Harlem, Chicago, Detroit, and St. Louis, according to State University of New York Professor David Lucander.[11]

"MOWM caught on quickly in Harlem, where Milton Webster said that African Americans with MOWM badges were proudly bought by people 'wearing them up and down the streets.' These buttons were widely distributed through a network of pre-existing 29 African-American social and political institutions and by the initiative of MOWM supporters. In Harlem, for example, 'young ladies on street corners and public spots' distributed 15,000 buttons throughout the New York metro area."

"Randolph's idea to march on Washington was well received in Atlanta, Savannah, Jacksonville, Tampa, and Richmond. His speeches struck a familiar chord because they emphasized cooperative self-reliance and racial solidarity. Randolph was certainly not the first to espouse the message, but his conclusion that 'The future of the Negro depends entirely upon his own action, and the individual cannot act alone' resonated with audiences who believed that this was a 'clarion call' for mass protest politics to address issues of racial inequality. It was a moment of awakening of a sleeping giant. MOWM was certainly Randolph's 'brainchild,' but it was grassroots activists who energized the organization he inspired and to successfully tackle pressing racial issues in their own communities.

Benjamin McLauren shared the podium with Randolph on this trip to promote the march and was he was present when the idea to march was first made public in Savannah. While spirits were high at the event, McLauren reminisced that Randolph's proposal 'scared some of them to death ... including myself.' Still, the moment was ripe for change and 'the plan caught on like fire' among a people who were certain that the war presented a crisis for a system of segregation and inequality that they bitterly called Jim Crow." MOWM's Executive Secretary E. Pauline Myers framed the organization's foray into nonviolent civil disobedience as one of the turning points in the American civil rights movement. Like James Baldwin, Myers saw the war years as a time of widespread change in the consciousness of African Americans. In her advocacy for a direct action campaign, Myers argued, "The old method of conferences, round table discussions, pink tea parties, luncheons and Black Cabinets has been exploded. The patience of Negro America is sorely tired." Myers continued, "The Negro has experimented for seventy-eight years with the education formula showing the white man why he should be free. He is not asking for a hand out. The Negro American has come to maturity and he wants to be free to walk as a man ... He is tired of being the white man's burden."[12]

Mrs. Roosevelt and LaGuardia met with Randolph and company on June 13 to ask him again to halt the march. He refused and five days later White and Randolph were again summoned to Washington. Once again they were asked to halt the march on the promise that the president would personally see to it that blacks were better treated in the future. Randolph again refused, saying nothing short of an executive order banning racial discrimination in the employment by federal contractors would do. This is the moment when negotiations generally break down if both sides are not willing to negotiate or compromise.

Randolph agreed to compromise when a satisfactory executive order signed by the president was drafted. Randolph helped draft the document in the Cabinet Room of the White House that day. After Randolph edited several drafts of the document, a final draft was agreed upon. Goodwin says, Joseph Rauh, a young attorney, asked to work with Randolph on drafting the order was later heard asking "Who is this guy Randolph? What the hell has he got over the president of the United States?"

On June 25, 1941, Executive Order 8802 was signed. It said, "There shall be no discrimination in the employment of workers in defense industries or government because of race, creed, color, or national origin." The order provided for the establishment of a Fair Employment Practices Committee (FEPC) to investigate reports of discrimination complaints[13] until the Korean War.

The march on Washington was called off and a rally of 20,000 was held in Madison Square Gardens in June Instead. Like a pageant only Marcus Garvey could have conceived, Randolph marched into the Garden led by 100 Pullman Porters ahead of him and 50 Pullman maids who walked behind him.[14]

According to Lillie Patterson, author of *A Philip Randolph, Messenger for the Masses,* the March on Washington movement had stirred the consciousness of militants who intended to use it as a springboard for making sweeping civil rights demands. When the march was called off, the momentum militants had gained was slowed too so not everyone in the Madison Square Garden crowd applauded the decision to halt the march. Randolph quelled detractors by saying the march had not been cancelled but merely postponed as a compromise to give the government time to follow through on the president's order. For the first time, he said, Negroes now had a watchdog committee to keep tabs on government promises to halt the discriminatory practices of federal contractors.

Randolph critics had complained that the FEPC was a toothless tiger established to appease Negro complaints, not to correct them. Defense contractors did hire blacks but they repeatedly failed to pay them fair wages or acknowledge worker seniority but Randolph had secured jobs that historically went to white workers.

The question of whether Randolph had been bluffing the president or not, remained unclear, even to some of his closest aids at the time. "NAACP leader Roy Wilkins suggested the whole thing may well have been a bluff on Randolph's part, but what an extraordinary bluff it was, he said. Described as a tall courtly black man with Shakespearean diction and the stare of an eagle, Randolph had looked the aristocratic FDR in the eye—'and made him back down.' It was the beginning of what Walter White would later call 'a rising wind.' "[15]

What had become clear for the first time was the fact that the tactic of nonviolent, civil disobedience, and the art of compromise had been tested and had at least won the attention of people in government who could enact civil rights, and the president of the United States.

Six years later, the Selective Service Act of 1947 instituted a nationwide military draft. Randolph immediately demanded that the military be integrated. When the government ignored his demand, Randolph again called upon the March on Washington movement Committee to begin planning another action. Simultaneously, Randolph created, The League for Nonviolent Civil Disobedience against Military Segregation. Operating out of offices Randolph set up on 125th Street in Harlem, the league urged black and white men to "refuse to cooperate with a Jim Crow conscription service. Needing black votes in a 1948 re-election campaign, President Harry Truman ordered an end to racial segregation in the armed forces. This was all made possible by threats to march on the White House made by the March on Washington movement in 1941. Their leaders, services and strategies would be called upon again and again throughout the next 20 years as the Civil Rights movement gained momentum and won various victories, always threatening to launch a dreaded black march on Washington.

CHAPTER EIGHTEEN

March on Washington II

An avowed socialist who began his activist career by giving speeches from a soapbox on Lenox Avenue, Randolph's revolutionary strategies years later would set the stage for future civil rights and antiwar movements in the United States. To acknowledge this role, he was named chairman of the 1963 March on Washington Committee, this one engineered by Randolph but led by the charismatic Rev. Dr. Martin Luther King.

The tactics used by the March on Washington Movement had been proven effective throughout the decades between 1940 and the turbulent 1950s in focusing the nation's attention on major black issues that cried out for immediate reform. The threat of an army of black people descending upon the nation's capital was seen as not only effective but also a necessary tactic in gathering federal support in civil rights issues. This was especially true for the March on Washington for Jobs and Freedom of 1963.

This time Randolph enlisted young community organizer Bayard Rustin to coordinate the many elements needed to bring a quarter million marchers to Washington that summer in 1963. A close aid, Rustin had once been the loudest critic of the compromise Randolph made in calling off the 1941 March on Washington. Rustin, an ardent speaker too, denounced Randolph as a reactionary sellout for choosing compromise over action but he softened his criticism and again joined Randolph in planning the 1963 march.

Rustin too knew how to compromise. Randolph said that the 1941 compromise could be a useful strategy if it produced gains. It was this kind of subtle leadership and patience in an era when black power movements were loud and sometimes shrill that would become the hallmark of Randolph's smooth, negotiating style that later gave him the potential to influence with future presidents.

Randolph had forced the national government to admit to the existence of widespread racial discrimination in employment opportunities by offering a settlement to remedy that condition. In 1963, Randolph was asked to again use the political action strategies he had devised and employed successfully 20 years earlier to make hard-to-imagine civil rights gains. A quiet, retiring man now 74 years old, Randolph's March on Washington Movement Committee had petitioned two presidents of the United States to end employment discrimination at federal agencies and among defense contractors. He won. He had also called for the end of segregated armed forces and by the start of the Korean War, he won that battle too. Now, he had organized and was about to dramatize black power for a third occupant of the White House, this time President John Kennedy, and asked him to support the most comprehensive civil rights legislation in American history, the Civil Rights Act of 1963.

On the eve of this historic March on Washington, I boarded a caravan train of passenger railroad cars in the northeast that would snake its way from Connecticut to New York. It was August 27, 1963, a date that was historic for another reason, W.E.B. Du Bois, one of Harlem's most ardent voices for five decades lay dying that night somewhere in Africa while the most effective civil rights plans in history was about to be born. In New York, our train was coupled with cars from other states and the train headed South toward the capital. When we arrived in Washington early the next morning, Du Bois has passed away almost without notice. No gathering of civil rights protesters like the one I had joined had ever been staged in American history. Our numbers were strong, we were told by March on Washington movement couriers who mingled throughout the crowd, delivering instructions about the day's events, lodging, water stations, food and where we could find toilet facilities. The passenger car we boarded the day before was shuffled, coupled, and uncoupled all the way to Washington and once in the city, we used it for sleeping and storing our belongings.

At just 16 years old, I was surrounded by the largest group of men in black suits, women in summer frocks, and clergy of every stripe and color who gathered with us in Washington that summer. I was president of a small youth group of the NAACP from Connecticut, a contingent that had joined this cavalcade of civil rights organizations from all over the world amassed to collectively demand passage of historic civil rights legislation in the nation's capital. Randolph's dream was not mentioned in the speeches we heard that day but it had come true. The head count of marchers that summer ranged from 200,000 to 250,000, according to the Congress for Racial Equality and *Dissent* magazine.

"Organized by a coalition of trade unionists, civil rights activists, and feminists—most of them African American and nearly all of them socialists—the protest drew nearly a quarter-million people to the nation's capital. Composed primarily of factory workers, domestic servants, public employees, and farm workers, it was the largest demonstration—and, some argued, the largest gathering of union members—in the history of the United States," the magazine said.

The event alone was of course an historic one for us because we marched, we sang, we cheered and together, we felt the power of the protest we had joined. Of course, Du Bois's passing also marked the passing of a long period of progressive, social advancement in America that this visionary had led for nearly a half century earlier, first as a Harvard-trained scholar and later as an activist and publisher perched in a Harlem bully pulpit of his own making.

Nevertheless, despite this broad history in black liberation movements worldwide, his death was barely mentioned above a whisper after a brief announcement about his passing was made at the march by Roy Wilkins, executive secretary of the NAACP. Du Bois died during the heyday of a movement that was fueled by the many narratives he had provided as one of the founding members of the NAACP and editor of *The Crisis*. Du Bois's many shifting stands on race, segregation, socialism, and Marxism were voiced throughout his life as a professor, as a lecturer supported by various academic institutions, and late in life as an independent scholar with no visible means of support from the scholars and elite he had once championed as the Talented Tenth.

In the sweltering, humid heat of that summer, we marched, not to the tune of this ailing American scholar anymore who had once led hundreds of thousands through the writings in the magazine he founded. We sang "We Shall Overcome," and marched behind the leadership of newer, younger civil rights Pied Pipers, now more visible and prominent than the exiled 95-year-old Du Bois had ever been. While Randolph & company had planned almost every detail of the march, we had now become followers of the Rev. King, the keynote speaker in 1963; of Malcolm X, the charismatic Nation of Islam leader now based in Harlem; and of Roy Wilkins. Months later

Randolph, King and Roy Wilkins met with President Kennedy urging him to sign the pending Civil Rights Act before Congress. Kennedy was assassinated in Dallas shortly after the meeting. A year later, Kennedy lay buried in Arlington National Cemetery. President Lyndon B. Johnson carried out the Kennedy promise and signed the Civil Rights Act of 1964 into law.

Unlike Malcolm X and King, who both died martyrs in their own time at the height of popularity at age 39, Du Bois's passing away was barely noticed in the crowd at the Mall and the Lincoln Memorial that morning in 1963.

By this time, Du Bois had become an exiled expatriate and a Communist, pledging his allegiance as a citizen of Accra, Ghana, not of America, he was in grave in danger of being forgotten.

"The manner in which the death of W.E.B. Du Bois was reported in some quarters here in the United States is itself a curious commentary on the extent to which the country of his birth was out of touch with him," historian John Hope Franklin wrote in *W.E.B. Du Bois: A Personal Memoir*. Writing in the autumn 1990 issue of *The Massachusetts Review*, Franklin said one newspaper that did report his death, said he was survived by his wife, Nina and a daughter. "As a matter of fact, he had survived both of them and, more than a decade ago, had remarried," Franklin said. "One of the great learned journals merely reported that he had died, thus indicating its own inability or unwillingness to come to terms with the impact of Du Bois on the field represented by the journal."[1]

Like Garvey, Dorothy West, and the so-called renaissance period itself, Du Bois too became one of the most maligned, illustrious, enigmatic figures of African American history who first grew the roots of modern African American culture from a Harlem storefront office. His political thought exists in nearly 50 years of writings as founder and editor of *The Crisis* and the many scholarly documents and books he wrote, including *Phylon*, a magazine founded by Du Bois and also still publishing scholarly articles in 2016 on race and culture. But the life and legacy of civil rights activist, Dr. W.E.B. Du Bois, is perplexing because determining what he thought and when must be deciphered with the ever-shifting politics and climate of a segregated America. The quiet way in which his passing went almost unnoticed that day on the most famous march of the American civil rights movement in Washington, in many ways, marks the way Du Bois's legacy only grew prominent over time after he died but had withered during his lifetime.

He died almost a forgotten man, Franklin said in his recollection of the man.

His arrival in Harlem in the early years of the twentieth century was applauded and chided by upstarts just like Du Bois himself in Harlem who had all pledged to uphold the loosely framed, often-chanted causes of a New Negro Movement. As I have said, all chose different and varied paths for creating this mythical New Negro. Many like Booker T. Washington believed a new respect could be cultivated for the black man through teaching trade vocations. Du Bois was his most vocal critic. Many of the men Du Bois walked with in Harlem veered off into socialism and more than a few toyed with the ideals of Marxism like Du Bois in attempts to chart a path to equality for American black men and women. The Communist Party was active in Harlem in the 1939s during the Depression. The party helped finance activities in Harlem, including the Federal Negro Theatre, which once employed more than 300 people in the Harlem Community Arts Center and other activities. Active members included novelist Richard Wright, Cyril Briggs, a writer for the *Amsterdam News*, and later, Du Bois himself.

Serving as *The Crisis* editor from 1909 until 1934, Du Bois resigned over artistic and political differences he had with the NAACP leadership. Returning to lecturing at Atlanta University, he established the journal *Phylon*. A decade later, he was forced to retire. He returned to Harlem as director of special research for the NAACP but was fired in 1948. Adrift as a scholar and editor, Du Bois worked to oppose nuclear weapons as chairman of an organization called the Peace Information Center (PIC). The center mainly worked to gather signatures to urge all governments to ban nuclear weapons. His association with PIC was a particularly dangerous activity in America in the 1950s.

This was during the Cold War between the United States and the Communist Soviet Union, when the U.S. government embarked upon a widespread witch hunt for Communist and Communist sympathizers in the United States. Many prominent blacks in Harlem became targets of federal probes, particularly investigations by the U.S. Senate, led by Wisconsin Sen. Joseph McCarthy who held an exhausting series of public hearings. McCarthy was infamous for making claims against actors, politicians, and other public figures labeled as Communist sympathizers. Du Bois's reputation became soiled under this cloud of suspicion. Branded a heretic, Du Bois was eventually arrested for his participation in Peace Information Center activities and stripped of his passport for nearly a decade.

Du Bois fought back, even at the advanced age of 82 in 1951, when he wrote, "Big business in the United States is forcing this nation into war, transforming our administration into a military dictatorship, paralyzing all democratic controls and depriving us of knowledge we need," he said in a speech in Chicago during a fund-raising tour he made for his own legal defense against charges that he was an agent of a foreign power. "The United States is ruled today by great industrial corporations controlling vast aggregations of capital and wealth. The acts and aims of this unprecedented integration of power, employing some of the best brain and ability of the land, are not and never have been under democratic control," he said. "Its dictatorship has varied from absolute monarchy to oligarchy . . ."[2]

Although history records the 1963 March on Washington as the largest civil rights assembly in the last century, this view is short-sighted if you simply measure its size to the appeal of just two men alone, Du Bois and Garvey. It is clear to me why both men were hounded into exile by the U.S. Justice Department. They were two of the most charismatic and persuasive black Americans of all time, despite the historic scourge inflicted upon them. The dark veil of scandal has been lifted from Du Bois by scholars and a Pulitzer Prize pair of biographies. Garvey remains a heretic of American history.

The appeal Du Bois enjoyed as both a public figure and leader was clearly demonstrated in the popularity of *The Crisis*, the general interest Negro publication soared beyond 100,000 in the first decade of publication.

The appeal Garvey garnered is even more impressive. Garvey launched and published the *Negro World* in 1918, a weekly with a circulation estimated to have been between 200,000 and 500,000 readers throughout the world, more copies than *Opportunity*, *The Crisis*, and *The Messenger* combined.

"Garveyism won massive support in the 1920s, and its intellectual and political legacies have been profound. It left its mark on every major black social and political movement of the twentieth century (here and abroad) and was an influence (often the dominant influence) on every form of popular black nationalism in the United States from the Nation of Islam to the Black Panthers," according to Steven Hahn of the University of Pennsylvania, presenting a paper titled "Marcus Garvey, U.N.I.A., and The Hidden Political History of African Americans."

"And there can be little doubt that Garveyism established a far more popular base among black Americans than the NAACP ever would, or that Garvey-inflicted black nationalist ideas continue to have great currency among black workers and the black poor," Hahn said to the Subaltern Citizens Conference, Emory University in October, 2006.

"Yet, for all of this, studies of W.E.B. Du Bois and the NAACP, of black union organizing and black communists, of black middle-class politics and institutions, and of the Civil Rights movement in its national, regional, and local incarnations abound … an immense world of politics, ideas, and cultural practices, which may complicate or confound our views of the past century, thereby remains largely hidden from us."

Although he had been the chief architect of the 1963 March on Washington, Randolph too was easy to miss in this pressing crowd of black and white civil rights marchers converging on the steps of the Lincoln Memorial in that hot, humid city. It was an emotional time for him. His wife Lucille had been his companion and chief supporter for nearly 50 years. She died in April, just four months before Randolph's biggest accomplishment occurred. The march was the cornerstone in a long career and sometimes agonizing confrontations with powerful entities—black and white—that had labeled Randolph as a troublemaker. One of his detractors was noticeably absent by those who knew Du Bois from their days together in Harlem. They weren't always friends, but in the struggle, they were colleagues.

Instead of his beloved Lucille, Randolph was flanked by younger, better known lieutenants of this civil rights movement he had nurtured for decades like the Dr. King, Ralph Abernathy, King's closest aide, and an outspoken black power Bayard Rustin, the Randolph protégé.

Almost all of these men were prime targets of ongoing FBI investigations on this unusually hot day in 1963, even this day when they were about to travel across town to the White House to meet with President John F. Kennedy in the Oval Office.

As founder of the March on Washington Movement, Randolph had risen to the peak of civil disobedience and nonviolent protest in America at this mass gatherings he built but no longer commanded. The march was seen as an *army of Negroes* by Justice Department operatives whose agents most certainly had joined we protesters for surveillance purposes. Although marchers around Randolph believed they were breaking new ground, a few close colleagues who knew Randolph from the old days on Lenox Avenue, and knew better.

Randolph was known to be among the best soapbox speakers in Harlem like Hubert Harrison and Marcus Garvey. Had been one of them himself. Now old, this slightly bent, grieving man had brought their kind of oratory to steps of the Lincoln Memorial in Washington and was about to get an audience with the sitting president of the United States to air their grievances. Randolph had journeyed to the White House before and walked away with a settlement he could live with. Almost single-handedly, Randolph had guided and carried out the legacy of the most important and necessary political turmoil that had long been debated on Lenox and Seventh Avenues in Harlem more than 40 years ago, civil rights in America.

"We are creatures of history, for every historical epoch has its roots in a preceding epoch," Randolph would later remark. "The black militants of today are standing upon the shoulders of the New Negro radicals of my day, the twenties, thirties and forties. We stood on the shoulders of the civil rights fighters of the Reconstruction era, and they stood on the shoulders of the black abolitionists. These are the interconnections of history, and they play their role in the course of development."[3]

Fire in the Crucible

World War I was in its final stages late in 1918. Noted Harlem author and activist James Weldon Johnson publically asked a question on the minds of blacks throughout the country at the time: Would black support for the war translate into improved status for the Negro in America.

That status, at best, was poor.

"At that historical moment, blacks' status in America could only be described as second-class—or worse. Their bill of complaints was painfully long: They were denied the vote in the South, trapped in a system of sharecropping that precluded economic mobility, excluded from countless workplaces, denigrated as biologically and culturally inferior, subject to harassment and violence, and relegated to segregated facilities that were palpably inferior to those of their white counterparts," Eric Anderson writes in a *Chicago Tribune* article. "Black wartime participation had raised 'many high hopes' about the possibilities for change."

"Now comes the test, Johnson announced."

The answer came the following year when race riots broke out in cities throughout the country, called the blood Red summer of 1919 by the NAACP.

After the Red summer, it became clear to race men and women of all stripes and temperaments that any future progress of blacks in America would be in jeopardy unless they urgently and immediately agitated for equal rights. That year was earmarked by marauding terrorism against blacks throughout the country that had sparked race riots and other violence. It reached a critical point when returning black soldiers were lynched in uniform in some Southern states.

Although solidarity among the so-called New Negro factions that had gathered in Harlem was a fleeting thing, one thing was clear to any observer who walked the length of Lenox Avenue, or lived on Edgecombe Avenue, or in the Sugar Hill neighborhood, or on Striver's Row, Harlem had acquired the real tug and feel of a welcoming, adopted homeland for black people like nowhere else on earth.

"By 1930, almost a quarter of Harlem's population was Caribbean-born. Even if they never traveled to Harlem, black Americans nationwide, and worldwide for that matter, turned their attention toward it and derived pleasure from the simple fact that it was there," Clare Corbould says *in Becoming African American.*

"In this volatile black cauldron of aspiration and expectation, a black public sphere flourished during the two decades following World War I. It comprised political and cultural organizations of all stripes ..." with large organizations like the NAACP, Garvey's U.N.I.A and the National Urban League. "Lesser known organizations included countless history and literature reading groups" that loaned their voices to the Negro causes of the day too, she said. "Churches ... continued to play an important role in black life. Black newspapers had existed for some time but urban weeklies expanded ... and were now joined by pamphlets and journals across the political spectrum." Black nationalist joined integrationist, Communists and civil rights activists in civic forums on Lenox Avenue and citizens up in the Sugar Hill district argued and debated their open wounds publically. Harlem, which had become the single most favored public space for blacks from around the world, made all of this argument possible.[1]

"Black public culture was suffused with debate about identity, representation, history and discussion about where black Americans belonged, Corbould said. The concerns of the artists and writers of the Harlem Renaissance, far from being a "vogue" made possible by white patronage that ended with the onset of economic depression, (their concerns) matched those of black Americans across the country, according to Corbould and David Levering Lewis, author of *When Harlem Was in Vogue.*[2]

It was in this crucible that the modern African American ethos was born, finally acknowledged decades later in the 2000 U.S. census that allowed respondents to check a box marked African American or black in the race category for the first time.

Notes

Epigraphs

1. Copage, Eric V., *Black Pearls: Daily Meditations, Affirmations, and Inspirations for African-Americans.* New York: Quill, W. Morrow, 1993.

2. Stowe, Harriet Beecher. *Uncle Tom's Cabin, Or, Life among the Lowly; The Minister's Wooing; Oldtown Folks.* New York: Literary Classics of the United States, 1982.

Introduction

1. Locke, Alain, *The New Negro: An Interpretation.* New York: Arno Press, 1968.

2. Locke, Alain, and Jeffrey C. Stewart, *The Critical Temper of Alain Locke: A Selection of His Essays on Art and Culture.* New York: Garland Pub., 1983.

3. Nugent, Bruce, "A Portrait of Harlem," *Federal Writers' Project.*

4. Ibid.

Chapter 1

1. Baldwin, James, and Francois Bondy, "James Baldwin, as Interviewed by Francois Bondy," *Transition,* no. 12. (Indiana University Press, Hutchins Center for African and African American Research at Harvard University, 1964).

2. Du Bois, W.E.B., *The Souls of Black Folk: Essays and Sketches.* Greenwich, CT: Fawcett Publications, 1961.

3. William S. Pollitzer, *The Gullah People and Their African Heritage.* University of Georgia Press, 1999.

4. Redding, J. Saunders, *They Came in Chains: Americans from Africa.* Philadelphia, PA: Lippincott, 1950; William S. Pollitzer, *The Gullah People and Their African Heritage.* University of Georgia Press, 1999.

5. Zinn, Howard, *A People's History of the United States.* New York: Harper & Row, 1980.

6. Locke, Alain, *Survey Graphic.* Harlem Edition (March 1925).

Chapter 2

1. Locke, Alain, *The New Negro: An Interpretation.* New York: Arno Press, 1968.

2. Vechten, Carl Van. *Nigger Heaven.* New York: Knopf, 1926.

3. Spiers, Fiona E., *The Talented Tenth: Leadership Problems and the Afro-American Intellectuals, 1895–1919.* Manchester, 1978; Gates, Henry Louis, and Cornel West, *The Future of the Race.* New York: A.A. Knopf, 1996.

4. Anderson, Jervis. *This Was Harlem: A Cultural Portrait, 1900–1950.* New York: Farrar Straus Giroux, 1982.

5. Locke, Alain, *The New Negro: An Interpretation.* New York: Arno Press, 1968.

6. Ibid.

7. *Universal Negro Improvement Association: And African Communities League: 51st International Convention, August 18th–24th, 2008: In Remembrance of President General Redman Battle and Marcus Garvey's Legacy: Our Future in the Present.* Philadelphia, PA: UNIA-ACL, 2008.

8. Andrews, William L., Frances Smith Foster, and Trudier Harris, *The Oxford Companion to African American Literature.* New York: Oxford University Press, 1997.

9. Hubert, Levi, "Whites Invade Harlem," *Library of Congress.*

10. Hughes, Langston, *Not without Laughter.* New York: Scribner Paperback Fiction, 1995.

Chapter 3

1. McKay, Claude, and Richard Wright, *Portrait of Harlem Circa 1937,* New York, New York Writers' Project, Work Projects Administration, 1937; *The WPA Guide to New York City the Federal Writers' Project Guide to 1930s New York: A Comprehensive Guide to the Five Boroughs of the Metropolis: Manhattan, Brooklyn, the Bronx, Queens, and Richmond.* New York: Pantheon Books, 1982; Pollard, Myrtle Evangeline. *Harlem as Is . . .* New York, 1936.

2. Bloom, Harold, *Richard Wright.* New York: Chelsea House Publishers, 1987.

3. "American Life Histories: Manuscripts from the Federal Writers' Project, 1936–1940." Accessed May 16, 2016. http://www.learnnc.org/bestweb/fpalifehistories.

4. Ibid.

5. Washington, Booker T., *Frederick Douglass*. New York: Greenwood Press, 1969.

6. Pennington, James W. C., *A Text Book of the Origin and History, &c. &c. of the Colored People*. Hartford: L. Skinner, Printer, 1841.

7. Hildreth, Richard, *The Slave; or, Memoirs of Archy Moore*. Upper Saddle River, NJ: Gregg Press, 1968.

8. McKay, Claude, *Harlem: Negro Metropolis*. New York: E.P. Dutton &, 1940.

9. Fortune15417/1881, Timothy. doi:10.

10. Fortune, Timothy Thomas, *Black and White; Land, Labor, and Politics in the South*. New York: Arno Press, 1968.

11. Kolmer, Elizabeth, Ida B. Wells, and Alfreda M. Duster. "Crusade for Justice: The Autobiography of Ida B. Wells," *American Quarterly* 23, no. 3 (1971): 294. doi:10.2307/2711740.

12. Ellison, Ralph, Whitney Young, and Herbert Gans, *The City in Crisis*. New York City, NY: A. Philip Randolph Educational Fund, 1966.

13. McKay, Claude, and Richard Wright, *Portrait of Harlem Circa 1937*, New York, New York Writer's Project, Work Projects Administration, 1937; *The WPA Guide to New York City the Federal Writers' Project Guide to 1930s New York: A Comprehensive Guide to the Five Boroughs of the Metropolis: Manhattan, Brooklyn, the Bronx, Queens, and Richmond*. New York: Pantheon Books, 1982; Pollard, Myrtle Evangeline. *Harlem as Is . . .* New York, 1936.

14. American Life Histories: Manuscripts from the Federal Writers' Project, 1936–1940." Accessed May 16, 2016. http://www.learnnc.org/bestweb/fpalifehistories.

15. Wright, Richard, and Claude McKay. *New York Panorama: A Comprehensive View of the Metropolis*. New York, NY: Random House; Federal Writer's Project, 1938.

16. Ibid.

17. *A Selection of Titles from the Schomburg Center for Research in Black Culture*. New York: Center, 1969; *The Schomburg Collection*. New York: Schomburg Collection of Black History, Literature and Art, 1972.

18. American Life Histories: Manuscripts Form the Federal Writers' Project, 1936–1940. Accessed May 16, 2016. http://www.learnnc.org/bestweb/fpalifehistories.

19. Ibid.

20. Bontemps, Arna. "2C." *American Scholar*, 1925. doi:10.15417/1881.

21. Ibid.

22. Valade, Roger M., "A Black Literary Guide to the Harlem Renaissance," *The Journal of Blacks in Higher Education*, no. 11 (1996): 102–109. JBHE Foundation, Inc. doi:10.2307/2963328.

23. Ibid.

24. Battle, Juan, and Earl Wright, "W.E.B. Du Bois's Talented Tenth: A Quantitative Assessment," *Journal of Black Studies* 32, no. 6 (2002): 654–672. Sage Publications, Inc. http://0-www.jstor.org.www.consuls.org/stable/3180968.

Chapter 4

1. Mitchell, Ernest Julius, "Black Renaissance: A Brief History of the Concept," *Amerikastudien/American Studies* 55, no. 4 (2010): 641–665. Universitätsverlag WINTER Gmbh. http://0-www.jstor.org.www.consuls.org/stable/41158720.

2. Holloway, Jonathan Scott, "Harlem Renaissance Scholars Debate the Route to Racial Progress," *The Journal of Blacks in Higher Education*, no. 8 (1995): 60.

3. Marable, Manning. *Columbia250*. Website. New York: Columbia University. http://c250.columbia.edu/c250_celebrates/harlem_history/marable_transcript.html.

4. *A Selection of Titles from the Schomburg Center for Research in Black Culture*. New York: Center, 1969.

5. Ibid.

6. Ibid.

7. Dickerson, D. C., "Witness: Two Hundred Years of African-American Faith and Practice at the Abyssinian Baptist Church of Harlem, New York," *Journal of American History* 101, no. 4 (2015): 1236–1237; Powell, Adam Clayton. "Black Power in the Church," *The Black Scholar* 2, no. 4 (1970): 32–34.

8. Miller, Arthur, *The Crucible: A Play in Four Acts*. New York: Viking Press, 1953.

9. United States. New York State Legislature. Joint Legislative Committee to Investigate Seditious Activities. *Revolutionary and Subversive Movements Abroad and at Home*. By Clayton R. Lusk and J. B. Lyon. Vol. I–II. Albany, NY: New York State Legislature, 1920.

Chapter 5

1. Bloom, Harold, *The Harlem Renaissance*. New York, NY: InfoBase, 2004.

2. Vechten, Carl Van, *Nigger Heaven*. New York: Knopf, 1926.

3. Hughes, Langston, *The Big Sea: An Autobiography*. New York: Hill and Wang, 1963.

4. Hurston, Zora, *American Mercury*. TS, New York, 1936; *You Don't Know Us Negroes*.

5. Diepeveen, Leonard, "Folktales in the Harlem Renaissance," *American Literature* 58, no. 1 (1986): 64. doi:10.2307/2925944.

6. Hughes, Langston, *The Big Sea: An Autobiography*. New York: Hill and Wang, 1963.

7. Watson, Steven, *The Harlem Renaissance: Hub of African-American Culture, 1920–1930*. New York: Pantheon, 1995.

8. Washington-Favors, and Sarah M. "The Harlem Renaissance, 1920–1940, Vol. 3, Black Writers Interpret the Harlem Renaissance," *African American Review*, 33, no. 4 December 22, 1999: 495–497.

9. Reed, Merl E., "The FBI, MOWM, and CORE, 1941–1946." *Journal of Black Studies* 21, no. 4 (1991): 465–479. Sage Publications, Inc. http://0-www.jstor.org.www.consuls.org/stable/2784689.

10. Hurston, Zora, *Color Struck*. MS, New York, 1926.

11. Hurston, Zora, *Sweat*. MS, New York, 1926.

12. Thurman, Wallace, *Intelligentsia*. MS, Schomburg Library, New York, 1926.

13. Ibid.

Chapter 6

1. Universal Negro Improvement Association. Raw data. Los Angeles. Universal Negro Improvement Association Papers Project.

2. Ibid.

3. Ottley, Roi, and William J. Weatherby, *The Negro in New York: An Informal Social History*. New York: New York Public Library, 1967.

4. James, Winston Anthony, *Claude McKay a Political Portrait in His Jamaican and American Contexts 1890–1920*. University of London, 1993.

5. Cooper, Wayne F., *Claude McKay: Rebel Sojourner in the Harlem Renaissance: A Biography*. Baton Rouge: Louisiana State University Press, 1987.

6. Van Deburg, William, L., *Modern Black Nationalism: From Marcus Garvey to Louis Farrakhan*. New York: New York University Press, 1997.

7. X, Malcolm, and Alex Haley, *The Autobiography of Malcolm X*. New York: Ballantine Books, 1992.

8. Miller, Wilbert, MS, Work Progress Administration Writer's History Project, Library of Congress, Washington, DC; New York, 1938.

9. Ibid.

10. Ibid.

11. Universal Negro Improvement Association Paper Project. Raw data. Los Angeles.

12. Cronon, Edmund David, *Black Moses: The Story of Marcus Garvey and the Universal Negro Improvement Association*. Madison, WI: University of Wisconsin Press, 1969.

13. United States. Federal Bureau of Investigation. *Marcus Garvey FBI Investigation File*. Washington: Publisher Not Identified, 1936.

14. Ibid.

15. "Look for Me in the Whirlwind, American Experience: Marcus Garvey." Public Broadcasting Service.

16. Kornweibel, Theodore, *Seeing Red: Federal Campaigns against Black Militancy, 1919–1925*. Bloomington: Indiana University Press, 1998; James, Winston, *Holding Aloft the Banner of Ethiopia: Caribbean Radicalism in Early Twentieth-Century America*. London: Verso, 1999.

17. "Look for Me in the Whirlwind, American Experience: Marcus Garvey." Public Broadcasting Service.

18. Vincent, Theodore G., *Black Power and the Garvey Movement*. Berkeley, CA: Ramparts Press, 1974.

19. Universal Negro Improvement Association Paper Project. Raw data. Los Angeles.

20. Kornweibel, Theodore, *Seeing Red: Federal Campaigns against Black Militancy, 1919–1925*. Bloomington: Indiana University Press, 1998

21. McKay, Claude, *Harlem: Negro Metropolis*. New York: E.P. Dutton, 1940.

22. Wilbert Miller, MS, Work Progress Administration Writer's History Project, Library of Congress, Washington, DC; New York, 1938

23. McKay, Claude, *Harlem: Negro Metropolis*. New York: E.P. Dutton, 1940.

24. Franklin, John Hope, *From Slavery to Freedom: A History of Negro Americans*. New York: Knopf, 1967.

Chapter 7

1. Jimoh, A. Yşmisi. "Mapping the Terrain of Black Writing during the Early New Negro Era," *College Literature* 42, no. 3 (Summer 2015): 488–524. *Academic Search Premier*, EBSCOhost (accessed May 19, 2016).

2. Franklin, John Hope, *John Hope Franklin: Selected Essays 1938–1988*. Baton Rouge: Louisiana State University Press, 1989.

3. Coombs, Norman, *The Black Experience in America*. New York: Twayne Publishers, 1972.

4. Cline, Andrew, In *Rhetoric of the New Negro*.

5. Locke, Alain, *The New Negro: An Interpretation*. New York: Arno Press, 1968.

6. Cline, Andrew, In *Rhetoric of the New Negro*.

7. Hughes, Langston, *The Big Sea: An Autobiography*. New York: Hill and Wang, 1963.

8. Lenz, Gunter, "2C." *Callaloo*. doi:10.15417/1881.

9. Ellison, Ralph, "Harlem's America." 1966. doi:10.1075/ps.5.3.02 chi.audio.2c.

10. Tennyson, Hallam, *Alfred Lord Tennyson: A Memoir by His Son.* New York: Macmillan, 1897.

Chapter 8

1. "Nikki Giovanni," Nikki Giovanni to Lionel Bascom.
2. Correll, Charles J., *Amos and Andy,* New York(?), 1935.
3. Carman, John, "Wrestling with an Albatross: 'Amos 'n' Andy'," *Electronic Media* 21, no. 35 (September 2, 2002): 12. *Academic Search Premier,* EBSCO*host* (accessed May 19, 2016).
4. Ibid.
5. Ibid.
6. Ibid.
7. Corbould, Clare, "Streets, Sounds and Identity in Interwar Harlem," *Journal of Social History* 40, no. 4 (2007): 859–894. Oxford University Press. http://0-www.jstor.org.www.consuls.org/stable/25096397.
8. Ibid.
9. Gilroy, Paul, *The Black Atlantic: Modernity and Double Consciousness.* Cambridge, MA: Harvard University Press, 1993.
10. Gosselin, Adrienne Johnson, "Beyond the Harlem Renaissance: The Case for Black Modernist Writers," *Modern Language Studies* 26, no. 4 (1996): 37–45.
11. "Foreword" Challenge, 1934.

Chapter 9

1. Carmody, Todd, "Sterling Brown and the Dialect of New Deal Optimism," *Callaloo* 33, no. 3 (2010): 820–840. http://0-www.jstor.org.www.consuls.org/stable/40962680.
2. Thurman, Wallace, Amritjit Singh, and Daniel M. Scott, *The Collected Writings of Wallace Thurman: A Harlem Renaissance Reader.* New Brunswick, NJ: Rutgers University Press, 2003.
3. Morris, Vivian, and Wilbert J. Miller. *[Almost Made King].* New York City: 1938. Manuscript/Mixed Material. Retrieved from the Library of Congress, https://www.loc.gov/item/wpalh001474 (accessed May 20, 2016).
4. Bercovici, Konrad, "Survey Graphic," *Survey Graphic* 6, no. 6 (March 1925): 679–680.
5. Ibid.
6. Morrison, Toni, *Jazz.* New York: Knopf, 1992.
7. Bercovici, Konrad, "Survey Graphic," *Survey Graphic* 6, no. 6 (March 1925).
8. Thurman, Wallace, Amritjit Singh, and Daniel M. Scott, *The Collected Writings of Wallace Thurman: A Harlem Renaissance Reader.* New Brunswick, NJ: Rutgers University Press, 2003.

9. Wright, Richard, *12 Million Black Voices: A Folk History of the Negro in the United States*. Viking Press, 1941; Holbrook, Stewart H., *The Story of American Railroads*. Bonanza Books, 1957.

10. Brotz, Howard M., "Negro 'Jews' in the United States," *Phylon (1940–1956)* 13, no. 4 (1952): 324. doi:10.2307/272569.

11. McKay, Claude. *Harlem: Negro Metropolis*. New York: E.P. Dutton &, 1940.

12. Ibid.

Chapter 10

1. Jackson, John G., *Hubert Henry Harrison: The Black Socrates*. Austin, TX: American Atheist Press, 1987.

2. Perry, Jeffrey B. "An Introduction to Harrison, Hubert: 'The Father of Harlem Radicalism'," *Souls* 2, no. 1 (2000): 38–54. doi:10.1080/10999940 009362198.

3. Jagessar, Michael, "Jeffrey B. Perry, Harrison, Hubert: The Voice of Harlem Radicalism, 1883–1918," *Black Theology* 8, no. 3 (2010): 387–389. doi:10.1558/blth.v8i3.387.

4. "Harrison, Hubert" *Columbia University Libraries Archives*. https://clio.columbia.edu/catalog/6134799.

5. Ibid.

6. Ibid.

7. Perry, Jeffrey B. "An Introduction to Harrison, Hubert: 'The Father of Harlem Radicalism'," *Souls* 2, no. 1 (2000): 38–54. doi:10.1080/109999400 09362198.

8. Solomon, Mark, *Science and Society*, 2004

9. Ibid.

10. Harrison, Hubert H., and Jeffrey Babcock Perry, *A Harrison, Hubert Reader*. Middletown, CT: Wesleyan University Press, 2001.

11. Ibid.

12. "Harrison, Hubert," *Columbia University Libraries Archives*. https://clio.columbia.edu/catalog/6134799.

13. Harrison, Hubert H., and Jeffrey Babcock Perry, *A Harrison, Hubert Reader*. Middletown, CT: Wesleyan University Press, 2001.

14. Ibid.

15. "Harrison, Hubert," *Columbia University Libraries Archives*. https://clio.columbia.edu/catalog/6134799; Heideman, Paul M. "Harrison, Hubert: The Voice of Harlem Radicalism, 1883–1918, Jeffrey B. Perry, New York: Columbia University Press, 2009," *Historical Materialism* 21, no. 3 (2013): 165–177. doi:10.1163/1569206x-12341315.

16. Rogers, J. A., *World's Great Men of Color*. New York: Macmillan, 1972.

17. Mitchell, Ernest J., *Amerikastuden/American Studies* (Winter 2010).

18. Harrison, Hubert H., and Jeffrey Babcock Perry, *A Harrison, Hubert Reader*. Middletown, CT: Wesleyan University Press, 2001.

19. Mitchell, Ernest J., *Amerikastuden/American Studies*, (Winter, 2010).

20. "Harrison, Hubert," *Columbia University Libraries Archives*. https://clio.columbia.edu/catalog/6134799.

21. Harrison, Hubert H., and Jeffrey Babcock Perry, *A Harrison, Hubert Reader*. Middletown, CT: Wesleyan University Press, 2001.

Chapter 11

1. West, Dorothy, *The Living Is Easy*. Old Westbury, NY: Feminist Press, 1982.

2. West, Dorothy, *The Wedding*. New York: Doubleday, 1995.

3. Hurston, Zora Neale, *Their Eyes Were Watching God: A Novel*. New York: Perennial Library, 1990.

4. West, Dorothy, *The Typewriter*. MS, New York, 1924.

5. Hellman, Lillian, *Pentimento*. Boston, MA: Little, Brown, 1973.

6. *Marcus Garvey*. Public Broadcasting Service. http://www.pbs.org/wgbh/amex/garvey/peopleevents/p_hoover.html.

7. West, Dorothy, and Lionel C. Bascom, *The Last Leaf of Harlem: The Uncollected Works of Dorothy West*. New York: St. Martin's Press, 2007.

8. Kingsolver, Barbara, and Katrina Kenison, *The Best American Short Stories, 2001: Selected from U.S. and Canadian Magazines*. Boston, MA: Houghton Mifflin, 2001.

9. *Porgy and Bess*. By Heyward.

10. Rashler, William, *The Bingo Long Traveling All-Stars and Motor Kings*. New York: Harper & Row, 1973.

11. West, Dorothy, "Black Women Oral History Project at Radcliffe College"; Bone, Robert, *The Negro Novel in America*. New Haven: Yale University Press, 1965.

Chapter 12

1. Meier, August, and John Bracey, "Thurgood Marshall's Best Years," *American Visions* 8, no. 5 (October 1993): 30. *Academic Search Premier*, EBSCO*host* (accessed May 24, 2016).

2. Particof, Susan, and Thelma Dye, "Obituary," *New York Amsterdam News*, (May 5, 2005), 34; *Academic Search Premier*, EBSCO*host* (accessed May 24, 2016).

3. Kirk, John, "The Long Road to Equality," *History Today* 59, no. 2 (2009): 52–58; *Academic Search Premier*, EBSCO*host* (accessed May 24, 2016).

4. Kirk, John, "The Long Road to Equality," *History Today* 59, no. 2 (2009): 52–58. *Academic Search Premier*, EBSCO*host* (accessed May 24, 2016).

5. Ware, Gilbert, "The NAACP-Inc. Fund Alliance: Its Strategy, Power, and Destruction," *Journal of Negro Education* 63, no. 3 (1994): 323; *Academic Search Premier*, EBSCO*host* (accessed May 24, 2016); Joiner, Lottie L., "Protecting the Rights of African Americans," *Crisis (15591573)* 120, no. 1 (2013): 10. *Academic Search Premier*, EBSCO*host* (accessed May 24, 2016).

6. Kirk, John, "The Long Road to Equality," *History Today* 59, no. 2 (2009): 52–58; *Academic Search Premier*, EBSCO*host* (accessed May 24, 2016).

7. James, Rawn, *Root and Branch: Charles Hamilton Houston, Thurgood Marshall, and the Struggle to End Segregation.* New York: Bloomsbury Press, 2010.

8. Davis, Thomas J., *Plessy v. Ferguson.* Santa Barbara, CA: Greenwood, 2012.

9. Browne-Marshall, Gloria J., "Houston, Charles Hamilton (1895–1950)," *Encyclopedia of Race and Crime.* doi:10.4135/9781412971928.n145.

10. Houston, Charles Hamilton, *Institute for Race & Justice.*

11. Ibid.

12. *Lyons v. Oklahoma* (1939).

13. Blevins, John F. " 'Lyons v. Oklahoma,' the NAACP, and Coerced Confessions under the Hughes, Stone, and Vinson Courts, 1936–1949," *Virginia Law Review* 90, no. 1 (2004): 387. doi:10.2307/3202431.

14. Ibid.

15. Ibid.

16. *Brown v. Topeka, Kansas Board of Education.*

17. "Brown v. Board of Education," *The Social History of the American Family: An Encyclopedia.* doi:10.4135/9781452286143.n71.

18. *Brown v. Board of Education* (1952) (testimony of Dr. Kenneth Clark).

19. Clark, Kenneth. White doll, black doll test. 1952. Raw data. Washington, DC.

20. *Brown v. Board of Education* (1953) (testimony of John W. Davis).

21. *Brown v. Board of Education* (1953) (argument of Thurgood Marshall).

22. *Brown v. Board of Education* (1953) (Opinion of Chief Justice Earl Warren).

Chapter 13

1. McNeil, Genna Rae, *Witness: Two Hundred Years of African-American Faith and Practice at the Abyssinian Baptist Church of Harlem, New York.*

2. Davis, Lenwood G., *Daddy Grace: An Annotated Bibliography*. New York: Greenwood Press, 1992; Dallam, Marie W., *Daddy Grace: A Celebrity Preacher and His House of Prayer*. New York: New York University Press, 2007.

3. Frantz, Douglas, and Brett Pulley, "Harlem Church Is Outpost of Empire," *New York Times* (New York), December 17, 1995, N.Y./Region ed. Accessed December 1995. http://www.nytimes.com/1995/12/17/ nyregion/harlem-church-outpost-empire-house-prayer-built-wide-holdings-devotion-sweet.html.

4. Davis, Lenwood G., *Daddy Grace: An Annotated Bibliography*. New York: Greenwood Press, 1992; Dallam, Marie W., *Daddy Grace: A Celebrity Preacher and His House of Prayer*. New York: New York University Press, 2007.

5. Watts, Jill, *God, Harlem U.S.A.: The Father Divine Story*. Berkeley: University of California Press, 1992.

6. "American Life Histories: Manuscripts from the Federal Writers' Project, 1936–1940." Accessed May 16, 2016. http://www.learnnc.org/ bestweb/fpalifehistories.

7. Ibid.

8. "American Life Histories: Manuscripts Form the Federal Writers' Project, 1936–1940." Accessed May 16, 2016. http://www.learnnc.org/ bestweb/fpalifehistories.

9. Walton, Jonathan, "African American Census," *Journal of African American Studies*, 2011. Accessed May 25, 2016.

10. Ibid.

11. Walton, Jonathan, "African American Census," *Journal of African American Studies*, 2011. Accessed May 25, 2016.

12. Spencer, Jon Michael, "Social Gospel Movement," *African American Review* 13, Fall (1996). Accessed May 25, 2016.

13. Ibid.

14. Newman, Judith, "Meet Reverend Adam Clayton Powell, Sr." *Scholastic*. http://www.scholastic.com/teachers/article/meet-reverend-adam -clayton-powell-sr.

15. Hayes, Alan L., *Anglican and Episcopal History; Abyssinian Baptist Church*. 2008.

16. McNeil, Genna Rae, Houston Byran Roberson, Quinton H. Dixie, and Kevin McGruder, *Witness: Two Hundred Years of African-American Faith and Practice at the Abyssinian Baptist Church of Harlem*.

17. Ibid.

18. Hamilton, Charles V., *Adam Clayton Powell, Jr.: The Political Biography of an American Dilemma*. New York: Atheneum, 1991.

19. Newman, Judith, "Meet Reverend Adam Clayton Powell, Sr." *Scholastic*. http://www.scholastic.com/teachers/article/meet-reverend-adam -clayton-powell-sr.

20. "American Life Histories: Manuscripts from the Federal Writers' Project, 1936–1940." Accessed May 16, 2016. http://www.learnnc.org/bestweb/fpalifehistories.

21. Zerner, Ruth, "Themes of Christ and Community," *Union Seminary Quarterly Review*, 1976.

22. Porter, Louis, "An Unlikely Alliance: Adam Clayton Powell Sr., Dietrich Bonhoeffer and the Seeds of Transformation," *Cross Currents* 64, no. 1 (2014): 116–122. doi:10.1111/cros.12063.

23. Ibid.

24. Elingsen, Mark, "The Church as a Strategic Place for Healing," *Journal of Church and State*, January 2001. doi: http://dx.doi.org/10.1093/jcs/43.2.235.

25. Haygood, Wil, *King of the Cats: The Life and times of Adam Clayton Powell, Jr.* Boston: Houghton Mifflin, 1993; Hamilton, Charles V., *Adam Clayton Powell, Jr.: The Political Biography of an American Dilemma.* New York: Atheneum, 1991.

26. Jakoubek, Robert E., *Adam Clayton Powell, Jr.* New York: Chelsea House, 1988; Powell, Adam C., Jr.; Powell, Adam Clayton, *Adam by Adam; the Autobiography of Adam Clayton Powell, Jr.* New York: Dial Press, 1971.

27. Jakoubek, Robert E., *Adam Clayton Powell, Jr.* New York: Chelsea House, 1988.

28. Leeman, Richard W., *African-American Orators: A Bio-critical Sourcebook.* Westport, CT: Greenwood Press, 1996.

29. Hamilton, Charles V., *Adam Clayton Powell, Jr.: The Political Biography of an American Dilemma.* New York: Atheneum, 1991.

30. McNeil, Genna Rae, Houston Byran Roberson, Quinton H. Dixie, and Kevin McGruder. *Witness: Two Hundred Years of African-American Faith and Practice at the Abyssinian Baptist Church of Harlem.*

31. Lucas, Ken. "Before Rev. King, There Was Adam Clayton Powell, Jr.," *Free Republic* (blog). http://www.freerepublic.com/focus/bloggers/2140109/posts.

32. "Powell, Adam Clayton, Jr. 1908–1972," *History, Art & Archives, United States House of Representatives* (blog). http://history.house.gov/People/Listing/P/POWELL,-Adam-Clayton,-Jr—(P000477)/.

33. Ibid.

34. Charles V. Hamilton, *Adam Clayton Powell, Jr.: The Political Biography of an American Dilemma.* (New York: Atheneum, 1991): 47–50.

Chapter 14

1. Christians, Clifford G., and Theodore Peterson, *Normative Theories of the Media: Journalism in Democratic Societies.* Urbana: University of Illinois Press, 2009.

2. Kimbrough, Marvin. "W.E.B. Du Bois as Editor of the Crisis." PhD diss., University of Texas at Austin.

3. Ibid.

4. Ibid.

5. Du Bois W.E.B., *Dusk of Dawn: An Essay toward an Autobiography of a Race Concept. Repr.* New York, 1940.

6. Ibid.

7. Kimbrough, Marvin "W.E.B. Du Bois as Editor of the Crisis." PhD diss., University of Texas at Austin.

8. Ottley, Roi, and William J. Weatherby, *The Negro in New York: An Informal Social History.* New York: New York Public Library, 1967.

9. Cooke, Marvel, *Journal for the Study of Radicalism,* Fall 2012.

10. "American Life Histories: Manuscripts Form the Federal Writers' Project, 1936–1940." Accessed May 16, 2016. http://www.learnnc.org/bestweb/fpalifehistories.

11. Ibid.

12. Bascom, Lionel C. *A Renaissance in Harlem: Lost Essays of the WPA, by Ralph Ellison, Dorothy West, and Other Voices of a Generation.* New York: Amistad, 2001.

13. Zinn, Howard, *A People's History of the United States: 1492–2001.*

14. Harris, LaShawn, *Michigan State University Journal.*

15. Ibid.

16. Du Bois W.E. B., *The Souls of Black Folks; Essays and Sketches.* New York: Allograph Press, 1968.

17. Harris, LaShawn, *Michigan State University Journal.*

18. Lewis, David L., *W.E.B. Du Bois.* New York: H. Holt, 1993; Lewis, David L., *W.E.B. Du Bois: Biography of a Race, 1868–1919.* New York: H. Holt, 1993.

Chapter 15

1. Seligmann, Herbert J., *The Negro Faces America.* New York: Harper & Brothers, 1920.

2. Ibid.

3. Ibid.

4. Hutchinson, George, "Mediating 'race' and 'nation': The Cultural Politics of the Messenger," *African American Review* 28, no. 4 (1994): 531; *Academic Search Premier,* EBSCOhost (accessed May 26, 2016).

5. Kornweibel, Theodore, *Seeing Red: Federal Campaigns against Black Militancy, 1919–1925.* Bloomington: Indiana University Press, 1998.

6. Bates, Beth Tompkins. *Pullman Porters and the Rise of Protest Politics in Black America, 1925–1945.* Chapel Hill, NC: University of North Carolina Press, 2001; Bates, Beth Tompkins. *Pullman Porters and the Rise of Protest Politics in Black America, 1925–1945 (The John Hope Franklin*

Series in African American History and Culture). University of North Carolina Press, 2001.

7. Wilson, Sondra K., *The Messenger Reader: Stories, Poetry, and Essays from the Messenger Magazine*. New York: Modern Library, 2000.

8. Randolph, Asa Philip. "Uncle Toms." Editorial. *The Messenger*, August 25, 1925; Stephen Railton; Institute for Advanced Technology in the Humanities, Electronic Text Center, Charlottesville, Virginia.

9. Bates, Beth Tompkins. *Pullman Porters and the Rise of Protest Politics in Black America, 1925–1945 (The John Hope Franklin Series in African American History and Culture)*. University of North Carolina Press, 2001.

10. Ibid.

11. Ibid.

12. PBS. In *Miles of Smiles*.

13. Bates, Beth Tompkins. *Pullman Porters and the Rise of Protest Politics in Black America, 1925–1945 (The John Hope Franklin Series in African American History and Culture)*. University of North Carolina Press, 2001.

14. Brotherhood of Sleeping Car Porters Record, 1925–1978. Raw data. Stuart A. Rose Manuscript, Archives, and Rare Book Library, Emory University, Atlanta.

15. Boehm, Randolph, and Blair Hydrick. *RECORDS OF THE BROTHERHOOD OF SLEEPING CAR PORTERS Series A, Holdings of the Chicago Historical Society and the Newberry Library, 1925–1969*. Bethesda, MD: University Publications of America.

16. Ibid.

Chapter 16

1. Boggs, James, "Uprooting Racism and Racists in the United States, *The Black Scholar* 2, no. 2 (1970): 2–10. http://0-www.jstor.org.www.consuls.org/stable/41202851; Vandal, Gilles. " 'Bloody Caddo': White Violence against Blacks in a Louisiana Parish, 1865–1876," *Journal of Social History* 25, no. 2 (1991): 373–388. http://0-www.jstor.org.www.consuls.org/stable/3788756; Brent M. S. Campney. " 'Light Is Bursting upon the World!'": White Supremacy and Racist Violence against Blacks in Reconstruction Kansas," *Western Historical Quarterly* 41, no. 2 (2010): 171–194; Olzak, Susan. "The Political Context of Competition: Lynching and Urban Racial Violence, 1882–1914," *Social Forces* 69, no. 2 (1990): 395–421.

2. McWilliams, Carey, "The Color of America," *The Antioch Review* 50, no. 1/2 (1992): 46–60.

3. Ibid.

4. Green, Victor H., *The Negro Motorist Green Book: An International Travel Guide*. New York: Victor H. Green &, 1949.

5. Loewen, James W., *Sundown Towns: A Hidden Dimension of American Racism*. New York: New Press, 2005.

6. Wright, Gavin., *Sharing the Prize: The Economics of the Civil Rights Revolution in the American South*. Cambridge, MA: Belknap Press of Harvard University Press, 2013.

7. Foster, Mark S. "In the Face of 'Jim Crow': Prosperous Blacks and Vacations, Travel and Outdoor Leisure, 1890–1945," *The Journal of Negro History* 84, no. 2 (1999): 130–149.

8. Green, Victor H., *The Negro Motorist Green Book: An International Travel Guide*. New York: Victor H. Green &, 1949.

9. Courtland Milloy, Jr., "Black Highways; Thirty Years Ago in the South, We Didn't Dare Stop," *Washington Post*, 1987.

10. Williams, John A., *This Is My Country Too*. New York: New American Library, 1965.

11. National Association for the Advancement of Colored People. 1969. *Thirty Years of Lynching in the United States, 1889–1918*. New York: Negro Universities Press.

12. O'Reilly, Kenneth. "The Roosevelt Administration and Black America: Federal Surveillance Policy and Civil Rights during the New Deal and World War II Years," *Phylon (1960)* 48, no. 1 (1987): 12–25.

13. Ibid.

14. Ibid.

Chapter 17

1. *FDR, A. Philip Randolph, and the Desegregation of the Defense Industries*. Website. Washington, DC: The White House Historical Association.https://www.whitehousehistory.org/teacher-resources/fdr-a -philip-randolph-and-the-desegregation-of-the-defense-industries

2. Goodwin, Doris Kearns. *No Ordinary Time: Franklin and Eleanor Roosevelt: The Home Front in World War II*. New York: Simon & Schuster, 1994.

3. Ibid.

4. *March on Washington Movement*. Web page. http://nvdatabase. swarthmore.edu/content/african-americans-threaten-march-washington-1941.

5. A. Philip Randolph Institute. Accessed May 31, 2016. http://www. apri.org/ht/d/sp/i/225/pid/225).

6. Rennebohm, Max, and Adriana Popa. African Americans Threaten March on Washington, 1941. Global Nonviolent Action Database. Accessed September 08, 2011. http://nvdatabase.swarthmore.edu/content/ african-americans-threaten-march-washington-1941.

7. Ibid.

8. Brinkley, David, *Washington Goes to War*. New York: A.A. Knopf, 1988.

9. Goodwin, Doris Kearns, *No Ordinary Time: Franklin and Eleanor Roosevelt: The Home Front in World War II*. New York: Simon & Schuster, 1994.

10. Barber, Lucy G., *Marching on Washington: The Forging of an American Political Tradition*. Berkeley, CA: University of California Press, 2002.

11. Lucander, David, *It Is a New Kind of Militancy March on Washington Movement, 1941–1946*. PhD diss., 2010.

12. A. Philip Randolph Papers. Raw data; Negro March on Washington Movement and Non-Violent Civil Disobedience, February 23, 1943 (Press Release) Reel 22, A. Philip Randolph.

13. Rennebohm, Max, and Adriana Popa, African Americans Threaten March on Washington, 1941. Global Nonviolent Action Database. Accessed September 8, 2011. http://nvdatabase.swarthmore.edu/content/african-americans-threaten-march-washington-1941.

14. Patterson, Lillie, *A. Philip Randolph: Messenger for the Masses*. New York: Facts on File, 1996.

15. Goodwin, Doris Kearns, *No Ordinary Time: Franklin and Eleanor Roosevelt: The Home Front in World War II*. New York: Simon & Schuster, 1994.

Chapter 18

1. Franklin, John Hope, W.E.B. Du Bois: A Personal Memoir. *The Massachusetts Review*, (September 1990).

2. Du Bois, David G. "The Du Bois Legacy Under Attack," *The Black Scholar* 9, no. 5 (February/March 1978): 2–12.

3. The Brotherhood of Sleeping Car Porters. http://www.religiousleftlaw.com/2015/08/the-brotherhood-of-sleeping-car-porters-bscp-1925-1978.html.

Epilogue

1. Corbould, Clare *Becoming African Americans: Black Public Life in Harlem, 1919–1939*. Cambridge, MA: Harvard University Press, 2009.

2. Lewis, David L., *When Harlem Was in Vogue*. New York: Knopf, 1981.

Index

About the Author

LIONEL C. BASCOM is a professor in the Department of Writing, Linguistics, and the Creative Process at Western Connecticut State University in Danbury, Connecticut. Author of numerous nonfiction books, including two about Harlem, Professor Bascom is a two-time member of the Pulitzer Prize Jury in Journalism at Columbia University.